The World of Golf

The World of Golf

Edited by Gordon Menzies

BRITISH BROADCASTING CORPORATION

Published by the British Broadcasting Corporation
35 Marylebone High Street, London W1M 4AA

ISBN 0 563 20018 9
First published 1982

Set in 11/13 Monophoto Photina and printed in England
by BAS Printers Limited, Over Wallop, Stockbridge, Hampshire

Contents

ACKNOWLEDGEMENTS

We wish to thank Liz Halliday for her research assistance.

Colour photographs
Page 33 top Sonia Halliday, bottom left The Bridgeman Art Library (Private Collection), bottom right National Trust (John Bethell); 34 top Christies, bottom Trustees of the British Museum; 51 top Royal Blackheath Golf Club (A. C. Cooper), bottom left The Mansell Collection, bottom right Royal Company of Archers (Tom Scott); 52 Scottish National Portrait Gallery (Tom Scott); 69 St Andrew's Golf Club, Hastings-on-Hudson (Graham Ross); 70 ILN Picture Library; 71 Picturepoint; 72 top, bottom left Peter Dazeley, bottom right Picturepoint; 137 and 138 Colorsport; 139 Golf Photography International; 140 Peter Dazeley; 141 top left and right Peter Dazeley, bottom Golf Photography International; 142 top left and right, bottom right Peter Dazeley, bottom left Colorsport; 143 Peter Dazeley; 144 top left and right Peter Dazeley, bottom Colorsport.

Black and white photographs
Page 7 Peter Dazeley; 8 Ron Wild; 9 top Svenskt Pressfoto, bottom Keystone Press; 11 Associated Press; 13, 14, 15 BBC Hulton Picture Library; 17, 20 J. M. Dent and Sons (from *A History of Golf* by Robert Browning); 18 Central Press Photos; 23 BBC Hulton Picture Library; 24 The Mansell Collection; 27 left *Golf Illustrated*, right Punch Publications; 29 left Christies, right G. M. Cowie; 30 *Golf Illustrated*; 31 *Golf Monthly*; 35 BBC Hulton Picture Library; 36 Colville Books (from *Five Open Champions and the Musselburgh Golf Story*); 37 top and upper middle BBC Hulton Picture Library, lower middle *Golf Illustrated* (Peter Dazeley), bottom Popperfoto; 38, 39 BBC Hulton Picture Library; 41 left *Golf Monthly*, right *Golf Illustrated*; 44, 45 top ILN Picture Library; 45 bottom Punch Publications; 47, 49 ILN Picture Library; 53 The Mansell Collection; 55 The Bettman Archive Inc.; 56 Associated Press; 57 Mary Evans Picture Library; 58 Colorsport; 60 Golf Photography International; 62 left Central Press Photos, middle Press Association, right Peter Dazeley; 63 left Action Photos (H. W. Neale), right Press Association; 65 USGA; 66 St Andrew's Golf Club, Hastings-on-Hudson (Joan Townend); 67, 68 USGA; 74 left BBC Hulton Picture Library, right USGA; 75 left Press Association, middle and right USGA; 76 left *Golf Monthly*, right BBC Hulton Picture Library; 77, 78 USGA; 80 BBC Hulton Picture Library; 82 top Popperfoto, bottom USGA; 83 left Keystone Press, right BBC Hulton Picture Library; 84 USGA; 85 top E. D. Lacey, bottom *Evening Times*, Glasgow; 86 Keystone Press; 87 left USGA, right Popperfoto; 88 Associated Press; 89 top E. D. Lacey, bottom George Ashton; 90 Tony Duffy/Allsport; 91 Popperfoto/UPI; 92 left Keystone Press, right Popperfoto/UPI; 93 left Popperfoto/UPI, right E. D. Lacey; 94 left USGA, right Peter Dazeley; 95 ILN Picture Library; 96, 97 BBC Hulton Picture Library; 98 The Mansell Collection; 99 Royal Portrush Golf Club; 101, 102 BBC Hulton Picture Library; 103 Central Press Photos; 104 top Frank Gardner, bottom *Evening Times*, Glasgow; 105 Sport and General; 106 Fox Photos; 108 Keystone Press; 109 left USGA, right Popperfoto; 110 USGA; 111 top Tony Duffy/Allsport, bottom E. D. Lacey; 112 top Peter Dazeley, bottom Don Morley/Allsport; 113 top Keystone Press, bottom Peter Dazeley; 114 left Tony Duffy/Allsport, right Peter Dazeley; 115 left Allsport, right Keystone Press; 116 Peter Dazeley; 117 BBC Hulton Picture Library; 118 Press Association; 121 BBC Hulton Picture Library; 123 top left USGA, top right and bottom left BBC Hulton Picture Library; 124 left USGA, right BBC Hulton Picture Library; 125 BBC Hulton Picture Library; 127 USGA; 129 right BBC Hulton Picture Library; 130 Fox Photos; 133 left Associated Press, right Popperfoto; 134 *Evening Times*, Glasgow; 135 top USGA, bottom Popperfoto; 136 left Popperfoto, right Central Press; 145 E. D. Lacey; 147 Colorsport; 149, 150 E. D. Lacey; 151 Peter Dazeley; 153 left USGA, right Golf Photography International; 154 left Peter Dazeley, right E. D. Lacey; 155 Popperfoto/UPI; 156 Colorsport; 157 E. D. Lacey; 158 left Peter Dazeley, right Popperfoto; 159 Peter Dazeley; 160 E. D. Lacey; 162, 163 Colorsport; 165 top Golf Photography International, bottom Peter Dazeley; 166 Golf Photography International; 169 Popperfoto; 172 Peter Dazeley; 174 left Popperfoto, right Peter Dazeley; 175 left Colorsport, right Popperfoto; 176 top left and right Colorsport, bottom Peter Dazeley; 177 top left Phil Sheldon, top right and bottom Peter Dazeley; 180 Peter Dazeley; 181 Popperfoto; 182 Peter Dazeley; 183 top left Peter Dazeley, top right Tony Duffy/Allsport, bottom IMG (Shimpei Asai); 186 Keystone Press; 189 BBC Hulton Picture Library; 190 Popperfoto; 191 Ian Joy; 193 USGA; 195 Aerofilms Ltd; 201, 204 top Ian Joy; 204 bottom BBC Hulton Picture Library; 205 Press Association; 206 E. D. Lacey; 208, 209 Ian Joy; 211 top Punch Publications, bottom BBC Hulton Picture Library; 212, Ian Joy; 213 top left Ian Joy, top right USGA, bottom G. M. Cowie; 215 Popperfoto; 217 Ian Joy; 218 left BBC Hulton Picture Library, right Ian Joy.

Map and diagrams by Bob Chapman.

Foreword

by Peter Alliss

Peter Alliss

Golf is a four-letter word. And it's probably caused as much passion, delight and anguish as some of the more notorious four-letter words. Its origins are hidden in the mists of time. Some say, 'Of course it began in Scotland'. Others say, 'Ah what about those ancient paintings depicting Dutch people, playing a game looking strangely like golf, on ice. Wasn't there a story about the Caesars in Roman times, playing with a round object and a stick and cracking it all round the hills of Rome?' Yet another form of golf has been reported from the days of the Persian Empire. But wherever this wondrous game began is not really of total importance. The great thing is it began, and over the last hundred years it has grown into staggering proportions.

Analysed, the game is a rather weird one. Perhaps a lot stranger than any other of the world's most popular games. Imagine trying to describe golf to someone who's never seen or heard of the game: put an assortment of metal and wooden tools of various lengths into a small bag; sling it over your shoulder; attach some sort of gripping shoes to your feet; find yourself a reasonably clean and round golf ball, and a few spares; place the ball on a little piece of wood or plastic for the opening shot; then begin a four- to five-mile hike and every so often attempt to get that ball into a hole $4\frac{1}{2}$ inches in diameter, in as few strokes as you possibly can. Ah yes, a strange game indeed, but one that has afforded millions of people hours of delight and despair in almost equal proportions.

I've often wondered why so many golfers continue to play the game so badly without making any effort to try and improve. Is it the camaraderie in the club house? Is it the walk in the fresh air? Is it to escape the household chores? Your guess is as good as mine. Golf clubs over the years have become a sort of bastion of a special type of society. But I think it would be totally wrong to say today that there is a large element of snobbery or prejudice at the majority of golf clubs. The evolution from that way of thinking in the last fifty years has also been quite staggering. In spite of its royal antecedents the game was never totally for the rich. There has always been a very strong undercurrent and collection of players who certainly did not come from privileged backgrounds. Scotland, for many

Peter Alliss, Jack Nicklaus and the Masters Trophy at Augusta National

the home of golf, has and still does provide very cheap golf, particularly in certain areas.

The most extraordinary thing about golf, in my opinion, is the unlikely countries in which the game has flourished. As far as Europe is concerned, people automatically think of the wonderful cluster of golf courses strung out like rich emeralds along the coastline of the Costa del Sol. Wondrous they are indeed! And I have very fond memories of them, being involved in the opening ceremonies in the sixties at Sotogrande and Atalaya Park, two of the early developments in that part of Spain. I remember my first visit in 1958 to Guadalmina, which was looked upon as a fun course for retired people to play on, or European folk, particularly British, Scandinavian and German, who enjoyed a game of golf and wanted to escape the rigours of their winter.

The growth of golf in Spain is well known, as are some of the remarkable golfers who have emerged and helped to make Spain into a powerful European golfing nation. But the real story in Europe in modern times is Sweden, a tremendous collection of golf courses of all standards. Some perched up in the hills with artificial tees. Funny little holes, down hills, round corners, over brooks, between boulders. A season which is desperately short, but then came the indoor golf school. Sven Tumba, the mighty man, one of the legendary ice hockey figures in Sweden, who turned golf professional when his ice hockey days were over, saw the potential and opened up indoor golfing centres.

Sweden is not often seen on the golfing circuit because, I suppose it would be fair to say, the majority of their courses do not reach a very high standard. Certainly most of them are not suitable for staging major events, although they do have several golf courses that would stand up in any company. So they do not get the publicity and few people know what is going on. But in terms of statistics, considering the number of golfers relative to total population, Sweden is rapidly climbing the world league.

Sven Tumba

Yet of all the phenomena that golf has created over the centuries the story of Japanese golf is – to put it simply – remarkable, astonishing, amazing, unbelievable. In the space of about thirty years, from about 1950 to 1980, the new mushroom cloud in Japanese life has been the golf explosion. More and more people are playing the game or wanting to play in the most expensive golf clubs in the world. Entrepreneurs are building courses in a country where only about seventeen or eighteen per cent of the land is suitable for agriculture, housing or industry. The rest is mountainous or considered to be unsuitable for development. Then along came golf: tops of mountains were blasted off, volcanic stone was ground up to make the base for fairways and greens. One-, two-, three-storey driving ranges were devised in the centre of Tokyo. One golf course has over 20,000 members – which in itself is a scandal – just memberships

The Shiba Park driving range, Tokyo

being sold and resold. Such was the enthusiasm of the Japanese for getting on to a golf course, they never stopped to inquire how many members there were going to be. The money was taken, and now, even though they are members of a golf club, one can imagine them balloting for a game fifteen years hence.

At the other end of the scale, there is the company membership. At a huge cost four, six, eight or ten memberships will be bought up by a major company. Part of the executive's perks would be this membership, where he plays and entertains the company's clients. The marketing of golf – the sale of clubs, gloves, shoes, shirts, caps with motifs on, etc. – is quite staggering. One of the most interesting sights for me on visits to Japan is watching an eager-beaver Japanese walking down the main street carrying a full bag of golf clubs, which would do credit to Jack Nicklaus, on his way to the driving range. And the thought must have crossed his mind that perhaps he may never ever, unless he goes away overseas for a holiday, get to play on a 'proper' golf course.

There has been talk of a company buying land on Penang Island off Malaysia and building six or eight golf courses and just having golfing tours down from Japan. In the Far East anything is possible and that may well happen.

America, although it's slowing down now, went through a tremendous golf and development boom. Retirement homes, condominiums, holiday complexes, country clubs were put up all through that mighty country. The rate of development has slowed down in recent years, of course, but with America being so vast, the rewards so high and the political temperature so different it is still possible there to develop golf, housing, retirement all in one area. The first time I went to Palm Springs, in 1954, there were only a couple of golf courses; now there are almost forty. And every one of them is oversubscribed. North Carolina and Arizona are other areas where the elderly and the holidaymaker can go, certainly in wintertime, in the safe knowledge that the temperature will be round about 70°, the cost of living relatively low and a game of golf always assured.

I remember a conversation with Henry Longhurst several years ago. I asked him what he would do if he had a magic wand and wished to retire. 'Well, if I have to leave my beloved windmills [those two wonderful structures he lived in high on the hills above Hassocks, 9 or 10 miles inland from Brighton], I would go to Sandwich,' he said. 'Ah! Why?' I asked, knowing that he had given up golf many years ago. 'Because Royal St George's is such a marvellous club,' he said. 'You see, there are so many wonderful chaps there it's impossible to be pompous or bogus, or to show off for too long, because no matter what you have, one of the other members will have it twice and threefold. That would be the hub of my life. Going down to the golf club, sitting in the wing window, reading the paper, having a conversation. Taking a walk in the summertime round the putting green, perhaps having the odd putt. Sitting on one of those benches having a pleasant drink. Availing myself of the excellent food. Strolling over to the Pro's shop, where the Whiting family have ruled unbroken since the club began. Oh,' he said, 'that would be my heaven.'

Golf has been very kind to the Alliss family. My father almost became a professional cricketer. In fact he was waiting for a reply from the Yorkshire Cricket Club and also from Royal Porthcawl where he had applied to the professional, Mr Hutchison, for the post of assistant professional. This was after he had come out of the Argyll and Sutherland Highlanders at the end of the 1914–18 War. Well, the letter from Royal Porthcawl came first, father's cricketing days were forgotten, and off he went. The rest is all part of the family history. I was introduced to the game, so was my brother, who no longer plays professionally but who was with me for a number of years at the Parkstone Golf Club, where I had my first post as a full professional.

The memories of all the clubs I've been to, that I've been attached to, come flooding back when I sit relaxed in a nice armchair in front of a log fire. Of course, it hasn't always been roses all the way. A golf professional's life is not always the easiest. I suppose that my father for most of his working life never did less than a 90-hour week, which by

Peter Alliss and Gene Sarazen, British Open, Royal Lytham, 1958

today's standards is almost laughable, but it was pleasant, with nice people in superb surroundings. And even the golf courses that are not in superb surroundings, and there are some that run alongside prison walls, some on the top of old slag heaps, some perched on the side of the Sussex Downs where the wind howls and the ball never stops rolling, usually away from you and into the rough, but wherever it is, it's usually the best bit of greenery around.

Golf! What an extraordinary game you are. It can be destroyed by those who wish to destroy it. Calling it a game for the toffs. A game for snobs. A game for racists. A stupid game. A good walk spoilt. And you would in some cases have to agree. Others, of course, present the game of golf as a great mirror of life. Watch and observe the people on the golf course, their movements quick and jerky, slow and easy, detached and aloof, eager to please, determined to win. Golfers! What an extraordinary lot they are, ranging from the born winners to the never-say-die hackers. I love the enthusiast who will try any new gimmick, new clubs, special golf balls, rain-resistant gloves, special visors to protect his glasses from the drizzle. The enthusiast who turns his garage into a driving range, his lawn into a putting green . . . even creates his own bunker in the corner so that he can practise, perhaps to win the Monthly Medal or the Captain's prize. Ah, for every detractor one can find ten supporters. For golf is something unique and rare. In these days of poor sportsmanship we are blessed indeed to follow a game where the players and spectators still are concerned to preserve the spirit of the game they love.

Crowds may be more noisily appreciative but they know when to be silent. And home-town crowds will always respect and applaud the skills of outsiders. Americans will acknowledge the talent of Seve Ballesteros; Britons will rise to the genius of Lee Trevino. Golf has a universal currency. And it is no respecter of persons. No one can win all the time, and all golfers in their heart of hearts know that. As my father once said to me, 'You can call a man anything but a cheat at golf.'

CHAPTER ONE

Royal and Ancient

by Pat Ward-Thomas

For a century and more learned research has sought to establish the precise origin of golf, but without success. In *The Golfers Manual*, one of the earliest books on the game published in 1857, H. B. Farnie wrote:

The simple requisites for the game, bat and ball of peculiar conformation, have been in common usage (fashioned it may be, in a rude and primitive way) amongst all races from time immemorial, as affording some species of athletic sport; and it needs little speculative enquiry to arrive at the belief that golf, as it is played in modern times, is but a refined and improved form of a very ancient amusement.

The first known instance of a game remotely resembling golf was paganica, played by Roman soldiers with a curved club and a leather ball stuffed with feathers. There is no evidence that paganica survived the departure of the Romans from Britain but a similar game, cambuca, in

which a small wooden ball was hit with a club or mallet, was played in the reign of Edward III. In 1363 an instruction was issued to sheriffs to ban all games including cambuca, which, conceivably, is illustrated in a stained-glass panel of the same period in the east window of Gloucester Cathedral (see page 33). It shows a figure about to strike a ball. The club resembles a hockey stick more than a golf club but the man's grip and backswing could be that of a competent golfer.

The French game of *jeu de mail* bore some resemblance to golf in that it was played in open country within a specific area with a target at the end. This was known as a touchstone and the player who struck it in the least number of strokes was the winner. The course, or goal as it was called, was about half a mile along a road. If a player's ball left the road he lost three strokes, possibly the origin of out of bounds. Another ancient cross-country game, chole, played in France and the Low Countries, was more adventurous. Two teams would agree on a target, such as a door or gate many miles distant. Each team would have three strokes, after which the other team were allowed one stroke to play their opponents' ball anywhere to create difficulty for them. The games must have taken an unimaginable time.

One popular theory is that golf originated in Holland. In his book *Early Golf*, published in 1972, Steven Van Hengel claimed that the game was played as far back as the thirteenth century in Loenen where there were four holes, and that it continued there until early in the nineteenth century. Evidence of the Dutch game of 'het kolven' being closely related

Aert van der Neer,
River Scene in Winter

to golf is in the numerous paintings by the great Dutch artists of the seventeenth and eighteenth centuries which show scenes on land and ice with players striking a ball towards a target, and in some instances a hole.

But golf had been played in Scotland long before then. In his *History of Golf* Robert Browning claims that the Scots were first responsible for the game in its present recognisable form: that they devised its essential features, 'the combination of hitting for distance with the final nicety of approach to an exiguous mark, and the independent progress of each player with his own ball, free from interference by his adversary'. Although a devoted Scot Browning was a meticulous historian, and there are no valid reasons for supposing that he was wrong.

Golf was a popular pastime in Scotland more than five centuries ago. In 1457 King James II, concerned as to the defence of his kingdom and determined that the people spend more time practising their archery, issued his famous decree 'that fute-ball and golfe be utterly cryed downe, and not be used'. If these games had only been the province of a few the King would hardly have troubled to make a law. His successors were of a

Adriaen van de Velde, *A Frost Scene*

like mind until, in 1503, James IV married a daughter of Henry VII and signed a treaty of peace with England. The golfers thus were reprieved, among them James himself. He was soon buying clubs and in the same year the new bridegroom drew on his Lord High Treasurer for forty-two shillings to pay a golfing debt, and nine shillings for clubs and balls. Doubtless he thought that golf expenses should be tax deductible, a precept which unfortunately was not maintained.

It is possible that the union between the two countries introduced golf briefly to England. In 1513 Queen Catherine of Aragon in a letter to Cardinal Wolsey regretted that she would not often be hearing from her husband, Henry VIII, but 'all his subjects be very glad I thank God to be busy with the Golfe for they take it for a pastime'. Golf has been an escape from many an unhappy marriage since. Presumably the Queen was referring to the Scottish game, for almost a century passed before James VI of Scotland succeeded to the English throne as James I and took the game to England.

Whereas originally golf seems to have been a game for the ordinary people, the Stuarts made it a royal pursuit as well. James V often played at Gosford in East Lothian where eventually an Earl of Wemyss had a private course. (With proper respect for his turf he would only allow wooden clubs to be used.) Golf may have contributed to the downfall of the King's beautiful daughter, Mary Queen of Scots. Whether in search of solace after the murder of her husband, Lord Darnley, or whether uncaring is not known, but she was seen playing golf and pall mall (*jeu de mail*) in the fields beside Seton a few days after his death in 1567. She probably learned *jeu de mail* in France and brought it to Scotland. In any event when she came to trial a poor view was taken of her games-playing at such a time.

James VI had considerable influence on the spread of golf. He learned the game in Perth on the tranquil meadows beside the Tay known as the North Inch, and appointed one William Mayne to be the royal clubmaker for the rest of his life. Ten years after arriving in England the King imposed an embargo on the import of feather balls from Holland and granted a 21-year monopoly for their manufacture to James Melvill. The sale of monopolies may have been a means of raising money for the crown but it also suggests that golf was sufficiently popular by then to justify granting one. A maximum price of fourpence a ball was fixed, whereas a century earlier James IV had paid only fourpence a dozen.

Clearly James VI thought that golf was a worthwhile recreation for the young. Both his sons, Prince Henry, who died of typhoid in his teens, and Prince Charles, later Charles I, were encouraged to play. Indeed, after he became king, Charles I was playing golf at Leith when news of an Irish rebellion was brought to him. One account states that he left the links immediately for Holyrood. This prompted Sir Walter Simpson, author of

Charles I on Leith links receiving news of the Irish rebellion (after the painting by Sir John Gilbert)

the masterpiece *The Art of Golf*, to comment that at the time the news arrived the King was being beaten and that he hurried away to save his half-crown rather than his crown. The other version has it that Charles insisted on finishing the match, perhaps recalling that Francis Drake had not panicked when the Armada crisis was at hand. Possibly the King's last golf was played when, as a prisoner of the Scots, he had a round on the Shield Field outside the walls of Newcastle-upon-Tyne.

Nothing is known of the golfing skill of the early Stuart monarchs but they all played. James VII of Scotland and II of England, when Duke of York and residing for a while in Edinburgh, was often on the links at Leith and took part in a famous contest. Apparently he had an argument with two English nobles as to the origin of golf and it was decided to settle the matter with a match. The Duke was to find himself a partner and, as there were no professionals in those days, a shoemaker, John Paterson, was chosen. He was a local expert, helped the Duke to victory, and was rewarded with such a handsome share of the wager that he built a house in Edinburgh.

Royal interest in golf faded with the passing of the Stuarts, although before the Jacobite rebellion in 1745 Bonnie Prince Charlie, while exiled in Italy, was seen practising in the Borghese Gardens. For all that golf in some form was played in Holland William III apparently wanted no part of it and neither did his Hanoverian successors. Royal patronage was not revived until 1833 when William IV bestowed the designation Royal on the Perth Golfing Society.

When news of this honour came to the ears of Murray Belshes, who was soon to be Captain of the St Andrews Society of Golfers, he wrote asking if the king would consent to be their patron. The king declined, saying that he had refused similar requests, but Belshes persisted, pointing out that his Society was almost a century older than the one at Perth and had a most distinguished membership. His persuasion had its effect. In 1834 William IV agreed to be patron and also that the Society be called The Royal and Ancient Golf Club of St Andrews. Three years later he presented the Club with the Gold Medal which is the main prize at the annual Autumn Meeting. On his death his widow, Queen Adelaide, became patron and gave a medal bearing her name, requesting that it be worn by the Captain on all public occasions to distinguish him from other Captains present.

When Queen Victoria became patron royal succession, so to speak, had been established. During the next hundred years Edward VII (as Prince of Wales), Prince Leopold, Edward VIII (as Prince of Wales), George VI (as Duke of York) and the Duke of Kent all became Captains of the Royal and Ancient. Thereafter royal patronage continued, but without active interest until the present Duke of Kent became Captain of the Royal West Norfolk Club in 1981.

The Prince of Wales, captain of the R & A, St Andrews, 1922

Although the edict of James II in 1457 is the earliest written reference to golf in Scotland, the game had been in progress before then as a simple exercise in hitting a ball from one point to another. The formation of clubs was centuries away and the players did not trouble their heads with elaborate rules and refinements of style. The game's growth can most readily be traced from 1552 when John Hamilton, Archbishop of St Andrews, was granted a licence to breed cunninggis (rabbits) within the northern part of the links next to the Eden estuary. The local community retained their right, among other things, to play at golf, football, shooting and other pastimes for all time. The links has remained a place for public relaxation, with obvious reservations agreed between the town and the Royal and Ancient, and for four centuries and more any golfer in the world has had a legal right to play the courses on payment of the green fee.

Golf in Britain was first played on links land along the eastern coasts of Scotland. The links were formed when the sea receded leaving wild, undulating wastes of sand. These became resting places for birds whose droppings helped to fertilise seeds borne by the winds, and gradually grass, gorse and other vegetation grew. The land was of little value except as a home for rabbits who made paths and burrows in the wilderness. In time these were widened into natural fairways by the passage of man. There were bunkers in profusion, many caused by digging for shells, and, as if providence had golf in mind, slightly raised areas suitable for greens.

Thus the Old Course at St Andrews evolved. Nature was its only architect; its design owned little to the hand of man and has stood the test of centuries apart from occasional alterations as equipment became more powerful and sophisticated. To a great extent the same was true elsewhere. In the seventeenth century Sir Robert Gordon, tutor to the Sutherland family, wrote of Dornoch 'that about this town are the fairest and largest links . . . fitt for Archery, Goffing and Ryding and all other exercises'. Every golfer who knows Dornoch realises that its greatness is founded on natural features.

As the game expanded in the nineteenth century, first in Scotland and later in England, Wales and Ireland, golfers turned to links as settings for their courses. The land was not suitable for agriculture, was comparatively remote from towns, and free to the elements which emphasised the challenge of the game. Grass and hazards were already there, the ground had natural movement, and fashioning a course needed no great imagination or labour. From the beginning the links has been the classic setting for the game in Britain and, with rare exceptions, the greatest courses lie on such land. For this reason, and also to preserve an ancient tradition, the Open Championship has always been played on a links course and will be for the foreseeable future.

A legend has long existed that Royal Blackheath, said to have been instituted in 1608, is the oldest golf club in the world. After James I and his

The Procession of the Silver Club. The Edinburgh Town Crier announces the date of the Competition, 1787 (after a drawing by David Allan)

court moved from Scotland to London in 1603 some form of golf probably was played near the palace at Greenwich, but in their history, *Royal Blackheath*, Ian Henderson and David Stirk find no evidence to support the formation of a golf club until well into the eighteenth century. Pride of seniority therefore belongs to the Honourable Company of Edinburgh Golfers, which came into existence in 1744. For some years previously several 'Gentlemen of Honour skilful in the ancient and healthful exercise of Golf' had been playing on the five-hole links at Leith. Anxious for formal recognition they approached the Edinburgh Town Council who presented them with a Silver Club to be played for annually. The Honourable Company was formed and the minutes kept from that date are the oldest continuous record of any golf club in the world.

The social spread of golf at that time was revealed in a statistical account of Scotland which declared that 'the greatest and wisest of the land were to be seen on the links of Leith mingling freely with the humblest mechanics in pursuit of their common and beloved amusement. All distinctions of rank were levelled by the joyous spirit of the game.' Each of the five holes was over 400 yards and, bearing in mind the equipment and the state of the ground, it is small wonder that the lowest score for ten holes, the distance for the Club Gold Medal contest, was 60.

The competition for the Silver Club in 1744 was the first ever held in golf, and a Code of Rules was agreed. The thirteen articles were:

1 You must tee your ball within one club's length of the hole.
2 Your tee must be on the ground.
3 You are not to change the ball you strike off the tee.
4 You are not to remove Stones, Bones or any Break Club, for the sake of playing your Ball, except upon the Fair Green and that only with a Club's length of your Ball.
5 If your Ball come among watter or any wattery filth, you are at liberty to take out your Ball and bringing it behind the hazard and teeing it, you may play it with any club and allow your Adversary a Stroke, for so getting out your ball.
6 If your balls be found anywhere touching one another you are to lift the first ball, till you play the last.
7 At Holing, you are to play your Ball honestly for the Hole, and not play upon your Adversary's Ball, not lying in your way to the Hole.
8 If you should lose your Ball, by its being taken up, or any other way you are to go back to the Spot, where you struck last, and drop another Ball, and allow your adversary a Stroke for the misfortune.
9 No man at Holing his Ball is to be allowed, to mark his way to the Hole with his Club or anything else.
10 If a Ball be stopp'd by any person, Horse, Dog or anything else, the Ball so stopp'd must be played where it lyes.
11 If you draw your Club, in order to Strike and proceed so far in the Stroke, as to be bringing down your Club: If then your Club shall break, in any way, it is to be Accounted a Stroke.
12 He whose Ball lyes farthest from the Hole is obliged to play first.
13 Neither Trench, Ditch or Dyke, made for the presentation of the Links, nor the Scholar's Holes or the Soldier's Lines, Shall be accounted a Hazard. But the Ball is to be taken out and Tee'd and play'd with any Iron Club.

The articles were signed by John Rattray, an Edinburgh surgeon, who won the Silver Club and thus became the Company's first captain. He defended successfully, but his golf was sharply interrupted the following autumn when he was ordered to act as surgeon to Prince Charles's troops at Prestonpans. While the Company presumably continued to enjoy their golf and claret, which was consumed in considerable quantities, the hapless Rattray was taken prisoner at Culloden. Only the intervention of a fellow member of the Honourable Company, Duncan Forbes, Lord President of the Court of Session, who had tried to prevent the rebellion, saved his life. When the competition was resumed in 1748 Rattray returned to the golfing fray.

The original rules included no penalties for violations. If a ball were lost or unplayable in what was the equivalent of a modern water hazard it could be lifted under penalty of one stroke. Otherwise it was assumed that Gentleman golfers would not attempt to take unfair advantage. As their number was small misdemeanors would soon have come to light. Also the rules were concerned with match rather than stroke play. Apart from Rule 10, referring to an outside agency, nothing is said about playing the ball from where it lies. Even as late as 1812 the only rule to that effect concerned a rabbit scrape, from which the golfer had to play as if from any common hazard. This probably meant any bad lie and was taken as such until clarified much later under the present Rule 16. Rule 6, regarding touching balls, was designed partly to prevent any malicious intent, as in croquet, but in 1775 when touching was defined as balls being within six inches of one another the stymie was born. Except for one year it remained a part of match play until 1952. Many, including Bobby Jones, regretted its passing, mainly because the delicate skill involved in trying to negotiate a stymie had been eliminated from the game.

It is remarkable that the vision of Rattray and his friends produced a code which embraces the essence and spirit of the modern rules in their vastly expanded version. There are golfers who believe that their purposes could still be served by the ancient code.

Ten years after the formation of the Honourable Company, in 1754, twenty-two Noblemen and Gentlemen gathered at St Andrews. Admiring the game as a healthy exercise, and having the interest and prosperity of their town at heart, they decided to contribute five shillings each for a Silver Club to be competed for each year. The St Andrews Society thus came into being and adopted the rules devised by their friends across the Forth with one small change. Under Rule 5 the player had to throw his ball behind him and not tee it as at Leith where the ground was softer.

A century and more passed before the number of rules was increased from thirteen to twenty-two. By then authority on matters of the rules had passed to the Royal and Ancient. In his history of the Honourable Company George Pottinger remarks that the Company had gracefully abrogated any residual authority to make laws or give authoritative interpretations on contentious cases. Among the new rules introduced in the nineteenth century was the right to identify a ball when covered by sand or vegetation, and to clear loose impediments from the green. Also the ball could be teed four to six club-lengths from the hole. The original one club-length indicated little concern for the putting surface. The general penalty of loss of hole (or two strokes) for infringements not covered by the rules lasted until 1933. By then, of course, competition had greatly increased and commercial influences were having their unfortunate effect on the game.

The St Andrews Society was determined that the first Silver Club competition would be properly organised. As the Old Course was public land where anyone could wander at will the Society forbade all kinds of wheeled machines, people on horseback and dogs from passing over the links while the golf was in progress. All went well and a local merchant, Bailie William Landale, was victorious and became the Society's first captain.

The Old Course then consisted of eleven holes out and the same number back, winding a perilously narrow path between dense banks of whin and sharing the same greens. In 1764, after William St Clair had mastered the twenty-two holes in 121 strokes, it was decided to make the first four holes into two. As the same fairways and greens were used going out and back the round was thus reduced to eighteen holes, which henceforth became the standard round. St Clair's score in effect was 99 for eighteen holes, a considerable performance for a man of 64, but he was an exceptional games player and one of the first great golfers. He won the Silver Club twice more at St Andrews and was Captain of the Honourable Company on four occasions (see page 51).

In those years much of the links was an almost untrodden waste and the greens untended. The breaking of 100 was an extraordinary feat but in 1767 James Durham won the Silver Club with a 94. This remained unbeaten for eighty-six years, surely the longest-standing record of all time, until J. C. Stewart returned a 90 to win the William IV Medal in 1853. Some thirty years before King William presented his Medal the Society had bought a gold one as a prize for the best player in a medal round. It seems there was doubt about the procedure of the Silver Club competition. In his *History of St Andrews* James Grierson claimed that the Captain was determined in advance of the event and that, as now, he alone is regarded as competing for the Club.

Towards the end of the eighteenth century, while golf at St Andrews was becoming solidly established, the Honourable Company were having problems. The five-hole course at Leith was becoming increasingly crowded with people and cattle, and military activities during the Napoleonic wars. Financial difficulties arose partly because there was no annual subscription and partly because many golfers were seeking their pleasures at Musselburgh. In 1836 the Company moved down the coast and shared the Musselburgh links with that Club. There they stayed until moving to Muirfield in 1892, but during the years at Musselburgh the Company organised six Open Championships.

In their researches concerning Blackheath Henderson and Stirk, authors also of the masterly *Golf in the Making*, drew the interesting conclusion that many of the early clubs were founded by masons, and that

A golf match on Blackheath, 1869

the date of their institution preceded by several years that of their foundation as golf clubs. Although the Honourable Company held its first competition for a Silver Club in 1744, twenty years passed before Club rules were framed and the competition was confined to members. The foundation stone for the Golf House was laid by William St Clair, Grandmaster Mason of Scotland, and all the members present were masons. When the Royal and Ancient decided upon its present clubhouse Murray Belshes laid the foundation stone with full masonic honours. The Royal Burgess Society of Edinburgh was instituted in 1735 but apparently no minutes exist as proof. In other instances minutes are missing, which suggests that as masonic affairs are secret the records were destroyed when the Societies opened their doors to golfers who were not masons. Similarly the minutes of Musselburgh do not start until 1784, ten years after the Club claimed to have been formed.

At the close of the eighteenth century there were only ten golf clubs. In 1818 William Mitchell, a local citizen, founded the Old Manchester Club at Kersal Moor which, after Blackheath, was the oldest club outside Scotland. Then the missionary zeal of the Scots, helped by strong trade links, led to the beginnings of golf in India. In 1829 the Calcutta Club was formed, followed thirteen years later by one in Bombay. Blackheath helped these clubs from the outset by sending copies of their rules and gold medals for competitions. The Calcutta Club inspired the Amateur Championship of India, the oldest national championship outside the British Isles.

The Victorians at golf, 1869

By the middle of the nineteenth century golf had spread steadily in Scotland, eventually reaching the west coast with the founding of Prestwick in 1851. For almost fifty years Blackheath and Old Manchester were the only English clubs but in 1856 the first Continental club was formed at Pau in southern France (see page 46). Meanwhile the long hiatus in England was drawing to a close. In the 1850s the Rev. I. H. Gosset and his family played golf on the burrows at Northam on the north coast of Devon. Local interest grew and in 1860 Tom Morris came from St Andrews and rearranged the course. By then so many people were playing that in April 1864 a meeting was held to arrange the 'preliminaries of a Golf Club for playing the fine Scotch Game of Golf on the burrows'. The Royal North Devon Club was formed and the links at Westward Ho is the oldest seaside course in the world outside Scotland. The Club was fortunate in having Horace Hutchinson, whose uncle had been one of the early golfers on the burrows. He became one of the great amateurs of his generation, was a felicitous and prolific writer on the game, and in 1908 was the first English captain of the Royal and Ancient.

The Clubs

Every golfer who swings a club is simply fulfilling the primeval instinct of striking an object with a stick. The implements are more elaborate, the settings more cultured and most, though by no means all, of the swings more sophisticated, but fundamentally the process is the same. The curved stick used by the Romans for paganica was in effect the prototype of the clubs used down the centuries for various games, notably those of the Dutch, and by the early golfers.

The first written record of clubs made specifically for golf is that of James IV buying several from a bowmaker at Perth. Whether this craftsman was the original club-maker can never be known and there is no further reference to the skill until, a century later, James VI/I gave a William Mayne the first Royal Warrant as fledger, bower, club-maker and spear-maker for life. No specimens of their work have come to light and probably the oldest clubs are preserved in the clubhouse at Troon. Their survival, almost certainly from Stuart times, was a remarkable accident of fortune. According to an account which appeared in *The Times* in 1889 a set of six wooden clubs and two irons was found in a boarded-up cupboard during alterations to an old house in Hull. Among documents was a Yorkshire newspaper of 1741 which, together with the length and weight of the clubs (one iron is 28 ounces), is evidence enough of their antiquity.

The earliest known club-makers after Mayne were the Dickson family of Leith and Henry Miln of St Andrews. Andrew Dickson had caddied for James II at Leith and one of his sons, John, is probably the Dickson referred to in Thomas Matheson's poem, 'The Goff', published in 1743:

Of finest ash, Castalio's shaft was made;
Pondrous with lead, and fenced with horn the head,
(The work of Dickson, who in Letha dwells,
And in the art of making clubs excels).

The clubs found in Hull could have been made by Dickson or Miln.

As the game grew more popular the making of clubs progressed from crude carpentry to a considerable craft whereby the clubs were beautifully made, finished and balanced. Simon Cossar, who followed the Dicksons at Leith, was club-maker to the Honourable Company. The quality of his work can be seen in the Royal and Ancient museum in the shape of two wooden clubs, dating about 1760, and a superb putting cleek which would be the envy of any modern golfer. The age of master club-makers had dawned.

Hugh Philp, born in 1782, was a carpenter by trade who turned his hand to repairing clubs. He was so successful that in 1819 he was appointed official club-maker to the Society of St Andrews Golfers (soon to become the Royal and Ancient). Previously the Society had paid an annual retainer of two guineas to the McEwans of Bruntsfield so that their agent, David Robertson, father of Allan, could attend the Spring and Autumn Meetings at St Andrews, but Philp had made such progress that this arrangement was cancelled in 1827. He was a quiet man, with a fund of dry caustic humour, a fine eye for a club and, it was said, exquisite taste. He used thorn, apple and pearwood for his heads and ash for the shafts. One of his admirers wrote that his clubs were to a golfer what a Toledo blade was to a swordsman. They soon became famous and are of increasing value to collectors as splendid examples of the craft. The Royal and Ancient has a complete set of his clubs, all wooden – play club, long spoon, mid spoon, short spoon, baffing spoon, driving putter and putter.

One of Philp's assistants, James Wilson, together with Cossar and Carrick of Musselburgh, was among the leading makers of irons. These were coming into use as cleeks, track irons (for extricating balls from railway lines, such as the one which used to border the Old Course at St Andrews), rut irons and play clubs. Allan Robertson and later young Tom Morris found the iron play club preferable to the baffing spoon for approaching, and for other shots which they were introducing to the game. When Wilson left to start on his own, Philp brought his nephew, Robert Forgan, into the business. In 1856 Forgan succeeded him and for over a century the family's shop overlooked the 18th green at St Andrews. Forgan was one of the pioneers in the use of hickory for shafts and for inserting the pegs holding the bone on a clubface at a slant instead of driving them in straight.

The McEwans' business was started in Edinburgh in 1770 by James who, like Philp, was a carpenter. His son Peter married a daughter of Douglas Gourlay, a feather ball-maker of Musselburgh, thus uniting two of the most significant names in the golf trade. Their son Douglas established the firm's rising reputation; his clubs were models of symmetry and shape, lacking nothing of the elegance of Philp's work and having perhaps a slight edge in the design of putters. Hugh Philp and Douglas McEwan were fittingly described by one historian as the Chippendale and Hepplewhite of golf. Their craftsmanship, imagination and devotion to the task of producing the finest possible clubs made them the foremost pioneers of an art which lasted deep into the next century.

For some years before the First World War experiments had been made with steel-shafted clubs but the Rules Committee of the Royal and Ancient decided that they were too great a departure from the traditional form. Although the United States Golf Association ruled that after April 1924 steel shafts were permissible for all their competitions, many of the great American golfers, Bobby Jones for one, continued to use hickory shafts. The set with which he achieved the Grand Slam in 1930 were all hand-made hickory. In May that year the Royal and Ancient finally approved the use of steel shafts. Previously they had been reluctant to do so except where the supply of hickory was limited. The Professional Golfers Association thought that steel would be detrimental to their trade but the trend was irresistible.

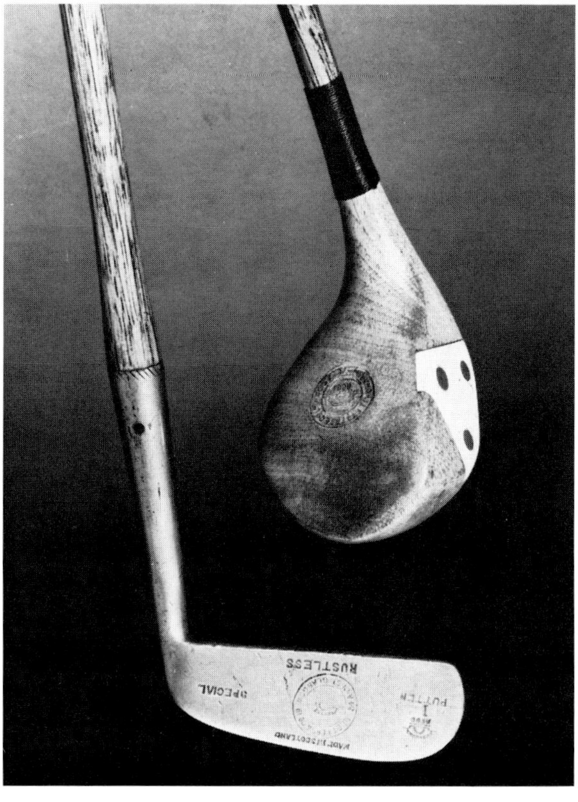

Left: The days of hickory
Right: INFURIATED FOOZLER (*after his first experience of a steel shaft*). 'G-r-r-r-h! The cursed thing won't even break.' (*Punch*)

The Balls

Most historians agree that the first balls to be used in the dark ages of golf were leather-covered objects filled with feathers, but it is possible that in the very beginning the balls were made of boxwood, similar to those used in chole and *jeu de mail*. Writing in the 1890s Horace Hutchinson said that he arranged for a ball to be made of this wood by a maker of balls for *jeu de mail*, or pall mall as it was known when played in England. They were of similar weight and grooving to a golf ball but were useless, flying no more than 100 yards. The experiment was conducted on grass whereas on hard, smooth surfaces such as roads or ice where other games were played it would travel much further. It is reasonable to suppose that the earliest golfers playing on grass soon abandoned the wooden balls in favour of the feathery which had been used in the Roman game of paganica.

The first written reference to the manufacture of featheries was in Matheson's poem 'The Goff':

The work of Bobson, who with matchless art
Shapes the firm hide, connecting ev'ry part,
Then in a socket sets the well-stitched void,
And thro' the eyelet drives the downy tide;
Crowds urging crowds the forceful brogue impels,
The feathers harden and the leather swells; . . .

Whether Bobson of the matchless art invented an ingenious process is a mystery but making featheries was an art. The leather usually was untanned bull's hide, softened, cut into strips and sewn together. A small hole was left through which the soft, boiled feathers, usually enough to fill a top hat, were stuffed. Before doing so the leather had to be turned inside out so that the seams were inside. The ball was then hammered into as round a shape as possible and painted. The task was laborious and hazardous because of inhaling dust from the feathers. Even an expert could only produce about four balls a day and they might cost as much as four shillings apiece. More by accident than design the seams acted in similar fashion to modern ball markings.

In dry conditions the feathery could be struck upwards of 200 yards. It has been recorded that on one legendary occasion Samuel Messieux, a Swiss who taught French at Madras College, St Andrews, drove from near the 13th green on the Old Course down the Elysian Fields into Hell bunker, a distance of some 360 yards. Even with a helping wind and hard ground this was an immense hit. The problem with the feathery was that when damp its performance declined, and when hit thin the cover would cut. Nonetheless it remained the standard ball until the gutty appeared in the late 1840s.

One of the first references to a ball-maker was the monopoly granted by James I. Some years later, in 1642, the town council of Aberdeen granted a licence to John Dickson, but the most famous early ball-makers

A top hat full of feathers – the amount required to fill a feathery.
Far left: An Allan Robertson feathery stamped size 30 (*top*) and a typical pre-1850 feathery

were the Gourlay family. They had moved from Edinburgh to Musselburgh in the 1840s and were so expert at their craft that a Gourlay ball, 'white as snow, hard as lead and elastic as whalebone', became a symbol of the very finest quality.

The Gourlays had rivals and prominent among them were the Robertsons, notably Allan, who was to become the first great professional golfer, possibly the first professional as such, for the calling had not been defined by then. He was born in 1815 and joined the family business in St Andrews. In 1844, with the help of Tom Morris who was apprenticed to him, he produced 2456 balls, almost doubling the previous year's output, but a shadow in the shape of the gutty ball was on their horizon.

No clear evidence exists as to the inventor of the gutta-percha ball (see page 46). Several people probably experimented with the substance because it could be fashioned into a ball easily and quickly unlike the elaborate process involved in making a feathery. At first the gutty, with its smooth, rolled surface, tended to duck in its flight, but it was found to fly much better after being nicked or cut. An enlightened saddler in St Andrews apparently was one of the first to realise this and hammered indentations all round the surface of the ball. Its performance was revolutionised and this method of marking was used until the appearance of moulds about 1880. The gutty flew further than the feathery, a prime virtue in every golfer's mind, and rolled more truly on the greens. As only one substance was involved it only cost about a quarter of the feathery, and could be remoulded if hacked about too harshly. By 1848 the feathery was doomed, much to the dismay of the Gourlays, Allan Robertson and other manufacturers who, after many years of learning the trade, saw their livelihood threatened. John Gourlay was soon making gutties but Robertson bought all that he could find in St Andrews and burned them, making an awful stench in the process. In his *Reminiscences of Golf and Golfers* Thomas Peter recalled asking Robertson to try the gutty and telling him how superior it was to the feathery. Allan deliberately topped the ball and said it would never fly.

The development of the golf ball. From the back: feathery, unmarked gutty, marked gutty, two early rubber-cores, the 'bramble' pattern, the 'lattice' pattern, the 'dimpled' pattern, the Dunlop 65 and the modern ball.

Robertson had made Tom Morris promise that he would never play in matches where gutties were used but one day discovered that Tom, having run out of balls in a match, borrowed one. This led to strong words and Morris set up his own ball-making business in St Andrews which he pursued until in 1851 he was persuaded to become custodian of the links at Prestwick. At the same time Robertson finally realised that he had been mistakenly obstinate and also took to making gutties.

For half a century the gutty remained unchallenged until Coburn Haskell, an American from Cleveland, revolutionised the game. Dissatisfied with the gutty, he experimented with rubber strips wound round a rubber core. Although harder to control than the gutty the Haskell went further and the golfer got more favourable results with an imperfectly struck shot. When at the last moment Alec Herd decided to use the Haskell for the Open at Hoylake in 1902 and won, the days of the gutty were numbered. For a while conflict raged between the manufacturers of the respective balls and advertisements for the gutty condemned the rubber-core for its lively, impish behaviour. Some of the experts, including Harry Vardon, claimed it would spoil the game, but they swam against an overwhelming tide and eventually recognised that it gave greater pleasure to the mass of golfers.

Adverts from early issues of *Golf Monthly*

The Professionals

The professional golfer naturally evolved from the caddie. For generations men or boys had been employed to carry clubs; it is hard to imagine the Scottish monarchs 'carrying their own'. Early in the seventeenth century the household accounts of the Duke of Montrose refer to a caddie as the 'boy who carried my Lord's clubbes to the field'. Andrew Dickson was only a boy when he carried for the Duke of York and is unlikely to have advised his royal employer, but gradually the caddie's status rose from that of a mere porter to golfer's friend, counsellor and coach.

Some caddies never played the game but they knew their links intimately and were well aware of their masters' strengths and failings. Of rough, humble origin they could be forthright and were no respecters of persons. Occasionally the caddie acted as steward if the crowds pressed too close. During one match they strained forward to see if a putt had dropped. The furious caddie seized the ear of the nearest spectator, who happened to be a magistrate, and forced his head down over the hole, declaring that if he could not see the ball he should stick his inquisitive nose in and he would feel it.

There were those who enhanced their income by other means. One such, known as 'Trap Door', pretended that one leg was shorter than the other and made a hollow sole in his boot which could accommodate twelve balls. During search in the fearsome gorse or whin he would ease a ball into his boot and declare it lost.

The first real concern for caddies at St Andrews was in 1771 when it was agreed that they should be paid fourpence for going the length of the Hole o' Cross, the present fifth, and sixpence but not more if they went further. This was meagre pay but later St Andrews was known for the exorbitant rates charged by caddies, some of whom would desert regular employers who had been generous to them in hard times, if a richer prospect appeared.

One of the first tributes to the caddie as a player was made of David Robertson, apparently in great demand as player and teacher although he was only a senior caddie. He was the father of the great Allan. It was said of Allan Robertson that from childhood his playthings were golf clubs. His style was easy and graceful and such was his control that he could appear to be hitting a powerful stroke whereas he was sparing it. Accuracy was his great strength and, as one observer wrote, 'his deadly steadiness was conspicuous with thoughtful consideration'. Tom Morris described him as 'the cunningest bit body of a player that ever handled club, cleek or putter. A kindly body with just a wealth of sly, pawky fun about him.'

Roberston was a small, sturdily built man with reddish side whiskers and an almost perpetual smile. He was unfailingly good-natured and never disturbed by his partner's mistakes in matches. This was notably so with beginners who invariably swore by him and became attracted to golf

Left: Stained-glass window, Gloucester Cathedral
Below left: Child Playing Golf, c. 1650, by Albert Cuyp
Below: The Golf Players, c. 1660, by Pieter de Hooch

Left: Allan Robertson
Right: Old Tom Morris

once and for all. He must have been a delight to play with. A myth arose that he was invincible but this was not so. Tom Morris beat him twice, and also challenged him to a match for £100 but the offer was refused. Robertson was not the last great golfer to realise that he had more to lose than to gain by such a contest, but he was happy enough to have Morris as a partner in foursomes. By then their dispute over the gutty ball had been healed. They played many famous matches, one over three courses against the Dunn brothers, Willie and James, when they won £400 after a desperate struggle. There was no mention of a prize for the losers.

In 1851 Willie Dunn became the first professional at Blackheath and therefore the first in England. His appointment may have been influenced by the appearance of the gutty ball because Sir Thomas Moncrieffe, a subsequent Captain of Blackheath, had sent Dunn, a skilled ball-maker, some gutta-percha when he was at North Berwick. Two years later Dunn was joined by his brother who started at 7/6 a week. After ten years at Blackheath Willie's salary had soared to 17/6. The brothers stayed there until 1864 when apparently alcohol was partly responsible for complaints against them and they returned to Scotland.

Robertson was undoubted master in his time. Sadly he died the year

Opposite
Above: Golf on the Ice, c. 1620, by Hendrik Avercamp
Below: View of Bruntsfield Links, Edinburgh, c. 1750, by Paul Sandby

before the first Open Championship in 1860 but the previous year he played the Old Course in 79, the first time 80 had been broken there, an astonishing score considering the well-nigh untended state of the course. It was no wonder that after his death a member of the Royal and Ancient remarked, 'They may shut up their shops and toll their bells, for the greatest among them is gone.'

Meanwhile Tom Morris had become established as custodian at Prestwick. He preferred the twelve-hole course to the Old at St Andrews, and not without reason. After finishing second to Willie Park in the first Open he was victorious the next two years. He had succeeded Robertson as the great player of the day, but professional golf then was dominated by a few families, notably the Parks, the Dunns of Musselburgh, the Morrises, and the Straths of St Andrews. All had a profound influence on the game.

Willie Park won the Open four times and his son, famed as one of the greatest putters, twice. Willie junior also designed many courses in various parts of the world. Tom Morris returned from Prestwick to St Andrews in 1863 and, as custodian of the Old Course and professional to the Royal and Ancient, remained a revered figure until his death in 1908. His son, Young Tom, won the Challenge Belt three times in succession and made it his own property. The championship was not held the following year but he won again in 1872.

Grand Golf Tournament by Professional Players, Leith Links, 17 May 1867. In the foreground Willie Park and Old Tom Morris. Behind, from left to right, T. Hunter, J. Hutchison, D. Park, R. Ferguson, R. Kirk, G. Paterson, W. Dunn, J. Campbell, Young Tom Morris, T. Brown, J. Anderson, G. Morris, W. Dow, A. Greig, A. Strath, R. Andrews, A. Brown, W. McDonald, R. Dow and J. Dunn

Beyond doubt Young Tom was the greatest golfer the game then had seen. In 1870 his winning score of 149 was an astounding achievement. The twelve-hole course measured 3800 yards, the equivalent of 5800 for eighteen holes, but Young Tom played one of his three rounds in 47. He won that Open by twelve strokes. Little is known of Young Tom's method of playing. His approach was said to be dashing and sometimes he waggled his driver so fiercely before striking that the head would snap off the shaft. Obviously he was extremely strong and a great iron player, notably into a gale of wind and with his niblick from the bad lies common in his day. And, withal, he was a fine putter, always attacking the hole, with an open stance and the ball almost opposite his right foot. Apparently he was as painstaking as Nicklaus in his approach to the shortest of putts. He was only twenty-four when, a few months after his wife died giving birth to their first child, he was found dead in bed on Christmas morning in 1875. He had never recovered from his wife's death, his health had declined, and he died from a burst artery in a lung.

Young Tom Morris and (*below, top to bottom*) J. H. Taylor, Harry Vardon and James Braid (*see also* p. 70)

After Young Tom Scottish professionals continued to dominate the game. The Park family, Jamie Anderson and Bob Ferguson, both of whom won three successive Open championships, were among the foremost. Then, in the early 1890s, John Ball and Harold Hilton, supreme amateurs of the time, became the first Englishmen to win the Open. The first English professional to win was J. H. Taylor in 1894. Harry Vardon won three of his six victories before the end of the century and, when James Braid joined their company soon afterwards, the 'Great Triumvirate' was born. Their command was almost absolute. From 1894 until the First War they won sixteen Open championships between them.

The birth of championship golf was the inspiration of the Prestwick Club only a few years after its foundation. In 1857 eight other leading clubs were invited to send teams for a foursomes competition. In the event eleven, including the Royal and Ancient, Musselburgh, Blackheath and North Berwick, took part. George Glennie and J. C. Stewart won the tournament for Blackheath, beating the Royal and Ancient by seven holes in the deciding contest. Matches then, and for many years afterwards, were determined by the number of holes up after a completed round. The following two years the tournament was played as an individual knock-out and could be claimed as the forerunner of the Amateur Championship. In any event it appears to have been the first open tournament in history, and in 1860 Major J. O. Fairlie, a member of Prestwick, proposed that a subscription be started to provide a medal for a professional competition. Eventually a Challenge Belt of red morocco leather was bought instead of a medal. On 17 October 1860 eight professionals played three rounds of the Prestwick links and Willie Park won with a total of 174, beating Tom Morris by two strokes.

Strictly speaking that first gathering was not an Open Championship because it was restricted to professionals. Major Fairlie therefore suggested that in 1861 Gentlemen golfers from eight of the leading clubs be allowed to enter. The tactless exclusion of several others led to a hasty change of mind. On the eve of the second championship it was decided that the 'Belt to be played for tomorrow and on all other occasions until it be otherwise resolved, shall be open to all the world'. In their wildest imaginings Fairlie and his friends could never have foreseen how far this would remain true, and that they stood on the threshold of an ever-expanding world.

The first Open, Prestwick, 1860: Charlie Hunter and Old Tom Morris (*right*)

CHAPTER TWO

Spreading the Gospel

by Peter Dobereiner

Golf is universal. There is hardly a country in the world which has not been touched by the twentieth-century epidemic of golf expansion. According to how you define a golfer, there are probably between forty and fifty million players in the world today. Oil men use portable fairways, in the form of mats which they carry with them between shots so that they can hit from a square of artificial turf in arid deserts where no grass can grow, and they play to islands of oiled sand called browns. In the Arctic crimson golf balls are struck over frozen tundra. Even the surface of the moon has been disturbed by the contact of iron head on golf ball. Nothing, it seems, can halt the spread of the golf virus.

Yet golf nearly disappeared from the face of the earth. In Holland, where the game almost certainly originated, it died out completely for more than 300 years. In America too it disappeared for the best part of a

Walter Hagen (winner) and Henry Cotton with their caddies, British Open, Muirfield, 1929

century. In Britain the survival of the game was threatened and it was preserved only by accident, as a means of working up a healthy appetite for gargantuan masonic feasts.

Regardless of where and how the game began, we know that by the middle of the fifteenth century it had taken such a hold of the population of eastern Scotland that it was considered a threat to national security. Men were ignoring their compulsory archery practice to pursue this absorbing pastime on the linksland. The game was banned by Act of Parliament so that the citizens' army could be kept in a proper state of readiness to withstand the English invaders. In those days the game was played by the common people, obviously enough from that Act of Parliament, and we may surmise that a ball of turned hardwood was in general use.

Sometime during the seventeenth century the game underwent a fundamental change. One of the very few written sources from this time is the royal account books, and we can see that the price of golf balls increased hugely. Of course the value of money changed, for inflation is not a modern invention, but in this case we have a comparison. Instead of being able to buy three golf balls for the price of one club the King was now paying the same amount for a golf ball (four Scottish shillings) as he had to pay for a club. Clearly the form of the golf ball had changed, and it is not difficult to put two and two together and conclude that this change was due to the introduction of the feather ball (see page 28), which was a vastly superior missile to the wooden ball. The lively feathery flew off the face of the club and on a frosty day at St Andrews with a light following wind a record drive with a feathery was established by Monsieur Samuel Messieux, a French master from Madras College. His drive was measured at 361 yards and years later, when the legendary big hitter Freddie Tait tried to emulate that feat over the same Elysian Fields with a gutta-percha ball, his best drive was twenty yards short of the feathery mark.

Golf clubs changed form to accommodate the feathery. Instead of the long, immensely cumbersome clubs of the wooden-ball era, club-makers now refined their craft to produce elegant wands with limber shafts. The only iron club carried in those days was a specialist rut iron to extricate the ball from cart tracks. For the rest the golfer's caddie carried perhaps five wooden-headed clubs to drive and spoon and baff and putt the spritely feathery. Iron clubs would have been far too harsh for general use on the leather cover of the feathery, which was all too prone to split anyway, especially in wet conditions.

The effect of this change in the game's equipment was to price the fishermen and labourers out of golf. For a while they probably continued to play golf with their wooden balls, but theirs would have been a different game, played on a different scale of distance, to the pastime of the Stuart kings and their courtly companions. The lords played and the commoners carried the clubs as caddies (a word derived from the French *cadet* which

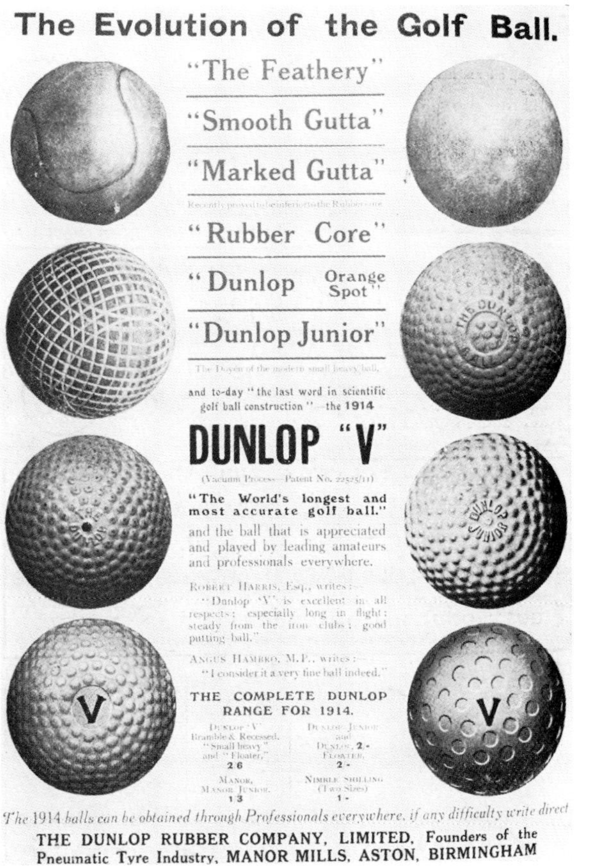

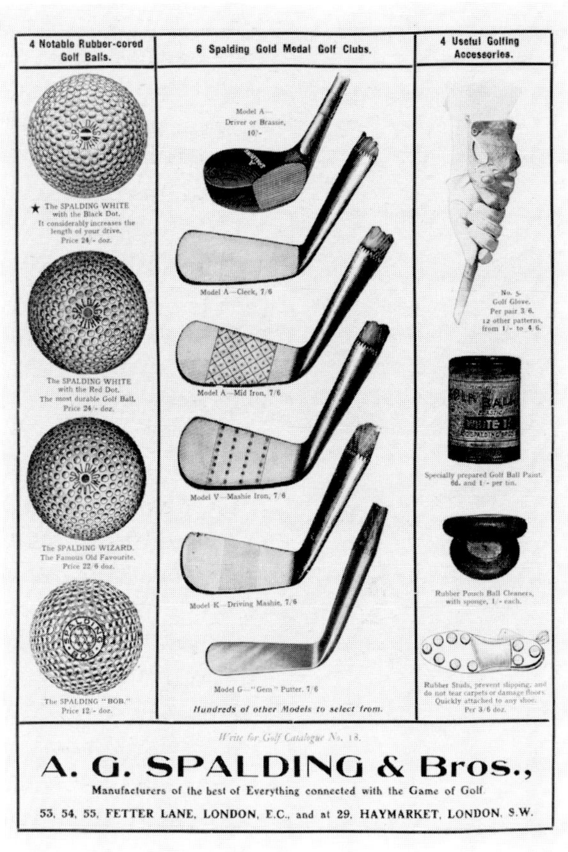

Left: The development of the golf ball according to a Dunlop ad, *Golf Monthly*, 1914
Right: Spalding's range of golf equipment, *Golf Illustrated*, 1907. The clubs are (from the top) brassie, cleek, mid-iron, mashie, driving mashie and putter

meant the son of a gentleman and which the Scots ironically adopted to describe loafers and scroungers). Caddie became the word for anyone who could be hired for a few pence to run errands or carry burdens, and thus came to be applied to the golfer's servant.

Another change during this period, a political one, had repercussions on the shrinking game of golf. In 1603, after years of sporadic warfare, the crowns of Scotland and England were united and James VI moved his court to London. With him came a vast retinue of courtiers and officials and naturally they brought their game with them, playing in the grounds of the royal palaces. Thus golf, which had been confined to the east coast of Scotland, sent out its first runner to take root in English soil and begin the slow process of spreading across the world.

It was a delicate shoot and might well have withered away, like real tennis, but for a nourishing influence from a surprising source, the freemasons. Only recently has research discovered the part played by the masons in keeping golf alive. For 200 years golf had been an informal game played on public recreational spaces. Players picked out likely areas to cut holes and away they went, negotiating their doubtless unpopular way past football matches, washerwomen hanging clothes on the whins, and archers. Friends might meet at regular times for golf but the sport was played solely as a match-play game so there was no reason to band into societies or clubs. The masons were, however, organised in their secret societies and so when they took up golf they brought to the game the concept of a club.

The secret nature of masonic tradition misled early golf historians in recording the origins of golf clubs. It was assumed that there were no clubs until the middle of the eighteenth century but we know that those official foundation dates represented the time when non-masons had joined the societies in such numbers that the nature of the clubs had to change. Unexplained and much earlier dates for the institution of those clubs now took on a relevant meaning because they represented the formation of golfing lodges whose records had to be destroyed under masonic rules lest the secrets of institution and ritual be revealed. And we also know that those early masons were not primarily interested in golf; they played the game to work up healthy appetites for their gargantuan feasts. In their excellent *Royal Blackheath*, Henderson and Stirk have pointed out that there were two clubs within the Blackheath club – the parent, or summer, club and the Knuckle club, which was the masonic section. The Honourable Company of Edinburgh Golfers was formalised as the first purely golfing club in 1744 but it clearly had an earlier masonic existence, just like Blackheath and the others.

One of the most influential members of the Honourable Company, and four times winner of the silver club which the city of Edinburgh presented as the world's first golf trophy, was William St Clair of Roslin, whose portrait (see page 51) remains one of the game's favourite prints and hangs in clubs around the world. St Clair was Hereditary Grandmaster Mason of Scotland and it was this association with a secret society which surely fuelled the contemporary notion that he derived his skill at golf and archery from witchcraft. Dame Margaret Ross, one of the pioneer women golfers at Musselburgh, was also believed to be a witch, using the black art to turn herself into a golf ball to frustrate her political enemies by deliberately rolling into hazards. She was also credited with becoming the ball of Sir Patrick Murray and, in return for political favours in parliament, directing herself unerringly into the hole.

By this time the first transplant of golf, or something akin to golf, had taken place in the New World. Court records of Fort Orange in New Netherland, known today as Albany, New York, tell of fines being imposed for playing golf in the streets as early as the year 1657. Were they golfers? The court proceedings were more concerned with the offence than describing the nature of the game and these records serve only to revive the debate about whether golf began in Holland or Scotland. There is persuasive if circumstantial evidence that the Dutch played a cross-country game with club and ball long before the first written record of golf in Scotland. A wooden ball about two inches in diameter has been retrieved from the mud of Amsterdam harbour, where it was buried under a pile driven into the silt to support a building, and metal club-heads have been discovered in what used to be the city dump. A village industry has existed for centuries for the making of leather balls, identical to Scottish featheries except that the filling was of uncombed lamb's-wool or sajet.

We know that the Dutch game was played over a formal course, the original target being an ornately carved post on each 'green' and that these posts were taken up after play for safe-keeping. What would have been more natural for Scottish officers serving in the Low Countries than to try their hand at this game? Perforce they would have had to play to the holes left in the ground. Probably we shall never know for sure just how and when golf began and it may well be that the game evolved gradually, through various transformations, from the Roman pastime of paganica. The Romans certainly made balls in the identical manner of the Dutch and Scottish craftsmen.

Whether it was golf or not which caused such displeasure among the magistrates of Fort Orange, it was certainly authentic golf which Scottish officers played in America during the revolutionary war. Before the end of the eighteenth century there were golf clubs in South Carolina and Savannah, Georgia, although some historians have questioned whether the members actually played golf. It might be that they were dining clubs, as a carry-over from the masonic style of the Knuckle club at Blackheath, and that they used the name of golf simply for the sake of tradition. At all events they disappeared without trace during the tumultuous growing pains of the republic, and the sound of club on ball was not heard again in America for seventy years.

At the dawn of the nineteenth century golf was at a low ebb, the exclusive preserve of a wealthy minority. The combined membership of the few clubs in Scotland and the one in England was a mere 500 players. It was the enthusiasm (or gluttony!) of the wealthy merchants and their feasts at places like the Green Man Tavern at Blackheath which kept golf alive until a fresh impetus was given to the game by another revolution in equipment.

Expatriate Scots, serving officers and merchants following the flag during the days of imperial expansion founded clubs in Calcutta (1829) and Bombay (1842) with the enthusiastic blessing of Blackheath, and clubs had been formed in Glasgow, Perth, Aberdeen, North Berwick and Manchester, but the year 1848 was the watershed for golf. One legend has it that a professor at St Andrews university accidentally stumbled on the possibilities of making golf balls out of gutta-percha after he had received a statue of Vishnu from India which had been packed in this resinous substance. Another theory has it that a Blackheath member received

Above: Opening day, Royal Calcutta, 1894

Opposite: Golf at Secunderabad, Madras, 1890

'The flies don't seem to have bothered you much, Major. What do you do for 'em?' 'Put treacle on my caddie!' (*Punch*) some sheets of gutta-percha from his agent in India in connection with his business and literally set the ball rolling. At all events, golf had a new ball.

Gutta-percha softens in hot water to a consistency which makes it possible to roll into a ball in the hands, and it then hardens as it cools. The early experimenters soon discovered that smooth, new balls dipped violently in flight, but that as the balls became marked by constant hitting they flew well. No doubt wooden-ball makers had found that their products improved with a roughening of the surface. These rudimentary experiments in aerodynamics produced more sophisticated surface patterns, a pimpled or bramble surface proving especially effective, and soon ball-makers had iron moulds and were producing gutta-percha balls like aspirins. The new ball was cheap and durable and golf retained its potential to become the game for Everyman. The golf explosion had dawned and by the end of the century the game had spread to every outpost of empire: Australia, Canada, India, Ceylon, New Zealand, South Africa, Shanghai, Singapore, Bangkok, Hong Kong – wherever the British (particularly the Scots) were stationed in any numbers, so they formed golf clubs.

One of the most interesting developments was the forerunner of what today we know as a tourist golf course. After the Duke of Wellington's victory at Orthez during the Peninsular War a group of his officers was stationed in the French town of Pau at the foot of the Pyrenees for rest and recuperation. They hunted for wild boar and those who had carried their golf clubs through the campaign played golf on a meadow. Clearly they enjoyed their stay at Pau, because some of them returned on holiday years later with their clubs. So Pau had a golfing tradition extending for forty-two years when the club was formally established in 1856 and became a popular resort for British families making the Grand Tour of Europe.

Although Pau is in France it is also, more importantly, in the Basque region, whose inhabitants acknowledge no boundaries except their own tribal limits in France and Spain. Nobody knows where the Basques came from originally, for their tongue is unrelated to any other European language except Cornish, but they are a race apart. Not least of their remarkable qualities is a natural aptitude for sport, which is perhaps best seen in their own game of *pelote*. However, they take to all ball games, not least golf. The Basque region embraced golf enthusiastically, especially at Biarritz, and every French golfer of note has been a Basque, including Arnaud Massy, who was the first foreign player to win the Open Championship.

Sweden proved to be infertile soil when the first seeds of golf were sown. A private six-hole course (later three more holes were added) was built by Robert and Edvard Sager on their estate at Ryfors in 1888 but it appears to have been a strictly family affair. A clergyman, the Rev. A. V. Despard, was the prime mover in the formation of the Gothenburg Golf

Opposite: Pau 1895

SKETCHES AT PAU
A
B
C
D
E
F

Club in 1891, the membership being mainly British and the club itself short-lived. Golf was not established on a permanent basis until 1904, after several more abortive attempts, near Gothenburg.

Development was slow and fifty years later there were only twenty-two courses in Sweden. However, the game received a remarkable stimulus through the example of the country's outstanding athlete, Sven Tumba. In Tumba the nation found a hero to rank among the gods of Norse mythology. This physically powerful giant with a debonair and fearless approach to sport represented Sweden in the Olympic Games at ice hockey, association football, water-skiing, skiing and ice-skating. The idolatry which he commanded was enhanced when he turned to the less physically demanding sport of golf, becoming a professional and representing Sweden in the World Cup. Tumba became a rabid evangelist of the game and, combined with the example of a golfing royal family, Sweden was won over to golf. During the 1960s the number of courses increased sixfold. Golf fever ensured continuing development and this process, combined with vigorous administration from the ruling bodies, made Sweden the strongest golfing nation in Europe outside the British Isles. This strength was manifested mainly by the successes of Swedish amateurs in international competition but it can be only a matter of time before Swedish professionals make their mark on the international scene.

Although there is fragmentary, and historically tantalising, evidence of golf on the North American continent in the eighteenth century and even earlier (in the form of newspaper items, court records and even advertisements for clubs and balls), such play seems to have been entirely informal. Presumably Scottish garrison officers took their clubs with them to America and Canada, for this was normal practice, and other expatriates, both Scottish and Dutch, maintained their enthusiasm for the game. However, formalised golf with purpose-built courses and properly constituted clubs, and continuity of those clubs, must be taken as the true birth of the game and here we are on firm historical ground.

The distinction, or blame as golf widows might prefer, for planting the permanent seed of golf on the North American continent belongs to Alexander Dennistoun, who was born in Edinburgh in 1821. As a young man he played at St Andrews and Musselburgh before emigrating to Canada to seek his fortune. In 1873, in association with two brother Scots, John and David Sidey, Dennistoun established the Royal Montreal Golf Club and became its first president. He had maintained close ties with his native land, becoming a member of several clubs in Scotland and England on visits home, and naturally he incorporated the Scottish club traditions at Royal Montreal. The club adopted the Royal and Ancient rules of golf, instituted an annual competition for a silver club, with the winners attaching silver balls in the manner of St Andrews, and the club uniform of red jacket was based on the form and design of Scottish clubs.

Opposite: Golf in Victoria, British Columbia, 1896

THE LINKS AT OAK BAY MOUNT BAKER (U.S.) IN THE DISTANCE

THE PAVILION.

DRIVING HOME.

SWAIN SC

SIWASH INDIAN SPECTATORS

"COOTZ" INDIAN WOOD

Less than two years later the Royal Quebec Golf Club was founded under the enthusiastic inspiration of Scottish regiments stationed in the ancient capital. The game spread and inevitably reached the maritime provinces where, in 1890, another St Andrews was founded in New Brunswick.

Thirteen years after the incorporation of Royal Montreal, golf took permanent root in the United States and by a similar process. John Reid, born in Dunfermline in 1840, had settled in Yonkers, New York, and had prospered with an iron foundry. In 1888 he and a few friends laid out a three-hole course in a cow pasture at Yonkers and a few months later, over dinner at Reid's home, the St Andrew's golf club was formally instituted. It appears that Reid was by no means consumed by missionary zeal. Golf thrived in spite of him rather than due to pioneering enthusiasm on his part. He opposed a move to a more spacious site and resisted an increase in the club's membership. Four years after the founding of St Andrew's, when the membership had grown to thirteen, progress in the form of a new road through the club's six-hole course on a butcher's meadow (to which it had graduated from the original cow pasture) forced another move. The club took over an apple orchard and thus became known as the Apple Tree Gang. One sequel to that move, as the game began to proliferate, was that novices at new clubs felt that apple trees were an essential element of golf and felt deprived if their courses were laid out on open meadows.

The real impetus for the expansion of American golf came from Long Island, where a group of enthusiasts commissioned the Scottish professional, Willie Dunn, to build them a twelve-hole course at Shinnecock Hills. The society architect Stanford White, who was to figure in a sensational scandal with a wealthy socialite, designed an imposing clubhouse and America thus had a standard which other clubs could follow. The pattern was set and even Reid had to bow to progress. St Andrew's moved again, creating a nine-hole course on a farm, but it was not until four years later, by which time golf had spread across the nation, that the country's premier club acquired its present location at Mount Hope and a proper 18-hole course.

It was a propitious time for golf to be introduced into America. The 1890s was a decade of ebullience and expansion, with a mood which might be compared with the 1920s. The motor car was coming into general use among the wealthy and golf, with its upper-class flavour, perfectly fitted the socially conscious times. During those ten years more than a thousand clubs were formed across the nation, some of them with courses which were rudimentary affairs indeed, for this was a great period for charlatans to climb aboard the golfing bandwagon. A Scottish accent was credentials enough to set up in business as a course designer, a process which often enough involved pacing a site and merely placing sticks in the ground at intervals with the instruction: 'Mow the grass for a

Left: 'Old Alick', portrait of Alick Brotherston, caddie and hole-cutter, Royal Blackheath, 1839, by R. S. E. Gallen
Below left: William Innes, Captain of Royal Blackheath, 1778, and caddie by L. F. Abbott
Below: William St Clair of Roslin, Captain, Honourable Company of Edinburgh Golfers, 1761, 1766, 1770–1, by Sir George Chalmers

Spanish-style clubhouse, Oak Knoll County Golf Club, California

tee here and a green here.' A really energetic and unscrupulous 'designer', like the notorious Tom Bendelow, could lay out two courses in a day.

The early attempts to regulate golf in America proved farcical. In 1894 the Newport GC invited twenty of the country's leading players to compete in a stroke-play tournament which was intended to be the inaugural national championship. Incredibly the tournament failed to gain that distinction simply because Charles Blair Macdonald did not win it (see page 68). Macdonald was an overbearing bull of a man who had been educated at St Andrews University and had become an accomplished player under the tutelage of Old Tom Morris, almost certainly good enough to endorse his opinion that he was the best native-born American golfer. Having inexplicably failed to win, Macdonald announced that it was not a proper championship and, such was the force of his personality, the organisers believed him. The St Andrew's club agreed to hold a match-play championship the following month and once again, owing to the after-effects of a premature victory party, Macdonald failed to win, losing in the final. Once more Macdonald dismissed the event as unworthy to be called a national championship.

Opposite: William Inglis, Captain, Honourable Company of Edinburgh Golfers, 1782–4, by David Allan

As a result of these unfortunate teething troubles, representatives of five clubs got together and founded the Amateur Golf Association of the United States, which duly became the United States Golf Association, responsible for the regulation of the game and its championships in America. An Amateur Championship was established, and Macdonald became its first winner. The same year the US Open Championship was established and the inaugural winner was a teenage assistant from Newport, Horace Rawlins. So the golf establishment was born and it was an establishment which had come to terms with Macdonald, and vice versa. He went on to create the National Links on Long Island, reproducing the challenge of the greatest holes he had played in Britain, and mellowed into the grand old man of American golf.

Another reason why the turn of the century was a propitious time for the introduction of golf into America was that it coincided with the development of the rubber-cored ball, although Spaldings, the sporting goods company, completely misjudged the importance of that development. In 1900 they brought over Harry Vardon on a promotional tour to boost the sales of the Vardon Flyer, one of the last brands of the doomed gutta-percha ball. If that was a commercial gaffe, the tour itself was a resounding success as a propaganda exercise. The English golfer astonished American galleries with his virtuosity and the precision of his play caused misgivings to the manager of a Boston department store where he was engaged to demonstrate golf by hitting balls into a net. Vardon quickly became bored by what he considered to be a fairly pointless exercise until he noticed the valve of a fire sprinkler projecting through the netting. It was about the size of a 10p coin and presented an interesting challenge as a suitable target. He hit it so often that the manager was afraid his store would be flooded and begged Vardon to desist.

On the more conventional part of his tour, Vardon played the better ball of a club's two best players, usually the professional and the club champion, and almost invariably won his matches handily. The tour was as significant in its way as the formation of the Shinnecock Hills club, for it provided a playing yardstick by which the professionals, many of them immigrants from Scotland, could measure their own progress. Another standard, and an extremely high one, had been set for American golf.

The Americans proved to be apt pupils and it was not long before the native-born professionals had surpassed the teachers. The growth of the game was arrested by a grim historical sandwich, a Depression between two world wars, but then circumstances combined to stimulate another era of rapid expansion. In the mid-fifties the nation was becoming enslaved by television and the new medium had a voracious appetite for all forms of entertainment, including sport. At this time a young man burst onto the golf scene who might have been created just for TV. Arnold Palmer brought the word charisma into the vocabulary of sport. In contrast to the

An early exhibition match – Joyce Wethered on her 1935 American tour, Columbia Country Club, Washington DC, with her partner Freddie McLeod (*left*) and her opponents Glenna Collett Vare and Roland Mackenzie

stern and conservative figures of professional golf, such as Ben Hogan and Byron Nelson, Palmer looked every inch the athlete, positively glowing with an animal vitality and built more like a middleweight boxer than a golfer. His game was also different, flamboyant, passionate, aggressive to the point of recklessness and, above all, powerful. He played golf which amateurs knew and understood, scorning danger and often putting his ball into impossible places. The difference with Palmer was that he then extricated it from trouble spots with massive recoveries. When things went well for Palmer his dashing tactics brought another word into currency: charge. Men saw in him an idealised version of themselves, the golfer they would like to be. Women saw another appeal, no less magnetic. Unprecedented crowds, Arnie's Army, flocked to follow this phenomenon and millions more followed his exciting progress on TV. Golf had never had such a recruiting sergeant. People who had believed golf to be a snobbish game for the country-club set watched Palmer, the kid from Latrobe whose father was a humble pro-greenkeeper, and decided that there must be something in this strange pastime.

It helped that there was also a golfer in the White House. Dwight D. Eisenhower was a national hero and TV showed him chipping balls around the lawns of No. 1 Pennsylvania Avenue and carpet-putting in the Oval office. So far as America was concerned the game was sold, respectable and universal. With Mark McCormack emerging as the most successful entrepreneur in the history of sport through his involvement with golf as Palmer's manager, the game spread like an epidemic to capture twenty million adherents.

In a global context America took to golf late. By the time those pioneers in Yonkers had established their founding club there were already 138 clubs in Britain and golf was thriving round the world. Precedence, however, meant little. It was America which inherited the kingdom of golf and dominated it, both in playing standards and in the fields of

Golfing buddies: Arnold Palmer and Dwight D. Eisenhower

organisation and innovation. The ancient Scottish game had well and truly been annexed by the New World.

The debate over the origins of the game may be lost in the controversial mists of history, with disputed claims for the Roman paganica, the Dutch kolf, an early cross-country version of Irish hurling, the French *jeu de mail* and, of course, the theory of pure Scottish invention. To that list we may add the further complication of the Patagonian Indians. There exists a print showing Araucanos Indians striking at a small sphere with implements which closely resemble early golf clubs, and they are being observed by an interested group of Spanish troops from whose uniforms the period has been determined as the early sixteenth century. But, since no further evidence of the game has survived, we are left with nothing but conjecture.

The Chilean game of El Sueca played by the Aracaunos Indians

However, with the coming of the industrial revolution we are on firmer historical ground. The latter period of the nineteenth century saw intense British commercial enterprise in South America, notably with massive investment in railway systems. British capital (much of it destined to disappear in a paper chase of worthless bonds) was poured into Argentina and Brazil, and with it went British engineers. They took their clubs with them on the voyage across the south Atlantic and played informal golf as the network of railways penetrated into the country. The distinction of being the first organised club belongs to the Buenos Aires Golf Club, formed by railwaymen in 1878, ten years before the St Andrew's club at Yonkers. Two more clubs were established within the next two years.

The native Argentinians soon took to golf and brought immense enthusiasm and a remarkable natural aptitude to the game, although in numbers strictly limited by economic considerations. The first club to be started by Argentinians was formed in Buenos Aires in 1908. Golf has never become a game for the masses in South America since its growth depends on social and economic development, and it is today at about the stage it reached in England between the two World Wars, as a minority pastime for the well-to-do middle classes, much as it is in continental Europe. There are fewer than 100 clubs in Argentina, for example, although the impact which Argentinians have made on the international scene is out of proportion to their modest numbers, with pride of place going to Roberto de Vicenzo, the most prolific international winner in the history of the game.

Roberto de Vicenzo

Railway engineers were also responsible for introducing golf to Brazil when, in 1890, a group of them commissioned Arthur Davidson to build a nine-hole course as an adjunct to the Sao Paulo Cricket Club. That same year Uruguay had its first club at Montevideo. Colombia, Mexico, Chile, Costa Rica and Panama have all joined the family of golfing nations. In general, it may be said that while South American golf is select, the courses are of remarkably fine quality and the club atmosphere a delightful compromise between native ebullience and sterner British traditions. The standard of play among the average club members is probably the highest in the world, with the possible exception of Scotland. The potential, especially in the world of professional golf, is enormous, for South America is one of the last bastions of the boy caddie.

Every major golfing nation has enjoyed a golden age of professional golf through recruitment from the ranks of caddies. Britain had the triumvirate of Harry Vardon, James Braid and J. H. Taylor, just as American caddies developed into Ben Hogan, Gene Sarazen and Walter Hagen. Golf's caddie tradition perfectly suited the sharply stratified social system of Spain, the land of Don Quixote and Sancho Panza, in the early years of the twentieth century when the game was in its infancy on the Iberian peninsula. Hardly a name appears on the honour boards of the pioneer clubs without the noble prefix of duke, count or marquis, and the clubs themselves, such as the founding Real Club de la Puerta de Hierro at Madrid, were few and far between. The Civil War had its repressive effects on golf, as on everything else, and it was not until the tourist boom following the Second World War that solid progress was made. The invasion by thousands of northern European tourists, hungering for the delights of sunshine and *rioja* at a penny a glass, nourished a building boom along the Costa del Sol, a concrete ribbon of hotels and apartments on the Mediterranean sward. For up-market developments a golf course was as essential as a swimming pool as a holiday amenity, and a chain of fine courses was built. The holidaymakers wanted caddies, a rare luxury at home but in Spain an indulgence costing only a few pesetas. Spanish golf, inheritor of a paternalistic tradition, provided schoolrooms at many clubs where the peasant lads could receive rudimentary education between their bag-carrying duties.

Inevitably, the boy caddies also spent their idle hours trying their hand at this alien game. Many became proficient and graduated as skilled professionals, notably the Miguel brothers who became popular and successful tournament players. Their example inspired other youngsters, such as Ramon Sota, Angel Gallardo, Manuel Pinero and, above all, Severiano Ballesteros. Spain thus had a forcing house of outstanding professional players, out of all proportion to the strength of the amateur game and exemplified by Spain's success in two World Cups. In 1976 Ballesteros and Manuel Pinero beat the world's best at Palm Springs,

Severiano Ballesteros, US Masters 1980

California, and the following year Ballesteros teamed up with Antonio Garrido to retain the trophy in Manila. By winning the British Open Championship and the US Masters, Ballesteros established himself in the very forefront of world golf.

Those apprenticeships for golf are now disappearing because of social progress, compulsory schooling and improved economic conditions, and for these countries the recruitment to professionalism has passed to the area of successful amateur players. In South America boys still have to supplement the family income, and those who do so by carrying the clubs of golfers are encouraged to develop their talents for the game. The possibility of more Roberto de Vicenzos appearing on the world stage of golf is an appealing prospect indeed.

The same possibilities exist throughout the East where native skills and local traditions have already introduced a beneficial influence on the game, particularly in the departments of dexterity, such as chipping, bunker play and putting. Any novice professional seeking guidance on the artistry of golf would be advised to go east. In the orient the touch game has been refined into the region of wizardry. It began, as we have seen, in India but it was not, as commonly supposed, Scottish garrison troops who planted the seed. Dundee was the great jute centre during the nineteenth century and the captains of the industry, known at St Andrews as the jute barons, sent factors to India to purchase and ship the raw material back to

Scotland. These were the men who, in 1829, established the first club at Dum Dum, Calcutta, now the site of the city's airport, making it the first golf club outside Britain. The success of the Taysiders in Calcutta encouraged the British colony in Bombay to start a club in 1842. This club, later to become Royal Bombay, had a chequered early history before becoming established on a firm and permanent basis. By the middle of the century there were as many clubs in India and Ceylon (now Sri Lanka) as there were in Great Britain, reflecting the growth of British influence and the capacity of the expatriates to impose British institutions on an alien environment.

With golf having established a strong bridgehead in India, the game now infiltrated further east. By the end of the century clubs had been established throughout the east. Enthusiasts laid out a few holes on the racecourse at Singapore, followed by a similar venture in Malaya. In Hong Kong a dinner party discussion resulted in a small advertisement being placed in the local paper seeking support for a golf club. There were only nine replies but that was enough to make a start with another racecourse golf club. The building of the Siamese railway system brought golfing engineers to what is now Thailand and it was here, and in the Philippines, that the game was to enslave the population. That is getting rather ahead of the story, because in those early days around the turn of the century, and for a further fifty or so years, golf was essentially a pastime for the British colony. A few locals, mainly wealthy men who had been sent to be educated in Britain, took to the game with enthusiasm, but at base it was a game which preserved one of the links with home for the administrators, businessmen and serving officers from Britain. The adoption of golf as a national game, albeit for the upper classes, came after the Second World War, and today in Thailand and the Philippines it can be said to have reached epidemic proportions – to the point where preferment in government service is jokingly said to depend on improvements in a man's handicap.

However, in this context of golf madness there is nowhere in the world like Japan. Here the game followed the traditional pattern, with a British enthusiast starting the ball rolling. Arthur Groom, a merchant, chose the unlikely site of the summit of Mount Rokko, near Kobe, to build the country's first course. That was in 1903 and getting to the course involved a 90-minute mountain climb. The fact that the golfer was borne on the back of a coolie took the labour out of the climb but adherence to the game still required exceptional enthusiasm. The Hirono club, possibly the finest golf course in the orient, was built in 1932 but, although Japanese caddies developed into fine professionals, the game remained basically a foreign diversion in a country firmly set in its established ways. There were fewer than twenty clubs in Japan at the outbreak of the Second World War.

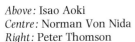

Above: Isao Aoki
Centre: Norman Von Nida
Right: Peter Thomson

This is not the place to ponder whether golf is good or bad for a nation. The facts are enough and the fact in this case was that after the war Japan went golf crazy. Most games prosper because they suit the geography and the working traditions of a country. Golf captured Japan in the face of a hostile environment. The country is small, overpopulated and mountainous; every square metre of fertile land is intensely cultivated and much too precious for the frivolous activity of hitting a golf ball. However, the game was not to be denied. Architects dynamited mountains to create ribbons of fairways in order to feed the growing hunger for golf. By western standards the costs were horrendous and reflected in membership dues, largely restricting golf to senior executives of Japan's flourishing business community. But the craze for golf permeated right through Japanese society, fed by twice-daily TV programmes and intense newspaper coverage.

The answer was the driving range. Look out over the rooftops of any Japanese city and you will see nets suspended from poles, as if an army of monster spiders had swathed the city in cobwebs. These are driving ranges – from modest, four-bay establishments, run by one man with a bucket of balls, to vast, multi-tiered golf centres with thousands of energetic Japanese beating golf balls into the floodlit night.

It is impossible to make an accurate head count of Japanese golfers. For a start there is the problem of defining what constitutes a golfer, since the normal statistics of club membership are meaningless. However, it has been estimated that Japan has ten million active golfers and half of them are condemned to spend their entire golfing lives on driving ranges, with

Left: Bobby Locke
Right: Gary Player with his American caddie Rabbit (Alfred Dyer)

never an opportunity to experience the unique thrill of hitting a shot off real turf. In Japan a green-fee ticket tied to your golf bag is a status symbol, proving that once in your life you played a real golf course.

Australia and South Africa have both made an impact on world golf out of all proportion to their populations. In both cases it was tough going in the early days because the climate was not conducive to the maintenance of large areas of prepared turf. We have seen in other parts of the world, however, that a temperate climate was less important than determination and enthusiasm among the founding fathers. Royal Adelaide (1870) is Australia's premier club but there is some doubt about whether the honour of primacy in South Africa should be bestowed on Royal Cape GC, founded by Scottish officers in 1885, or on Maritzburg, which may have come into existence the previous year. New Zealand saw the formation of its first club at Christchurch in 1873.

In all these areas the British tradition was strong because of the immigrant population, and the development of the game followed the same steady pattern as at home. With advances in irrigation and greenkeeping techniques the Australians, New Zealanders and South Africans were able to build more and better courses as the years went by. What is more, once the problems of agronomy had been overcome these countries were able to make huge advances in playing standards because of favourable climatic conditions.

The game of golf comes from hardy stock, weathered in the chill nor'easters of Fife and hardened by the frosts and snow of Britain. Whatever its origins, it was here that the game became established and playing standards were set by the pioneers of the early years. And it was exiled Britons, mostly Scots, who, as we have seen, drew the game to the furthest corners of the earth. Given a more amenable environment, it is hardly surprising that this sturdy plant should flourish ever more vigorously, as it clearly has in Australasia, South Africa and the southern areas of the United States. These are the parts of the world which set the pace in playing standards because these are the places where opportunities and conditions for improvement flourish most strongly. Social and economic progress will surely bring more areas into the list of forcing grounds of golf. The Far East and South America in particular could well join the superpowers of the game; Japan has already achieved that distinction.

What further worlds has golf left to conquer? The Communist nations have largely set their hearts against a game which they brand as an élitist activity, an assessment which was never completely true and which is demonstrably less true with each passing week as adherents from all walks of life take to the links. As with the earlier periods of expansion, penetration by golf behind the Iron Curtain must await auspicious social, ecomonic and political conditions. The question may now perhaps be asked whether, if golf followed détente into the Communist world, it would be able to play a beneficial part in international relations. The ideal of international brotherhood through sport has been compromised in football, the Olympic Games and other games. So far, golf has escaped such animosities. Is it, then, different from other games? Is true sportsmanship more deeply rooted in golf? Does the very nature of the game promote good will?

Certainly the fact that golf is a self-regulating game, which cannot be played without a marked degree of self-discipline and honesty, sets it apart from sports in which contestants are tempted to take advantage of the rules. Be that as it may, whether golf enhances the nobler qualities of human nature and subdues the worst or not, it is self-evident that the game has become the *lingua franca* of international sport. A Japanese businessman, an American diplomat and a Swedish academic may have nothing in common and be unable to exchange the simplest idea in each others' languages. But put them on the first tee of a golf course and at once they achieve a rapport through the agency of golf. By sharing the triumphs and disasters of this great game they can form sure judgements of each others' characters and establish a bond. They are members of a worldwide fellowship which transcends national prejudices, class bigotries and the divisive influences of race and religion. Perhaps bond is the wrong word. On reflection the role which golf has to play in international relationships is better expressed as a lubricant. In itself it may not be the cog in the machinery of world relationships which some have claimed for it, but it certainly makes that clanking machinery turn more smoothly.

CHAPTER THREE

America Gets the Bug

by Ross Goodner

The game of golf, like the pilgrims of an earlier day, didn't gain a permanent foothold in America on the first attempt. But when golf did come to stay, in 1888, not surprisingly it was because a Scotsman sent for it. The gentleman was John Reid, a native of Dunfermline (see page 69), who asked his friend Robert Lockhart to pick up some clubs and balls on his next trip to Britain. These items were duly purchased in the shop of Old Tom Morris in St Andrews and delivered to Reid, who tried them out with some friends on a rude, three-hole course across the street from his home in Yonkers, New York. The date was 22 February 1888.

The first golfers at Yonkers, New York

Reid's group soon moved around the corner to a 30-acre plot, where they laid out six holes and organised themselves into the St Andrew's (with an apostrophe) Golf Club. Their 'clubhouse' was for some years a large apple tree, from whose branches hung jugs of liquid refreshment and whence came the name by which they are known in the history books: the Apple Tree Gang. By the time the club made its final move, in 1897, clubs were springing up everywhere and golf was beginning to play an important role in America's social life.

St Andrew's Golf Club, New York, today

It is difficult today to realise just how slowly the word got around in those days – on both sides of the Atlantic. Horace Hutchinson has written about the time he and Leslie Balfour were asked if they would give a game to two stonemasons from Elie. The pair turned out to be Jack Simpson and Douglas Rolland, who finished first and second in the Open Championship later that year – yet they had been virtually unknown in St Andrews only a few miles from Elie. It was the same in America a century ago, except that fledgling golfers there not only hadn't heard of 'two stonemasons from Elie', they hadn't, so to speak, even heard of Elie itself.

This was demonstrated in 1892 when John C. Ten Eyck, one of the pioneers of St Andrew's, visited the offices of Samuel Parrish, a founder of the new Shinnecock Hills club on Long Island. Ten Eyck said he had heard they were playing golf down on Long Island, to which Parrish, astonished, replied: 'Why, yes. Does anyone else play golf in this country?' Shinnecock Hills, which had come into being in 1891, was to become in many ways even more significant than St Andrew's. It was designed by Willie Dunn, who had hit a few shots for some American travellers while laying out a course at Biarritz. They were so taken with the game that they engaged Dunn to create a course on Long Island and, in so doing, they set in motion the migration of Scottish professionals across the Atlantic.

Shinnecock Hills Golf Club, *c.* 1900

Shinnecock also led the way in other areas. It was the first to have a clubhouse (designed by the eminent Stanford White), the first club to be incorporated, and the first to have a waiting list of those wanting to join. And, if the truth were known, because of its seaside location and the man who designed it, Shinnecock was the first American course that actually looked like a golf course.

After Dunn arrived, his nephews Seymour and John came. Then there were Tom Anderson and his sons, Willie and Tom Jr, and then the Smiths from Carnoustie – Alex, Willie, George, James and Macdonald. American golfers were eager to learn about this new game from the Scottish experts,

The Smith brothers: Alex (*left*) and Macdonald

Charles Blair Macdonald

but they had little idea of how to go about it. Fred McLeod, who came from North Berwick, recalls those early years:

Americans had no golf tradition then, unlike baseball, and they really had very little idea of how they should swing the club, so we had to teach them almost from scratch. I gave plenty of lessons. If someone came and asked for a set of clubs, I made them usually. That's what a pro was for; you weren't hired as a good player.

Once the professional left the course, however, he wasn't always treated with respect. Alex Smith told of being pelted with rocks by neighbourhood boys on his way home from work at Washington Park in Chicago. And golfers for years were ridiculed for wasting their time on 'cow pasture pool'.

But at the clubs themselves golf was serious business, so serious that soon the inevitable cry arose for a tournament to determine a national champion. This drive was led by Charles Blair Macdonald, a strong-willed man who had learned the game while a student at St Andrews. Macdonald, probably the best player in the country in those formative years, also was to become famous as a course architect. When he laid out the Chicago Golf Club's course in 1893 it was the first in America to boast eighteen holes.

Two tournaments in 1894 – one stroke-play and the other match-play – were held to determine a national champion. Macdonald finished second in both events and in each case he contrived reasons why it could not possibly qualify as a championship (see page 53). As a direct result a meeting was held to establish a governing body for American golf. Nine delegates, representing five clubs, met in December of 1894 and formed what is now the United States Golf Association.

An immediate result was the first sanctioned Amateur Championship, held at Newport in October 1895. And to the surprise of some and the disappointment of many Macdonald emerged as America's first champion. His victim was Charles Sands of Newport, who was dispatched by 12 and 11. Almost as an afterthought an Open Championship was held the day after the Amateur. It was won by Horace Rawlins, a 21-year-old Englishman who had come to America the previous January. He scored 173 for four trips around the nine-hole course and that was two strokes better than Willie Dunn.

Golf in America progressed quite nicely over the next few years. Then, in 1900, it took a quantum leap. In that year A. G. Spalding, a sporting goods firm that had taken up the manufacture of golf clubs in the 1890s, put on the market a new ball, the Vardon Flyer, and brought the great Harry Vardon himself to the United States to promote it. Vardon played countless exhibition matches up and down the country from February to November, losing only twice to a single opponent. His other defeats, and there weren't many of them, came when he was playing the best ball of two or more. He played virtually non-stop, except for a hurried

Opposite: John Reid, c. 1900, by Frank Fowler

Page 70: The Great Triumvirate: J. H. Taylor, James Braid and Harry Vardon, by Clement Fowler

CLEMENT
FLOWER

Previous page: The eighteenth green and the R & A clubhouse, St Andrews

Right: The sixteenth hole, Augusta National, during the Masters
Below: The sixteenth hole, Cypress Point, California: the most photographed hole in golf
Below right: Indoor golf range, Osaka, Japan

visit home for the Open Championship, won by J. H. Taylor. By coincidence, Taylor also was in the United States in 1900 and both entered the US Open that autumn at the Chicago Golf Club. Vardon won it by two strokes from Taylor and the next player was seven strokes adrift.

Vardon's visit not only stimulated existing American golfers, it also gained converts from the thousands who came out to see his exhibitions. Thus it was a great artistic success. However, it wasn't so profitable for Vardon. Never of robust health, he seemed to lose vigour during his rigorous trip and many felt he was never quite the same again after returning home. A final indignity was the failure of the Vardon Flyer to gain lasting success. The rubber-cored ball was introduced not long after Vardon's tour, and the gutties became obsolete virtually overnight.

The game was changing in other ways – at least in America. Unlike the golf clubs of Britain, American clubs became known as 'country clubs', attracting all members of the family and sometimes utilised for social functions as much as for golf. Only at a few men-only clubs, known at the time as Eveless Edens, was a man able to enjoy a round and lift a glass with friends without having women and children underfoot.

Golf was not a seaside game in America, with few exceptions, and courses might be laid out anywhere, usually near the more affluent sections of towns and cities or near the summer homes of the well-to-do. As the game became more fashionable, more and more people took lessons from pros who then sold more clubs and balls. Nearby farms were then purchased and subdivided into lots on which fine homes were built, better roads were constructed and the wealthy suburb was born. Then, as the automobile began to replace the horse and carriage, people could travel greater distances to play the game, and thus began a trend that continues to this day: members sell their club to real-estate developers for a handsome profit, then purchase land farther away from the city and build a new course, usually with a clubhouse whose size and appointments far exceed the members' needs.

While Americans were, typically, putting their own distinctive mark on the trappings of the game, the good scores still were being turned in by transplanted Scots and Englishmen. In the decade following Vardon's 1900 visit, the United States Open was won four times by Willie Anderson, twice by Alex Smith, and once each by Laurie Auchterlonie, Alex Ross, Fred McLeod and George Sargent. Americans were playing the game better and better, but not well enough. When Walter Travis went to Sandwich in 1904 and won the British Amateur – and made few friends in the process – it wasn't strictly an American triumph since Travis himself had migrated to the US from Australia. Chick Evans went over in 1911 and won the French Amateur, but the same year Harold Hilton more than restored the balance by winning the US Amateur at Apawamis.

However, it was in that year of 1911 that Johnny McDermott became the first home-bred professional to win the US Open. He repeated his triumph in 1912 and was so full of himself that he went to Muirfield in search of bigger game but was decisively repulsed. But the stage was set for a historic breakthrough.

Harry Vardon was touring the United States again in 1913, this time in the company of Ted Ray and under the aegis of Lord Northcliffe. As before, innumerable exhibition matches were played, with the visitors winning the vast majority of them, but unlike Vardon's previous visit the centrepiece of the trip was the US Open, which had taken on somewhat more importance in the 13-year interval. Not only had more good players migrated from Britain, but the home-breds, as they were called, were beginning to display a talent for the game. McDermott was looking for a third straight title and among the newcomers at The Country Club was Walter Hagen, on hand 'to help the boys beat Vardon and Ray'.

The field also included a 20-year-old amateur named Francis Ouimet, and his surprise victory over the British pair in a play-off is now familiar even to casual dabblers in golf lore. It has often been said that Ouimet's triumph 'put golf on the front pages' of America, and there is no doubt it had a great impact. Not only did the victory serve as an inspiration to countless American youngsters who might have passed the game by, it also gave the game its first common touch. Previously golf was thought to be a diversion for the rich, and while it continued to be known as a 'rich man's game' for many years, it nevertheless gained a large measure of respectability with those who had not been born with a silver spoon – or brassie – in their mouths.

Left: Ted Ray and Harry Vardon
Right: Francis Ouimet and his caddie Eddie Lowery, US Open 1913

Left: Walter Hagen
Centre: Bobby Jones aged 14
Right: Gene Sarazen

Although Hagen won his first US Open in 1914 and Jim Barnes won the first championship of the newly-formed Professional Golfers' Association in 1916, golf in America still was a game dominated by amateurs. Jerry Travers won the Open in 1915 and Chick Evans in 1916, and it was they the crowds came out to see at the many Red Cross exhibitions held after America entered the war in 1917. Another attraction in those matches was a group of teenage players that included Bobby Jones, a 15-year-old who already was making galleries sit up and take notice.

Jones had made his championship debut in 1916 when only fourteen years old and had astonished everyone with his play in the Amateur at Merion. Only a violent temper seemed to stand between him and success. He conquered the temper, of course, just as he conquered all his opponents, but his successes had to wait a few years. Meanwhile Walter Hagen won the Open again when competition was resumed in 1919. And in 1920 Harry Vardon returned to the United States for his last visit and Hagen made his first visit to Britain. The 1920 US Open, at Inverness, was won by Ted Ray, but Vardon might have won it. He was leading in the last round, but a storm arose and the strong winds cost him valuable strokes. That Open also was significant as being the first for Jones and Gene Sarazen, both just eighteen years old. Hagen's debut in Britain was ignominious, but it marked the beginning of an American invasion that continued intermittently for decades, like the Hundred Years War.

Vardon, Ray and Hilton weren't the only British golfers making successful visits to America. Dorothy Campbell, of North Berwick, became the first to win the championship of both countries in the same year when she won the US Women's Amateur in October of 1909. The first US Women's Championship had been held in 1895, just a few weeks after Horace Rawlins' victory at Newport, and by the time of Miss Campbell's arrival American women were playing with a measure of skill as well as enthusiasm. At the same time Bobby Jones was emerging as a golfing prodigy, another Atlanta youngster, Alexa Stirling, was doing the same. Alexa won the Women's Amateur in 1916, then made many friends for women's golf during those wartime exhibitions with Jones. She won the national championship again in 1919 and 1920 before being supplanted at the top by an even greater prodigy, Glenna Collett.

Above: Dorothy Campbell
Right: Glenna Collett with Alex Smith, 1925

Glenna owed much of her success to the teaching of Alex Smith, and she was considered the first American woman to 'attack the hole rather than play to the green'. She entered her first championship in 1919, at the age of sixteen, and scored the first of her six victories three years later. Glenna was a popular figure during the 1920s, a decade when America virtually conferred sainthood on its sports heroes. Many of these, such as the baseball stars Babe Ruth and Ty Cobb and the football star Red Grange, were not famous outside the United States. Others were international figures, such as Jack Dempsey and Bill Tilden. Jones, Hagen and Sarazen were in this class, as a result of their frequent trips to Britain and, in the case of Hagen and Sarazen, because of their extensive exhibition tours to all parts of the globe. It was, after all, exhibitions that provided for the great players what today would be called discretionary income.

From the earliest days of the game in America club professionals in colder climates headed south when their clubs closed for the winter. Many of them gravitated to southern California and even more became regular winter residents of Florida, and it was only natural that competitions sprang up. In the beginning these events were promoted by owners of resorts, who saw tournament golf as a means to attract people to their watering holes, and as the idea caught on more resorts and holiday communities sought to capitalise on this popular activity.

Although there wasn't a professional tour worthy of the name until the late 1920s, nevertheless a series of winter events was being played a decade earlier. And by the early 1920s players who had been in California were stopping in Texas and Louisiana for tournaments on the way east to compete in Florida events. This catch-as-catch-can circuit usually wound up at Pinehurst, North Carolina, in late March and the pros began heading back north to the club jobs that would occupy them until the next winter.

Donald Ross on a sand green at Pinehurst

Pinehurst, a pioneer golfing resort developed by the Tufts family around the turn of the century, was the headquarters of Donald Ross, a native of Dornoch who had become America's most sought-after course architect. After Charles Blair Macdonald opened his National Golf Links in 1911, course architecture came into its own in America. Once they got a look at the National, club members never again would be satisfied with a course laid out in an afternoon with eighteen stakes and some string. People could see at once that course design, done properly, was an art in which the architect sought to match wits with the golfer rather than bludgeon him.

Some outstanding courses were designed by amateurs, such as Pine Valley (George Crump), Merion (Hugh Wilson), Pebble Beach (Douglas Grant and Jack Neville) and Oakmont (Henry and William Fownes), but in general prospective buyers sought out the best professional architects, which in the 1920s and 1930s meant Ross or A. W. Tillinghast, or perhaps Alister Mackenzie, who did Augusta National and Cypress Point (see page 72). Ross claimed to have designed or remodelled some 600 courses during his career, although probably no more than half of these were projects in which he was heavily involved. At the height of his fame he would 'lay out' courses with no more knowledge of the property to be developed than the topographical maps sent to him at Pinehurst. But people were willing to settle for this in order to say that they had a Donald Ross golf course. To this day it is a matter of pride for a club to boast of its 'original' Ross course. Ross did marvellous work and his credits include such outstanding courses as Oakland Hills, Inverness, Scioto, Aronomink, Oak Hill, Seminole, Interlachen, Salem, Wannamoisett, Winchester, Plainfield and many more. Tillinghast, who was every bit as talented as Ross, designed such courses as Winged Foot, Baltusrol, Ridgewood, Shawnee, the Five Farms course at Baltimore Country Club, Quaker Ridge and San Francisco Golf Club.

Following World War II Robert Trent Jones came to the fore, designing dozens of courses and also doing substantial remodelling jobs, often at the request of clubs seeking to make their courses tougher for upcoming

Spyglass Hill, California, and its designer Robert Trent-Jones

championships. Jones is as well known for his remodelling of Oakland Hills, Baltusrol and Firestone as he is for such original work as Hazeltine, Spyglass Hill, Bellerive, Dorado Beach, Mauna Kea and Sotogrande. Although Jones became known for extremely long teeing grounds and large greens well guarded by bunkers – and drew much criticism for the severity of his courses – he almost single-handedly raised course architecture to its present level of esteem. A resort developer who could advertise 'a 7000-yard championship Robert Trent Jones course' was almost guaranteed success.

Jones' chief rival was Dick Wilson, who designed Pine Tree, Doral, Laurel Valley, Bay Hill, LaCosta, Meadow Brook and many more. Wilson had worked for the firm of Toomey and Flynn, helping design such courses as Shinnecock Hills, before going out on his own. Today course architecture is such a desirable profession that Jack Nicklaus, Arnold Palmer and Gary Player devote much time to it, with Nicklaus, particularly, having done good work at Muirfield Village, Shoal Creek and elsewhere.

Trent Jones is still active and his sons, Robert Jr and Rees, are also doing good work. Wilson is gone, but his style is seen in the courses of Joe Lee and Bob Von Hagge, both of whom trained under Wilson. Also prominent are George Fazio and his nephew Tom, and Pete Dye, whose distinctive use of railroad ties and large waste areas has surely reached its limits in the controversial Players Club in Florida.

All this sophisticated design was far from the minds of those pioneer pros of the 1920s who gathered in Pinehurst for their final winter competition. Doubtless they admired Donald Ross' courses, but they had to have been more concerned with getting back to a regular job – and a regular pay check. The point was that playing tournament golf all winter was a pleasant diversion and might even keep the better players in groceries for a time, but it was only that – a diversion. The club job, with its lessons, club-making and club repair, remained the principal source of income for all but a few professional golfers. Those few, such as Walter Hagen, who chose not to pursue the life of a club pro, soon found that exhibition tours were the only means of bringing in enough money to keep the creditors from the door.

Whatever Hagen's original reasons for going to Britain to play in the Open Championship, he quickly learned that victory was the entrée to a world of fast cars, beautiful women and champagne. His disregard for money was legendary and whether or not he actually gave his first-prize cheque to his caddie on one occasion in Britain doesn't really matter. People believed such stories because they wanted to and this suited Sir Walter just fine. He repeatedly said a championship meant a title he could take on the road; it was the exhibitions that paid the bills. Sarazen, who was thrust into stardom and a friendly rivalry with Hagen almost before he was old enough to vote, wasn't all that flamboyant, but he was shrewd enough to follow the trail Hagen was blazing. Travelling with a variety of playing companions, but most notably with Joe Kirkwood, both Hagen and Sarazen took the game around the world and into places where even Scottish soldiers had never taken it.

Jones, the biggest hero of them all, bore little resemblance to Hagen and Sarazen. He was, in the first place, an amateur, a Southern gentleman who not only read books but wrote them. Furthermore, unlike most leading amateurs Jones played in but a handful of tournaments a year and in some years played only two – the US Open and Amateur. Yet he won thirteen championships in eight seasons, and so dominated the American scene that many pros all but conceded victory to him whenever he entered a tournament.

When Jones won his first championship – the 1923 US Open, after a play-off with Bobby Cruickshank – his backers breathed a sigh of relief that he had finally broken through after seven years of trying. Yet he was only twenty-one at the time. When, in 1930, he won the Open and Amateur Championships of America and Britain in the same year he was only twenty-eight, but the strain of the competition was apparent and he looked to be much older. Then he retired, full of memories if not of years.

'Welcome home.'
Bobby Jones, July 1923

During his eight championship seasons American golf underwent substantial changes. At the beginning of the decade such stars as Jock Hutchison and Jim Barnes continued the domination of the foreign-born pros, but over the years such personalities as Leo Diegel, Johnny Farrell, Al Watrous, Joe Turnesa and Bill Mehlhorn (and another Scottish transplant named Tommy Armour) joined Jones, Hagen and Sarazen in moving America toward a dominant position in the game. As native-born players moved to the fore the game became more popular, and soon everyone seemed to be trying to look like a golfer – or what they thought a golfer looked like. At country clubs everywhere men lounged on the veranda or in the bar wearing plus-fours, argyle stockings and pullover sweaters, parting their hair in the middle and sticking it down in the style of Valentino – and Hagen. At the end of the decade the stock market collapse had made the Era of Wonderful Nonsense a little less wonderful, but there remained enough ticker tape to shower on Jones in a parade along Broadway after his Grand Slam in 1930.

The Great Depression, the advent of steel shafts and the absence of Bobby Jones gave the golf scene a different appearance as the 1930s began. A bona fide professional tour had emerged, but the players were out there for the love of the game as much as for the money, because the latter had virtually disappeared. Paul Runyan was the leading money winner in 1934 with $6767, and when Sam Snead won almost $20,000 in 1938 it seemed like all the money in the world to a nation that only recently had trouble in finding someone who could spare a dime.

The first US Open without Jones was in 1931 at Inverness, Ohio, where Jones had made his debut in the event eleven years before. Without Jones to set the pace it appeared for a time that there wouldn't be a winner. Billy Burke and George Von Elm tied after 72 holes and remained tied after a 36-hole play-off the next day. Still another 36 holes were played before Burke won by a single stroke. Things returned somewhat to normal in 1932 when Sarazen, who people were surprised to learn was still only thirty years old, won both Opens finally to solidify his place in the game after a decade of spotty play. In the US Open at Fresh Meadow he played the last 28 holes in 100 strokes. Hagen, despite his four British Opens and five PGA Championships (four of them in succession) in the 1920s, had not won the US Open since 1919 – in fact he had never finished ahead of Jones in any championship. And now that Jones was gone, Hagen had lost the great powers of recovery with niblick and putter that had taken the heart out of countless opponents. He was fourth in 1933 and third in 1935, but there were to be no more championships.

A lot of good players emerged in the 1930s, men like Runyan, Denny Shute, Craig Wood, Harry Cooper, Horton Smith, Henry Picard – and especially Lawson Little who won the Amateur Championships of the US and Britain in both 1934 and 1935 before turning professional amid

Sam Snead

considerable fanfare, and Ralph Guldahl, who almost quit the game in 1935 only to come back and win two Opens and a Masters in three years before disappearing as quickly as he had emerged. But in 1937 two men who were to attain even greater stature first came to prominence.

After several years of struggling and honing his game, Byron Nelson entered the public consciousness by winning the Masters, a tournament founded three years earlier by Bobby Jones. That same spring Sam Snead had come out of West Virginia to make a spectacular debut on the tour and he went on to finish a close second to Guldahl in the US Open. Guldahl won again in 1938, then it was Nelson's turn in 1939 after Snead took a tragic 8 on the final hole. Attracting almost no notice in that 1939 field was the man in sixty-second place: Ben Hogan.

Ben Hogan was the same age as Nelson and Snead (all were born in 1912), but his development as a great player was much slower. While Snead's skills apparently came out of the cradle with him and Nelson's developed systematically but inevitably, Hogan's came reluctantly, tortuously. He had tried to make it on the professional tour two or three times during the Depression years, but his small stake always disappeared as rapidly – and regularly – as his chronic hooks disappeared into the rough. But Hogan was dogged, and almost certainly he hit more practice balls than anyone before him had done. Suddenly, in 1940, he began to win, and once he got the hang of it it appeared he might never stop winning. He was leading money winner in 1940, 1941 and 1942 – then the war intervened.

Bob Hope and Bing Crosby

In World War II, as in its predecessor, countless exhibitions were played on behalf of the Red Cross and other war relief agencies. Two of the most tireless performers were Bing Crosby and Bob Hope, two golfomaniacs who played at every opportunity. Crosby began to sponsor his own tournament in 1937 and Hope was to follow suit in 1960. It would be difficult to name anyone who did more to promote the game.

There was no professional golf to speak of in 1943, but the circuit was revived in 1944 with a cast of players who were too old for conscription or had failed to pass their military physical examinations. In this latter group was Nelson, a 'free bleeder' whose blood required almost four times as long as normal to clot. He won a number of events in 1944 and was leading money winner, but his performance, fine as it was, paled before his work in 1945. In that year he won nineteen tournaments, eleven of them in succession, and averaged 68.33 strokes per round. He was awesome, and it was a cruel twist of fate that he hit his peak at a time when his great natural rivals were not on the scene. Hogan and Snead returned to golf late in 1945 and won tournaments, but only a brief, intense exchange of victories by Nelson and Hogan near the end of the season hinted at what might have been. Midway through 1946 Nelson, bone-weary as Jones had been sixteen years before, retired from regular competition. He had won five championships. Shortly after, at the age of thirty-four, Hogan won his first championship, the 1946 PGA.

Another significant development in 1946 was Snead's triumph at St Andrews. Although members of the American Ryder Cup team had

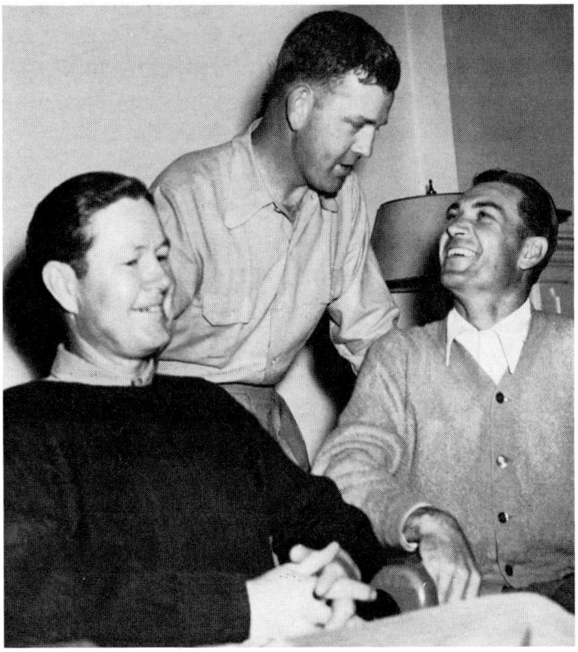

Left: Byron Nelson (*left*), who beat Ben Hogan (*right*) in a play-off for the 1942 US Masters. Sam Byrd, who finished fourth, is between them
Right: Sam Snead and Ben Hogan, Canada Cup, 1956

Jimmy Demaret

played in the Open at Carnoustie in 1937 – without great distinction – there had been no strong US entry in a dozen years when friends persuaded Snead to go over. His victory didn't launch another invasion of the magnitude of the 1920s, but it reminded Americans that golf was still an international game – and it may have had an influence on Hogan's decision to go to Carnoustie seven years later.

Snead was such a natural that he didn't need anyone to tell the world how good he was; the word would have gotten around soon enough. However, it got around a little sooner because of Fred Corcoran, who had taken on the job of directing the professional tour early in 1937, at precisely the same time Snead arrived. Corcoran, whose promotional abilities did much to build the tour into a thriving operation, immediately saw that Snead was a potential gold mine. He quickly reached an agreement with the young man to represent him in financial dealings, and the arrangement lasted until Corcoran's death some forty years later. It is a colossal understatement to say the relationship was worth a great deal to both parties.

Eventually Snead was to win more than 150 tournaments, including seven major titles, and even at the age of seventy he was still shooting scores less than his age. This work of art was, however, flawed in the eyes of some because of his failure to win the US Open, a title he came close to again in 1947 only to lose in a play-off with Lew Worsham. It became a *cause célèbre* and over the years more stories were written about Snead's Open 'jinx' than about some of the players who won.

In 1948 Hogan finally won his first Open, at Riviera, breaking the tournament record and winning by two strokes from Jimmy Demaret, his friend and fellow Texan. Demaret, whose outgoing personality and apparent inability to take life seriously made him the very antithesis of Hogan, was himself quite a player, ultimately the winner of three Masters. More significantly, Demaret's penchant for unusual – even bizarre – clothing on the golf course singlehandedly stormed the Bastille of American sporting fashion and led the way to a freedom of dress that put apparel manufacturers in his debt for ever.

In the immediate post-war years, despite numerous victories by Snead, Demaret, Lloyd Mangrum and the barnstorming Bobby Locke, it was Hogan who dominated. In 1948 he won eleven tournaments, including the Open and the PGA Championship, was the leading money winner and took the Vardon Trophy for low stroke average. When he began 1949 by winning two of the first four tournaments and losing another in a play-off with Demaret it appeared that another long season was ahead for the rest of the pros. Then, while driving home to Texas for a rest, Hogan and his wife were struck head-on by a bus that loomed out of the early-morning mist, and the face of American tournament golf changed abruptly.

There was talk at first that Hogan's life was in danger, but those

Bobby Locke

reports were erroneous. It was true, however, that he faced a long, painful recovery period, and the consensus was he would never play the tour again. Everyone knows that he came back only a year later and went on to write further indelible chapters in the game's history, but in the early months of 1949 such a thing seemed impossible, and people were wondering, as they had done on Jones's retirement, who would emerge as the next golfing hero. There was Sam Snead, of course, and Sam did indeed win ten tournaments in 1950, but he had been around a long time, eclipsed first by Nelson and then by Hogan, despite having perhaps more native talent than either. Perhaps Hogan's successor might come from such promising young players as Dr Cary Middlecoff, a dentist who forsook the profession in favour of golf and who won the US Open in 1949, or Julius Boros, a 29-year-old accountant who had just turned pro after considerable success as an amateur.

Julius Boros

This was a period of change in other respects as well. For one thing there was a budding women's professional tour, under the direction of the enterprising Fred Corcoran, who had Babe Zaharias and Patty Berg – and precious little else – to sell. There was only a handful of players in the beginning and the tour was underwritten for several years by Wilson, whose clubs Zaharias and Berg played. And just emerging were two elements that were to change the game mightily: television and George S. May.

Babe Zaharias

However, the game's followers didn't have long to ponder these developments because Hogan rendered everything academic by making a remarkable comeback. He returned in January of 1950 at the Los Angeles Open, the first event of the season, and miraculously tied for first. The fact that he lost a play-off to Snead did nothing to dim what he had achieved. He tied for fourth in the Masters, five strokes behind Demaret, then came all the way back in the Open at Merion, where he pushed his battered body through the closing 36 holes to tie with Mangrum and George Fazio, whom he defeated soundly in a play-off.

If anything, Hogan was an even better player after his accident. His flat swing repeated itself time after time, leaving such an impression of inevitability that someone described it as looking 'like a machine stamping out bottle caps'. He won the Masters in 1951, then triumphed over the extremely difficult Oakland Hills course to win the Open two months later. His closing round of 67 is considered by many to be the best he ever played and afterward he said, 'I'm glad I brought this monster to its knees'. Robert Trent Jones, the course designer, had been brought in to modernise the old Donald Ross course, and his punitive changes prompted Hogan's statement. The notoriety Jones received at Oakland Hills gave impetus to his highly successful career as a course architect.

Hogan won no major titles in 1952, but the following season he won the Masters, the US Open and – in his only appearance in the event – the

Ben Hogan, British Open winner, 1953, is received by New York's mayor Vincent R. Impellitteri after his ticker-tape welcome

British Open. He was unable to play in the PGA Championship because its dates conflicted with the British Open, but he might not have played in it anyway because the strain of 36-hole matches on his patched-up body had caused him to pass up the event after his accident. Even so, his feat of winning the only three majors available to him caused fans everywhere to draw comparisons with Jones's Grand Slam, and led to general agreement that a modern 'Slam' couldn't logically include the two amateur championships as it had in Jones's day.

After his great year Hogan was certainly expected to add to his laurels, but in fact it was not to be. He came close in several more US Opens (he was tied by Jack Fleck and lost a play-off in 1955, tied for second in 1956 and had a chance to win in both 1959 and 1960), but his run was ended. Besides his memorable triumphs, Hogan left another legacy: a single-mindedness and passion for practice that set a higher standard of excellence, and that meant the days were gone for ever when a sportsman-golfer could enter a championship as a lark and have any hope of winning. Before Hogan tournament golf was a lot of fun. After Hogan it was a business.

By the early 1950s a Chicago entrepreneur named George S. May had also set some new standards for the game. He had devised an event he modestly labelled the 'World Championship' and which carried with it a first prize of $25,000 – soon to be increased to $50,000 plus an additional $50,000 for fifty exhibitions at $1000 each. Not surprisingly, the winner of May's tournament was, *ipso facto*, the year's leading money winner. All

Left: The Tam O'Shanter World Trophy is presented to Bob Toski (*left*) by George S. May, 1954
Right: President Dwight D. Eisenhower

this was brought to public notice in 1953 when the event became the first ever to be seen on nationwide television. And to mark the occasion, in a finish so melodramatic no author would dare to try to sell it, Lew Worsham holed a full wedge shot of just over 100 yards for an eagle 2 and a one-stroke victory over a stunned Chandler Harper, who had been standing beside the green accepting congratulations.

Another development in 1953 had as much impact on the game as Hogan's heroics and the advent of televised golf. That was the arrival in the White House of Dwight D. Eisenhower, a devout golfer who often went off to Augusta for golfing weekends and who even had a practice green constructed on the White House lawn. Ike, who had won a great popular victory at the polls, legitimised golf in the eyes of the general public in a way nothing else ever could. People who wouldn't have dreamed of playing golf now could be seen down at the local sporting goods store inquiring into the price of a set of clubs. Then, for the *coup de grâce*, Arnold Palmer came along and converted those Americans not already brought into the fold by Eisenhower and TV.

Palmer made his first mark in 1954 by winning the US Amateur, and the proof that golf was a game for Everyman was there for all to see. Palmer, young and aggressive, shirt-tail hanging out, hitching his trousers before a shot, defeated socialite Bob Sweeny and for ever laid to rest the notion that golf was a rich man's game. He joined the professional tour the following year and scored a notable victory in the Canadian Open, and it was to be another seventeen years before he went through a year without winning a tournament. Boros had won the US Open in 1952 and Cary Middlecoff won his second in 1956 to go along with a Masters triumph a year earlier. Palmer won the 1958 Masters and then a stout young man with a decisive putting stroke – Billy Casper – broke through in the 1959 Open. It was at this point that the Age of Hogan ended and the Age of Palmer formally began.

In the Masters of 1960 Palmer birdied the final two holes to defeat Ken Venturi and establish himself as a popular hero. He also took over as the swashbuckling leader of 'Arnie's Army', a raucous, fiercely loyal horde

Opposite
Top: Billy Casper
Bottom: Arnold Palmer

Arnie with his 'Army'

that had been growing over the past few years and was now at full strength. The second half of Palmer's two-stage conquest of the golfing public came two months later, in the US Open at Cherry Hills. There, with the adrenalin flowing like a torrent, Palmer began the final round by driving the first green, 346 yards away. He played the first nine holes in 30 strokes and finished with a 65 that won the tournament as well as the allegiance of those stragglers who hadn't previously enlisted in the Army.

Arnold Palmer was not all-conquering, despite his hold on the public. Far from it. Besides Billy Casper, who had come to prominence in 1959, others were emerging who would play even greater roles. An unknown (in America) Gary Player had been runner-up to Tommy Bolt in the 1958 US Open and was to continue to be a major figure for the next two decades. And the winner of the 1959 US Amateur was a strong, self-assured young man of nineteen named Jack Nicklaus.

Palmer's rise had its effects off the course as well, principally in the area of player management. This wasn't anything new; after all, Bob Harlow had managed the affairs of Walter Hagen as far back as the 1920s and Fred Corcoran used his promotional talents on behalf of Sam Snead and others. But there now appeared on the stage Mark McCormack, a Cleveland attorney who was to make a science of representing golfers. McCormack was himself a fine amateur golfer and it was as a player that he had first met Palmer and others. A number of pros approached him for advice on exhibitions, endorsements and the like, and he began to devote considerable time to this activity. Then Palmer began to loom larger in the public eye and McCormack soon found himself handling Palmer's business exclusively. McCormack left no stone unturned if he thought there might be a dollar under that stone. Besides endorsing such traditional things as clubs and balls, not to mention apparel, Palmer was soon into everything from junior golf camps to laundries, and people began saying all this frantic business activity was hurting his game. No one could say for certain, but Palmer himself claimed he thrived on a full schedule and in fact began to pilot his own plane from tournament to exhibition to corporate outing to testimonial dinner. One wonders what the stonemasons in Elie would have made of it all.

Part of Palmer's appeal was that his emotions were there for all to see, in defeat as well as victory. Thus millions anguished with him when he made a double-bogey 6 on the final hole of the 1961 Masters, allowing Gary Player to win by a stroke. The next year he shot 31 on the back nine to beat Player and Dow Finsterwald in a play-off. As much as anything, it was the dramatic way in which Palmer both won and lost the Masters during those years that made it the popular event it became.

Palmer did something else significant in the early 1960s. He did permanently what Hogan had done temporarily back in 1953: he made Americans aware of the British Open and its significance. In going over for

Nancy Lopez-Melton

the Opens of 1960, 1961 and 1962 – and coming close to winning all three – Palmer demonstrated how much history and tradition meant to him, and his actions went a long way towards making his followers feel the same way. From those pilgrimages of the early 1960s can be traced the growth of American participation that now is comparable to the 1920s' voyages of Hagen, Sarazen and their contemporaries. Whatever effect the invasion had on the British, it was good for the always insular Americans because it gave them needed perspective.

Led by Palmer the professsional tour was booming, with purses increasing so much that Palmer and Nicklaus each won more than $100,000 by 1963. Meanwhile the Ladies PGA was working the back roads of America, providing the public with good golf – if only the public had been there to watch it. To the nucleus of Zaharias and Berg the LPGA had added such outstanding players as Louise Suggs and Betsy Rawls. Babe Zaharias came back from cancer surgery to win the US Open in 1954 by 12 strokes, and that same year a young woman named Mickey Wright joined the tour.

Mickey Wright won eighty-two tournaments in her career, including four US Opens and four LPGA Championships. She won thirteen times in 1963 alone but collected only $31,269 for her troubles. Here was one of history's greatest players, but it was one of the best-kept secrets in sport. Kathy Whitworth, who joined the tour in 1959 and so far has won eighty-two tournaments, was equally anonymous. It would take the impact of a Nancy Lopez in 1978 before the women began to make up lost ground financially and in public awareness.

Meanwhile, almost as soon as the Age of Palmer began the seeds of its destruction were being sown. When Palmer was carrying all before him at Cherry Hills in 1960 and Ben Hogan was making his final bid in that same tournament, Jack Nicklaus was finishing second while still an amateur. After winning his second Amateur Championship in 1961 he turned professional and had the colossal effrontery to defeat Palmer himself in a play-off for the 1962 US Open at Oakmont. Nicklaus – overweight, outspoken and hardly charismatic – now found himself the villain of the piece, the crew-cut Hun who represented a threat to life and liberty.

The rivalry between Palmer and Nicklaus was friendly but nonetheless intense. Nicklaus won the Masters in 1963, Palmer in 1964, Nicklaus in 1965 and 1966. In the Open Palmer lost another play-off in 1963 – this time to Julius Boros – and was fifth behind the gallant Ken Venturi in 1964. Then he lost still another play-off in 1965 at the Olympic Club: Billy Casper made an astonishing rally on the final nine holes to tie a Palmer who had gotten careless and had begun trying to break the tournament record. In the play-off the next day Palmer built another huge lead, only to lose as the strokes melted away once more on the back nine. Although no one could have known it – or believed it – Palmer would never again

Jack Nicklaus, 1968

come that close to winning a championship. Nicklaus, meanwhile, won the first of his five PGA Championships in 1963, while Palmer was second three times during the decade but never won. It remained the only major title to elude him.

The PGA Championship Arnold Palmer sought in vain was not the same event he knew as a youngster. The match-play format that had existed from the beginning in 1916 disappeared after 1957 and it became a 72-hole stroke-play event. Some blamed the change on television, which was becoming an important element in the game. Mark McCormack, never slow to seize an opportunity, was managing the affairs of Nicklaus and Gary Player as well as Palmer by the mid-1960s, and the three could be seen regularly on weekly filmed-for-television specials. In those years Shell's Wonderful World of Golf took the game over the globe and beamed the result into American living-rooms.

Because golf didn't lend itself readily to television, much of the coverage had to focus on the putting green. In no time at all Americans were lining up their putts with the care of surveyors and the length of a round – never as fast in the US as in the UK – soon stretched to five hours. One of the culprits, if one must assign blame, was Nicklaus, who took an inordinately long time over his putts. They generally went in, whether one liked it or not, and there began to develop a sense of inevitability about Nicklaus. People who resented his overthrow of Palmer early in the 1960s began at least to tolerate him. Then, ever conscious of his image, Nicklaus with great self-control lost twenty pounds, let his hair grow modishly long, and emerged transformed into a genuine hero. By the end of the decade, when he ended a lean period by winning at St Andrews, his followers perhaps outnumbered Palmer's. At this stage the guard was changing somewhat, and Nicklaus was facing new challenges.

Ken Venturi's star never rose as it might have; the insouciant Tony Lema was gone no sooner than he had arrived; Casper's last hurrah was the Masters of 1970; Tom Weiskopf's promise remained unfulfilled; and Palmer – though he and the Army never knew it – would win no more major battles. Gary Player was at his peak, and joining him in the front lines against Nicklaus was Lee Trevino, the very antithesis of a hero. Trevino had first come to public notice when he finished a surprising fifth in the 1967 US Open at Baltusrol, a tournament in which Nicklaus broke Hogan's record and in which Palmer was runner-up. Nevertheless

Below left: Tony Lema
Below right: America retains the Ryder Cup, Royal Birkdale, 1965. Byron Nelson, non-playing captain holding trophy, flanked by Gene Littler (*left*) and Dave Marr and (*behind, left to right*) Tommy Jacobs, Johnny Pott, Ken Venturi, Billy Casper, Arnold Palmer, Julius Boros, Don January and Tony Lema

Trevino captivated the press who soon learned this Mexican–American was the grandson of a gravedigger, had served in the Marines, and had honed his game on the public courses of Texas with such devices as hitting the ball to par-3 holes with a soft-drinks bottle covered with tape, much to the dismay – and expense – of his opponents. All this biographical material

Above: Tom Weiskopf
Left: Lee Trevino

gushed forth amid a welter of jokes, jibes and general bonhomie. The world has always had its quota of fine fellows, but this one was different – he could play. Between 1968 and 1974 he won five Championships and Nicklaus was the runner-up in four of them.

While all this was going on Nicklaus won the Masters and US Open in 1972 and came close in the British Open at Muirfield in what was to be his strongest bid for the modern Grand Slam. Then the following year he won the PGA Championship. It was his fourteenth major title, one more than the total of Bobby Jones, the man he sought to emulate. And that wasn't all. He won twice more in 1975, scored another memorable triumph at St Andrews in 1978, and then won still another pair of titles in 1980 when

Left: Johnny Miller with US Open trophy, 1973
Right: Tom Watson and Jack Nicklaus, partners in 1981 Ryder Cup

many of his fans were giving him up for lost. After this last burst there were few if any who would bet he wouldn't win another.

And still the challengers came forth. First there was Johnny Miller, whose future seemed limited only by his own reluctance to come to grips with it. Then came Tom Watson, whose early failures when he was on the threshold of victory made his subsequent triumphs more satisfying. Watson, a man with an unusually keen intelligence, has eyes that combine the directness of Nicklaus and the intensity of Hogan. His work habits, too, remind one of Hogan's, both in hours spent on the practice tee and in fierceness of concentration. The lustre of his victories in Britain and in the Masters has been dimmed only by his failure to win the US Open. But there is plenty of time.

As American golf approaches its centenary it appears to be sound in mind and body. The LPGA is thriving under the direction of its energetic commissioners, until recently Ray Volpe and now John Laupheimer; the men's tour is prospering under the equally vigorous direction of Deane Beman; a budding senior tour features such stars of the past as Snead, Boros and Gene Littler. Jack Nicklaus, long since divorced from McCormack and master of his own empire, is heavily involved in course architecture. Palmer and Player also dabble in it from time to time.

And the loyal fan? He's about given up on Palmer, but he still seats himself regularly in front of his television set, ready to lend support should Nicklaus decide to win another championship.

CHAPTER FOUR

The Ladies

by Lewine Mair

If today's popular papers had existed in the year 1567, it is not too difficult to imagine just how much they would have made of the fact that Mary Queen of Scots was spotted playing golf in the grounds of Seton House only days after her husband, Lord Darnley, had been murdered. Her Highness had by all accounts first learned the game while at school in France but her golfing career was dramatically cut short when 'she failed to maintain that basic relationship between head and shoulders which golfers from time immemorial have deemed essential'.

In a game which, down the centuries, has been accepted as one in

Mary Queen of Scots playing at St Andrews, 1563

which 'a king may play with a cobbler', it is hardly surprising to find in the record books that the Fish Wives of Musselburgh follow closely on the heels of Mary Queen of Scots. In the late 1700s these Fish Wives formed their own golfing society, the following reference being made to their sporting predilections in a publication entitled *The Statistical Account*: 'On holidays they frequently play at golf; and on Shrove Tuesday there is a standing match at football between married and unmarried women in which the former are always the winners.' In the Fish Wives' minutes in 1810, mention was made of how the winner of the golf competition on New Year's day would receive 'a handsome new creel and skull together with two of the best Barcelona silk handkerchiefs'. Unfortunately there are no longer any fisherwomen in Musselburgh – and one can therefore assume that these good ladies long ago decided that it was rather more fun to compete for such things as silk handkerchiefs than shoals of fish.

What every lady golfer needs

Up in St Andrews, at the time when the first Ladies' Club was being started, a golfing female was viewed as a woman of ill repute. 'A damsel with even one modest putter in her hand', noted one Miss A. M. Stewart in *The Gentlewoman's Book of Sports*, 'was labelled a fast and almost disreputable person, definitely one to be avoided.'

It was in the 1880s, at the Royal Wimbledon GC, that a group of women golfers began to occupy themselves with thoughts of a standard handicapping system. Among them was a Miss Issette Pearson, and it was she who became the first secretary of a Ladies Golf Union founded in 1893. The ladies wasted no time in organising a British women's championship and some idea of just what these pioneers were up against can be gauged from the reaction of Horace Hutchinson, a leading light in men's golf at that time and noted essayist on the game. 'The first women's championship,' warned Hutchinson, 'will be the last . . . They are bound to fall out and quarrel on the slightest, or no, provocation.'

Since Hutchinson's views on women golfers had the support of most of his contemporaries and would, I wager, meet with a nod of approval from many a man today, they are maybe worth recording. In the first place, he felt strongly that women did not belong on a true golf course:

> Ladies' links [he recommended] should be laid out on the model, though on a smaller scale, of the long round; containing some short putting holes, some longer holes, admitting of a drive or two of seventy or eighty yards and a few suitable hazards. We venture to suggest seventy or eighty yards as the average limit of a drive advisedly; not because we doubt a lady's powers to make a longer drive but because that cannot well be done without raising the club above the shoulder. Now we do not presume to dictate, but we must observe that the posture and gestures requisite for a full swing are not particularly graceful when the player is clad in female dress.
>
> Their right to play, or rather the expediency of their playing the long round is much more doubtful. If they choose to play at times when the male golfers are feeding or resting, no one can object. But at other times – must we say it – they are in the way; just because gallantry forbids to treat them exactly as men . . .

On the subject of ladies playing a full round of golf with men as their partners, Hutchinson merely cited the sorry instance of a young man whose score suffered as he was torn between flirting and playing the game. 'It's mighty pleasant,' the young man had said, 'but it's not business.'

Teeing up for the Warwickshire ladies, 1889

Hutchinson may have been right when he said that the ladies would quarrel and fall out on the slightest or no provocation, but the fact remains that, far from being a one-off, the British women's championship has flourished to a point where it nowadays draws top players from all corners of the globe. Cecil Leitch, a legendary figure in British women's golf who died but a few years ago, was justifiably proud of the fact that she had met all but one of the winners of the British women's championship. Of Lady Margaret Scott, who won the championship in each of its first three years, Miss Leitch had this to say: 'She was a gentle soul, very quiet both on and off the course. Her manners were impeccable and she was universally admired.'

Lady Margaret, who had the advantage of a golf course in the family's park, learned her golf from her father, Lord Eldon. In a feature in a *Golf Illustrated* of 1899 the writer told how it was from Lord Eldon and her brothers that Lady Margaret 'acquired that graceful yet powerful style which has been so immensely admired but unfortunately never

Ladies Championship medallists, Royal Portrush, 1895. Seated: Lady Margaret Scott (*left*) and Miss Lythgoe. Standing: Mrs Ryder Richardson (*left*) and Mrs H. C. Willock

successfully imitated'. Mention was made of her sudden departure from the golfing scene:

It is a matter of general regret among all golfers that Lady Margaret has not appeared since 1895 at any subsequent championship competitions, and still more that within the last two years she has practically given up playing and has resigned her membership of the Cotswold, Cheltenham and Westward Ho! clubs.

Lottie Dod was another charismatic champion from those early years. Labelled by Lord Aberdare as the first 'infant prodigy' of tennis, she was fifteen when first she played at Wimbledon in 1887. She won the Championship that year and did so every year until 1893, save on the two occasions when she had too many commitments to compete. Having had enough of playing tennis by the time she was twenty-one, for all that she was to go regularly to Wimbledon as a spectator all her days, Lottie Dod turned to golf. In the space of two years she was playing for England against Ireland at Portrush and, in 1904, she won the British women's

Left: Ladies Championship, Royal Portrush, 1911. Seated: Dorothy Campbell (winner, *left*) and Violet Hezlet
Right: May Hezlet

championship at Troon, defeating May Hezlet on the last green in what must have been the closest final she had known in either sport.

Paradoxically, although Miss Dod was to be remembered in tennis for the strength of her smash and volley – unusual armoury in the game of a Victorian lady – she yet served underarm on the disarming grounds that an overarm service placed too great a strain on a woman player. In golf she excelled with her woods, while her powers of recovery were by all accounts uncanny for one of her sex. Miss Leitch's verdict on Miss Dod was that she was 'a still greater sportswoman than Babe Zaharias'. Away from tennis and golf, Miss Dod was a champion skater, a skilful archer, a fine billiards player and 'a noteworthy member of the Alpine club'.

The aforementioned May Hezlet, who lost in the 1904 final, was one of four golfing sisters who hailed from Portrush (the others being Emmy, Violet and Jackie). She won three British and five Irish titles, while her sisters collected a haul of nine runners-up medals from those two championships. There are many at Portrush today who can remember listening to the sisters talk of the days when they would cycle the ten or twelve miles up to the course and play morning and afternoon before cycling home. Interestingly, when Ireland won the Home Internationals in 1979 for the first time since the early 1900s, one of the first telegrams opened by the Irish captain, Maureen Madill, came from the sole surviving Hezlet sister, Violet. In offering her congratulations, Violet recalled how she had played in the last winning Irish side.

The Hezlet sisters had been taught by their mother, a marvellously enthusiastic soul who played in the Irish championship no fewer than thirty-one times, her last appearance being when she was only three years away from her eightieth birthday.

It was in 1908, the year after May Hezlet beat Frances Hezlet in the final of the British at Newcastle, County Down, that Cecil Leitch came to the fore. She had started to play golf at Silloth in 1900, when she was just nine years of age. As she remembered it, her membership cost but five shillings a year, while she learnt the game by means of hammering a guttie ball around the course with an old cleek. That she taught herself maybe had much to do with the fact that her game was so different from that of her contemporaries. At a time when women were expected to observe a certain amount of decorum in making their swings, the young Miss Leitch had no compunction about giving the ball a masculine thump. Indeed, it was said that her crisp shots with the iron clubs set an entirely new standard for her sex.

By the time she was seventeen, Cecil Leitch was a good enough player to cause something of a sensation by reaching the semi-finals of the British women's championship at St Andrews. She won her first British title in 1914 but, with no championship played between 1915 and 1919, first because of the war and then because of the railway strike, she had to wait until 1921 to complete her hat-trick of titles. In 1926 she won again and also collected two English women's titles. Her greatest rival, as the whole of the golfing world knows, was Joyce Wethered (subsequently Lady Heathcoat-Amory). She played a very different game to Miss Leitch for, while the older player was hitting the ball as hard as she could, Miss Wethered had a swing which was at once graceful and relatively compact. Walter Hagen, when he watched her play, owned to envying 'the strong, firm type of stroke she played', and added that, to him, the greatest strength of her game lay in its strictly feminine characteristics. Bobby Jones paid her a unique tribute when he said that she was the best golfer – man or woman – he had ever seen.

The first of the legendary Wethered–Leitch matches was in the final of the English at Sheringham in the summer of 1920. This was Miss Wethered's initiation into the world of championship golf. A friend by name of Molly Griffiths had suggested they make the trip to the championship and the Wethered parents, though they had no particular ambitions for their daughter at that point, did not oppose the idea. Miss Wethered was nineteen and her game was at a stage where she would be good one day and indifferent the next. She finished well down among the qualifiers but, in the match-play stages, had a trouble-free run to the final. Just as Cecil Leitch had shaken everyone by coming from nowhere to make the semi-finals of the British at St Andrews some years before, so Miss Wethered's progress created a real stir. Early on in the final, Miss

Left: Cecil Leitch
Right: Joyce Wethered

Leitch was in full control against the youngster. Four up at lunch, she went six ahead after the first two holes of the afternoon. But Sheringham in June was dry and playing short and, all of a sudden, Miss Wethered played three flawless holes – each one in three – to unsettle her vastly more experienced adversary. Not so long ago Lady Heathcoat-Amory recalled how she suddenly sensed, very keenly, that the winning of this game meant very much more to Miss Leitch than it did to her. But, if her thoughts were momentarily less than positive, she was still in a very much better frame of mind than an opponent who had seen so commanding a lead disappear. She holed a good putt to take the sixteenth and a straightforward par won her the match at the seventeenth.

There is a railway running alongside Sheringham's seventeenth and, though the story has been solemnly attached to almost every links course she ever played, Lady Heathcoat-Amory confirmed that it was here that 'the train incident' took place. When she was talking to the press at the end of the championship, the party of golf writers had asked how much she had been disturbed by the train which had rattled down the line as she was settling to her putt. Her reply, which has become part of golfing folklore, was 'What train?'

In 1921 Miss Wethered and Miss Leitch met twice – in the final of both the British championship and the French. On both of these occasions it was Miss Leitch who prevailed and, with the tally between the two of them then standing 2–1 in her favour, it was hardly surprising that so much interest attached to their meeting in the final of the British at Sandwich the following year. In the morning the match more than came up to expectations and the two lunched all square. After lunch, however, Miss Leitch became unnerved against an opponent who had the ability to wrap herself in a cocoon of concentration, and the holes slipped through her fingers to such an extent that the match was over on the eleventh green, Miss Wethered having won by 9 and 7.

They met again in the fifth round of the 1924 British Championship and in the final of the 1925 edition. Each time Miss Wethered was the winner and now she had proved herself to be the better player. She retired from championship golf after winning three British titles and five successive English titles, but when she learnt that the British championship of 1929 was to be played at St Andrews, she could not resist making a comeback. To her, there was a certain magic about the little grey town: 'I have always loved the way you meet the same people on the streets as on the fairways, the way in which town and course are one . . .'

With Cecil Leitch now past her best, Glenna Collett Vare, a six-time winner of the American Amateur Championship, and far and away the best woman golfer that America had to offer, came through to the final to meet Miss Wethered, indisputably the outstanding player on this side of the Atlantic. The oft-repeated story of how the local postman, during the course of his morning round, informed a total stranger, 'She's five doon', related to Miss Wethered's position after her opening nine holes against

Joyce Wethered (*left*) and Glenna Collett, Troon, 1925

Miss Collett. However, the home player proceeded to play her next eighteen holes in 73 strokes and finally closed out her opponent on the 35th green. That this comeback should have such a fairy-tale ending is something which provided Joyce Wethered with her happiest golfing memory. 'It was a wonderful moment,' she confided. 'I had wanted to win at St Andrews so badly and, with Glenna being such a good sport, that match was everything a good match ought to be . . .'

Joyce Wethered worked in the golf department of Fortnum and Masons for some time after her retirement from championship golf and gave more time to other interests such as fishing and tennis. In 1935, though, she was persuaded to tour America as a professional, and it is said that she earned some £4000 over a stay embracing fifty-two matches with all the top amateurs and professionals.

Enid Wilson would undoubtedly have received a very much better press down the years for the three successive British women's championships she won from 1931 had she herself not been responsible for the major part of women's golf coverage. She wrote with great distinction in the *Daily Telegraph* for many years, seldom giving herself any sort of a mention. Indeed, in the foreword to her book, *A Gallery of Golfers*, she was gently chided by that legendary scribe, Bernard Darwin:

I have only one fault to find with this capital book. I can find no mention among the great lady golfers of that eminent player, Miss E. Wilson, who won the championship for three years running – 1931, 1932, 1933 – and then retired trailing clouds of glory. I do wish she had not been quite so modest, as it would have been interesting to hear of her early days at

Enid Wilson (*left*) and Madeleine Fyshe, Gleneagles, 1933

Hollinwell and her hard work under the eye of Tom Williamson. Also, I would have liked to have known how she felt in meeting her illustrious contemporaries. Did she fear some more than others?

As Donald Steel and Peter Ryde noted in their *Encyclopedia of Golf*, Enid Wilson was 'a devoted and model pupil willing to apply herself wholeheartedly to practice'. She had a sound and solid swing and, far better than most women, was able to come up with her best golf in the most critical of situations. She may have retired early from the championship scene, but her genuine love and feel for the game are apparent in the way in which, even now, she hates to miss a day's golf round her beloved Crowborough.

Pam Barton, who won the British and American amateur titles, was tragically killed in a plane crash when still only twenty-six, but another golfer from that era with great staying power was Jessie Valentine, née Anderson. She won the British three times between 1937 and 1958 and then, in the 1960s, won a hat-trick of Worplesdon foursomes alongside John Behrend. She was one of those golfers for whom that triple Open Champion, Henry Cotton, had a profound admiration:

While I have always had the normal appreciation for the play of the power-house types, I have admired more the accurate play of what might be called weaker feminine stars. . . The weaker the golfer, the more accurate needs to be the hit to get decent results. Power players, in contrast, can get satisfactory results from blows, say, 80% perfect – and I myself have even broken a course record when continuously striking the ball poorly, mishitting it but managing to keep out of trouble.

One player who certainly did not come into the 'fragile female' category was Babe Zaharias. It was just after she had won gold medals at the 1932 Olympics for the 80-metres hurdles and the javelin that Grantland Rice, a noted sports scribe of the day, suggested that Babe should join him and a couple of other journalists for a four. Her drives averaged a startling 240–250 yards and, though there were inevitably a number of bad shots, Grantland Rice had no hesitation in writing in his weekly column that he had never seen a woman who could hit a golf ball the way she did – and that she had the ability to be a great golfer.

In the aftermath of those Olympics the Babe became a professional athlete and, as soon as she had put some money on one side, she elected to turn her hand to golf on a serious basis. 'I have enough money to last me three years,' she said. 'My intention is to win the women's Amateur Championship before those three years and my bankroll are gone.' In 1934 she came out top in the qualifying stages of the Fort Worth Invitation Tournament and the following April won the Texas State women's championship.

The Babe may have been one of the greatest natural woman athletes the world has ever known, but her insatiable appetite for practice was arguably as much or even more of a gift. In her autobiography, *This Life I've Led*, she noted down the details of her golf programme:

> Weekends I put in between twelve and sixteen hours a day on golf. During the working week I got up at the crack of dawn and practised from 5.30 till 8.30, when I had to leave for the office. I worked until lunch-time, then had a quick sandwich and spent the rest of my lunch hour practising in the boss's office, which was the only one that had a carpet. I practised putting on the carpet and I chipped balls into his leather chair.

On leaving work at 3.30, the Babe would have an hour's tuition from her coach, George Sulback. Then she would 'drill and drill and drill on the different kinds of shots. I'd hit balls until my hands were bloody and sore. I'd have tape all over my hands and blood all over the tape. After it got too dark to practise any more, I went home and had dinner. Then I'd go to bed with a golf rule book.'

Her professional activities in the realm of athletics led to the golfing authorities ruling that she was a professional in their game as well, but in due course she regained her amateur status and, after winning the US Amateur of 1946, set out for Britain in search of the 1947 British Women's title. The affection and interest she inspired among golfing folk in Britain were apparent long before she teed off in the first round of the championship. The weather at Gullane was very much colder than she had anticipated and, with clothes rationing still the order of the day, she was unable to supplement the outfits she had with her. Only hours after the local papers had mentioned her plight, the lobby of her North Berwick hotel was stacked with parcels of clothing from well-wishers.

Jean Donald

Opposite
Top: Jessie Valentine
Bottom: Babe Zaharias

Aside from the weather, another thing which took the Babe aback was the traditional Scottish caddie. She was issued with a gentleman in his eighties who insisted on offering advice, especially when it came to the little shots around the green. The two disagreed since she wanted to use a wedge for her little pitches and he asked for the ball to be run up to the hole with a three- or four-iron. The story goes that the Babe went up to the caddie master and asked, 'Don't you have any younger caddies around here?' Whereupon he produced a man who, at best, was only five years younger. In truth, she stayed with the octogenarian all week and, despite the fact that he was somewhat set in his ways, succeeded in winning him round to do things as she wanted.

In the semi-finals the Babe came up against Jean Donald, the reigning Scottish champion, and when the newspapers reported that the Scottish champion was out to slay the American, the crowds grew to 'almost unmanageable proportions'. Figures put about ranged between five and eight thousand, while there were no fewer than a hundred marshalls. In her book the Babe summarised the match as follows:

> Jean Donald was hitting her drives almost as far as mine for a while, but I beat her with my short game. The match only lasted thirteen holes and I was one under the men's par for as

far as we went. I had just one three-putt green, and there were six times when I was able to hole out with a single putt.

Jacqueline Gordon, who had disposed of Jessie Valentine in the other semi-final, was something of an unknown quantity and everyone was surprised when, after eighteen holes of the final, she was still level with the Babe. The Babe, though, had her attention diverted in the morning because her shoes had come unstuck and the outfit she had chosen for the occasion was not warm enough. During the lunch break she attended to both these things and in the afternoon polished off her opponent in the space of fourteen holes.

Having won the trophy, the American stayed over to play some of the more famous Scottish courses before returning home – and everywhere she went she was pursued by the kind of crowds which had not been known since Joyce Wethered's heyday. At the end of that year the Babe turned professional from choice, and won the American Open Championship in both 1948 and 1950. In all she collected thirty-one titles on the women's professional circuit, the last of them in 1955 just a year before her death from cancer.

Jacqueline Gordon (*left*) with Babe Zaharias, Wentworth, 1951

Mrs Bunty Smith, who won the British championship just two years after the Babe, was similarly a cancer victim. The daughter of a professional, she had a pronounced pause at the top of her backswing with every club from a driver to a putter. Perhaps her most famous championship round was the 1954 English final at Woodhall Spa when, over the front nine of the morning round, she reached the turn in an astounding 30 against the par of 39, having had an ace at the fifth.

Her victim in that championship was Elizabeth Price Fisher, but though the two were keen rivals, they will more likely be bracketed together in history for their success in Curtis Cup matches between 1950 and 1960, a period in which Britain twice won and once halved with the Americans. The Curtis Cup match had started in 1932 when the Misses Harriet and Margaret Curtis of Massachusetts presented a simple silver bowl 'to stimulate friendly rivalry among the women golfers of many lands'. The idea had been prompted by their involvement in a friendly and impromptu match between America and Britain played at the time of the British women's championship in 1905. Other informal matches followed, but the success and interest of a 1930 encounter in which that much-loved English golfer, Molly Gourlay, led a team of British players against a side got together by America's Glenna Collett, suggested the time was right to make the match an official concern.

Among the Scots, the forties and early fifties belonged to Jessie Anderson, Jean Donald and Helen Holm. Indeed, the Scottish trophy circulated exclusively among this trio between 1937 and 1953. Across the Irish Sea they had Philomena Garvey who, between 1946 and 1970, won what is surely a never-to-be-beaten tally of fifteen Irish championships. But the later fifties and the sixties in England were the era of Marley Spearman and Angela Bonallack.

At a time when women golfers had, to say the least, a somewhat drab image, Marley Spearman's arrival on the scene can only be compared with the advent of colour TV. I remember seeing her for the first time at the English women's championship at Liphook. Where everyone else's golf shoes were black or brown, Marley's were fashioned from red suede. Her trousers were beautifully cut in emerald-green silk and, to complete the outfit, she wore an immaculate white sweater which most others would have put on solely for the prizegiving – and then only if they had won. As this former dancer herself confessed, she saw the golf course as an excellent platform for sporting the latest fashions. 'After all,' she would say, 'it's not like gardening. You're not going to get muddy or anything.'

From the beginning Marley found golf breathtakingly easy. For example, when first she joined her husband for a four at Sudbury, only a matter of weeks after she had started the game, she could not comprehend how it was that, while she hit the ball up the middle, the other members of the party kept arriving on the greens by way of bunkers and trees. 'I could

Marley Spearman watched by Angela Bonallack, Avia Ladies Foursomes, Berkshire, 1971

not understand why they were making life so difficult for themselves.' She had opened that day with a four and, so well did she continue to score, that one of the men jotted down her figures on a piece of paper from a cigarette packet. The final total was 81 – and it was on the strength of that extraordinary round that she set about joining the club.

Though she met with opposition from sister golfers who felt that their colleague from the stage was wielding a set of magic wands rather than golf clubs, Marley soon worked her way into the international arena. She played for England for eleven successive years from 1955 and represented Great Britain in the Curtis Cups of 1960, 1962 and 1964. In the 1964 match at Royal Porthcawl she gave the home side an inspired lead by winning both her foursomes with Angela Bonallack and halving her singles against Barbara McIntire and Jo-Anne Carner.

The halved game against Jo-Anne Carner, who was to amass no fewer than five American Amateur Championship titles before moving across to the professional circuit, was a match she picked out as one of the most memorable of her career. Another which she still remembers was a semi-final tangle with Angela Bonallack in the English at Lytham in 1964. In 1962, at Birkdale, Mrs Spearman had beaten Mrs Bonallack by one hole to win the British women's championship for a second successive year. At Lytham their match was still closer, going to extra holes. 'As I remember it,' said Marley, 'that match was played in a marvellous spirit. I always felt myself lucky to have played at the same time as Angela. She was a terrific golfer, one of the best competitors I ever met.' Mrs Bonallack, whose husband Michael has won both the Amateur Championship and the English Championship five times, had two wins in the English and was twice a runner-up.

The American women's professional scene was by now strong enough for it to be arguable whether the winners of the American and British Amateur championships were any longer the best women golfers in the world. Babe Zaharias apart, the two players whose golf had contributed most to the credibility of the professional circuit in its earliest years were Patty Berg and Louise Suggs.

Left: Patty Berg
Right: Louise Suggs

Patty Berg, who was taught by a father who made a hobby of studying and analysing the form and methods of famous golfers, won the US Women's Amateur Championship in 1938 before turning to a professional career in which she gathered forty-one titles. She was the first-ever president of the LPGA, which she helped form with eleven charter members, and is even now actively involved in committee work. Always less interested in making money than spreading the gospel of the game, she was at one time travelling some 60,000 miles a year conducting clinics and playing exhibition matches at clubs and colleges. She was employed by the Wilson Sporting Goods Company, and it was typical of her that, when she won the 1948 Women's Western Open, she promptly handed over her $500 cheque to the amateur officials of that region, asking that they should use it to help with the promotion of junior golf.

Louise Suggs won both the US and British Amateur Championships by way of preparing for a professional career which featured precisely fifty titles including two US Opens. The daughter of a golf professional, she was a thorough student who accepted from the start that golf was not so much a game of 'hit and hope' as one in which the player had to know and understand exactly what he or she was trying to do. 'The average player', she once explained, 'is too anxious to see good results on the scoreboard before she has fully absorbed the principles of the golf swing in mind and muscle on the practice tee . . .' Ben Hogan once described her swing as one which combined 'all the desirable elements of efficiency, timing and coordination' and insisted that there was none better for the aspiring player to emulate.

Perhaps the outstanding professional of all time, though, was Mickey Wright, a shy, retiring woman who hit the ball a prodigious distance with a seemingly effortless swing. She turned professional in 1954 and went on to win a record eighty-two tournaments including four US Opens and four LPGA Championships. In one spell of five years from 1960 she won fifty of the 130 tournaments in which she played. Only Kathy Whitworth has matched these achievements. Miss Whitworth, nowadays a tall, slim woman, won nine tournaments in her first years as a professional – and that in spite of the fact that at least one LPGA official had advised her against turning professional on the grounds that she was carrying too much weight, had an indifferent swing and no amateur record. In 1982 she recorded her eighty-second tournament win – equalling Miss Wright – and in the previous season went over the $1 million mark in career earnings. Yet where Mickey Wright's career is very much the complete article, Kathy Whitworth's is something of an unfinished symphony in that she has still to capture a US Open crown.

Mickey Wright

The fact that Jo-Anne Carner chose not to turn professional until she was past thirty for long helped to keep the amateurs in the forefront, while it similarly did the amateurs' standing no harm that in 1967 the leading French amateur, Catherine Lacoste, crossed the Atlantic and won the American Women's Open at Hot Springs, Virginia, from the professionals. Miss Lacoste, who had by that time won most of the titles Europe had to offer, was the daughter of René Lacoste and Simone de la Chaume, who had won Wimbledon and the British women's golf championship respectively. The Lacoste parents had wanted to accompany their daughter on her mission to the States, but Catherine was adamant that she had to go on her own and do it all for herself.

The American women professionals were a somewhat insular sect and the young French girl was left out in the cold to an extent which even she had not visualised. But, as luck would have it, she met up with a Mr William Preston and his family who were holidaying at her motel. Catherine remained sane amid the pressures by playing with the Preston children. Indeed, so interested did that family become in the progress of their new-found friend that they prolonged their holiday in order to give her their support throughout the week.

Kathy Whitworth

Miss Lacoste put together a book of cuttings around her American Open win and takes a mischievous delight in showing off the first three pages of previews in which she was given not a single mention among possible winners. Only one writer, who had asked the host professional for his views about the girls' play, brought Catherine into his story. He quoted the professional as saying that Catherine had been particularly good in practice in that, in their games together, she had always scored in the sixties. But he had added: 'I don't really know what this means . . . All sorts of funny things happen in practice.'

A shot off the lead at the end of the first round, Catherine was five shots ahead at the half-way stage. She came within a shot of being caught with two holes to play in the final round but made a birdie at the dog-leg seventeenth and finished with a par at the last. Many of the professionals were embarrassed at being thus beaten by an amateur, while it goes without saying that the American journalists made the most of their discomfort. As for the American amateurs, they could not conceal their

Catherine Lacoste

Jane Blalock

Judy Rankin

delight. 'If it can't be one of us,' they said, 'then why not a French girl. Mind you, it kind of makes you feel funny when someone from Europe comes over and wins our biggest tournament just about as easily as a Sunday fourball.'

Two years later Catherine was back in the States to try for the premier title on the amateur front. Here, she insisted, there was still more pressure than there had been in the American Open in that she was unofficially engaged at the time and knew that this was probably her last chance to make a full-scale bid for the title. In the semi-final she recovered from having been three down to defeat Anne Sander and then, in the final, she won a close encounter with Shelley Hamlin.

Though she never made that oft-quoted remark to the effect that she no more wished to play as a professional than have her appendix out, Catherine made it pretty clear all along that she had no intention of turning professional. A year or so ago, as Catherine Lacoste de Prado, she was included as Bernhard Langer's partner in the World Series in Japan. As the only amateur in the field of men and women professionals, she had the chance to see, again, what might have been. But, as you may have guessed, all she was conscious of missing that week were her husband and four small children back home in Madrid.

Nancy Lopez, who has done so much to bring women's professional golf to life in the last five years, has many of the same qualities of character and determination as had Catherine Lacoste de Prado. In her amateur days she had exactly the same relish for the game and, thankfully, lost none of this when she moved in among the professionals. As Marley Spearman once said: 'Nancy stands out like a diamond on the LPGA tour. She is alive, vibrant, and clearly sees golf for what it is – nothing more than a game.'

The daughter of a farm labourer who was to become an autobody dealer, Nancy started golf at the age of seven. With no funds for a babysitter – her elder sister, Delma, was by then married – her parents took Nancy up to the golf club each afternoon and, handing over a cut-down four-wood, would offer the following advice: 'Aim at the hole and don't fall behind.' Domingo Lopez pushed his daughter, but at the same time he always made it fun. A good morning's work was always rewarded with some small gift, while it says volumes for her parents that, in spite of their daughter's extravagant talent, they brought her up more girl than golfer. Nancy won her first tournament at the age of nine, beating a field of twelve and unders by a little matter of one hundred and ten shots. At twelve she won the first of three successive New Mexico state championships and, by the time she finished in junior golf, she had stowed away two US junior titles. She arrived on the professional scene just as that business-like little mother, Judy Rankin, was coming to the end of her ascendancy.

The compelling thing about Judy Rankin, whose haul of tournament wins included two Colgate European Opens at Sunningdale, was that she was slight compared to her rivals. At five foot three and a half inches and weighing less than eight stone, she yet contrived to hit the ball with exactly the right amount of draw to ensure that she was never far behind even the longest of hitters. The draw was brought about by an ultra-strong grip. Early on in her career Bob Toski, her coach, had suggested that she should switch to a more orthodox grip on the club but he did not press the matter since she was unwilling. Indeed, he eventually came to realise that it would have been a crime to have altered something which was such an integral part of her game, especially when her low, hooky flight was not only giving her extra yards but contributing to her reputation as one of the best bad-weather golfers in the game. Mrs Rankin had won a record $150,000 in 1976 and $122,000 in 1977, and was in each of these years ranked one. In 1978 she had recurring trouble from a back injury and it came almost as a relief when Nancy Lopez stole the limelight.

Nancy Lopez-Melton

Nancy's feats in her first twelve months as a professional were nothing short of remarkable. The week before she tried for her player's card at the LPGA school, she finished second in the 1977 US Open. Then, having come third in the qualifying school, she wound up second in each of her next two events, the 1977 Colgate European Open and the Long Island Charity Classic. It was a start which made every ounce of sacrifice on the part of the Lopez family worthwhile, though sadly her mother was to die in the September of that year, only months before her daughter launched into that spectacular winning spree of 1978. In the early spring she took two events back to back, then, after a lull of some six weeks, she ran up a historic sequence of five successive titles including the LPGA. Jane Blalock, one of her keenest rivals, said it all when she observed that Nancy was dominating the tour in the same way as had the Babe, Mickey Wright and Kathy Whitworth, 'only now it's more difficult in that there is so much more strength in depth on the tour'.

Beth Daniel

Nancy failed to convert those five wins into six but, by way of compensation in that sixth week, she met her husband, a TV commentator by name of Tim Melton. They were married in the winter of 1978. Since then she has cut down somewhat on her schedule, without in any way seriously affecting the family's combined income. In 1979, for instance, she tucked away $193,000 and in 1980 in excess of $200,000. In 1981, a year in which the 25-year-old Beth Daniel finished atop the money list for a second successive year, she took home the tidy sum of $165,679.

Where Nancy's cheerful disposition has always been one of her greatest assets, Beth Daniel has had to contend with a somewhat fiery disposition. This marvellously long hitter of a ball was twice in trouble for flinging clubs in the early part of 1980 but had things sufficiently under

Left: Jo-Anne Carner
Right: Donna Caponi

control in the latter part of the season to win three tournaments in a row. After a similarly slow start to 1981, she warmed up in time to take home the $50,000 winner's cheque for the so-called World Championship. This was far and away the biggest prize on offer in 1981 and it led to Beth Daniel earning $206,977 over the year against $206,648 for the runner-up, Jo-Anne Carner – a little unjust perhaps in that Miss Daniel had only two actual tournament wins to Mrs Carner's four.

This 'photo-finish' apart, what made the 1981 money list such interesting reading was that the top twelve contained such variety. Not for the first time South Africa's Sally Little and Australia's Jan Stephenson – two of the most decorative professionals on the circuit – were right up there among the best Americans, while the ages of those involved ranged from the forty-two years of both Jo-Anne Carner and Kathy Whitworth to the twenty-four years of Nancy Lopez-Melton. (Patty Sheehan, who won the Mazda Classic at the end of the season to finish eleventh on the money list and take the Rookie of the Year award, was twenty-five.)

One competitor from that first dozen whose wins have multiplied to an extent where she, like Lopez, Carner and Whitworth, cannot but go down as one of the most successful players in the history of the LPGA is the 36-year-old Donna Caponi Young. Mrs Caponi, who marked up the first of two US Open titles back in 1969, had fourteen titles to her name at the end of 1979 and twenty-four at the close of 1981. One of the most likeable

Left: Sally Little
Right: Jan Stephenson

players on the tour, she has a golf swing which is every bit as sound as her personality. Straight driving is her trademark and many will remember how, when she won the Colgate European Open at Sunningdale in 1975, she only twice strayed from the fairway over the four rounds.

Though the thriving Japanese professional tour has Chako Higuchi of the swaying swing, there is as yet no answer to these Carners, Lopez-Meltons and Caponis on the British women's professional circuit, which was started in 1978 by Barry Edwards, an ace in the realm of marketing. What the British tour does have, however, is the support of such considerable players as Michelle Walker, who tucked under her belt two British championships and one English before turning professional, and Jenny Lee Smith, a hard-working and marvellously level-headed professional who has often prompted Edwards to remark that he wished he had 'thirty more just like her'. As she collected her £1000 cheque for winning the 1981 Hambro Life Order of Merit ahead of such as Scotland's Cathy Panton and Muriel Thomson, Miss Lee Smith remarked that she had never believed that the British girls would have their own professional tour in her lifetime. In official and unofficial earnings Miss Lee Smith must have made in excess of £15,000 in 1981, while there were several others who pocketed around £10,000. Most have been quick to acknowledge just what miracles Edwards has wrought in terms of finding sponsors for WPGA events. But there have been some who, it is felt, have been playing with fire by asking for still more money at a stage when, as that eminently

Belle Robertson

sound professional, Neil Coles, has said, the women's approach should be one of 'softly, softly'.

Meanwhile in the amateur ranks pride of place in recent years must go to the Scot Belle Robertson, whose championship career has spanned four decades. Having lost to Elizabeth Price in the final of the British Women's Championship at Royal Berkshire as long ago as 1959, in 1981 after having been five up with five to play she ultimately beat Wilma Aitken at the second extra hole finally to get her hands on the British trophy.

At forty-five Mrs Robertson could have been forgiven for sitting back and achieving this ambition of a lifetime, but in 1981 she went out to Madrid where she was the only member of the British team to stand up to the Continentals right through the weekend of the Vagliano Trophy match. In all, she took three and a half points out of four, winning both her singles against the Continent's No. 1, Marta Figueras Dotti. The overall result of this match was a comfortable win for the Continent. But the immediate impression that, aside from Belle Robertson and Ireland's Mary McKenna, the British team was relatively short of experience took something of a knock when the story unfurled of the revolutionary approach to golf in Sweden.

In that northern land where golf is almost out of the question in most parts for five months out of the twelve, there is a coach by the name of There Holmstrom who is saying to his pupils 'to hell with experience'. He is indoctrinating them with the notion that they, like swimmers, must win while they are in peak physical condition – in other words, in their teens. All this could be easily dismissed as so much nonsense but for the performance of a fifteen-year-old, Liselotte Neumann. She first came under Holmstrom's wing in Swedish junior training sessions, but had not been considered good enough to play for her country in the side which, in August 1981, came to Wentworth and won the Junior European Team Championships. Nor had she ever previously played in a senior national championship when she played in the 72-hole Swedish Open stroke-play championship at Jönköping in the late summer of 1981. She opened with rounds of 70 and 75 and then, with everyone making the virtually foolproof forecast that she would crack, finished with scores of 69 and 68 to win the championship by a record nine-shot margin. Her four-round aggregate of 282 was a personal best by a matter of thirty shots, while it was the lowest-ever total by any Swedish woman golfer in the history of the event.

It is, indeed, an extraordinary tale, but if There Holmstrom's theories are to survive, he would do well to keep his young Swedes in some kind of golf monastery lest they should ever learn from the world at large just how devilishly difficult the game can be.

CHAPTER FIVE

The All-Time Greats

by Michael McDonnell

The question of a golfer's greatness depends ultimately on whether he left the game better than he found it and in what manner the game benefited because he played it. In such terms a legion of famous players down the years fail to qualify because, even though their skills impressed, their achievements were accumulative rather than contributory. But those rare individuals who enriched the game with new ideas, techniques and standards have earned a permanent place in its history. Each in his era created a climate and set levels of performance which inspired others.

This story of champions must begin with Harry Vardon, for while the Parks of Musselburgh, the Morrises of St Andrews and even J. H. Taylor and James Braid were dominant figures of their day, none influenced the sport in the manner of this former Jersey gardener who elevated it to the exercise of skill we know today. Until he began to play the sport had developed little in terms of skill from its primitive cross-country hitting origins. But Vardon, quite unintentionally, changed all that and

Harry Vardon beats Ted Ray in the final of a £400 professional golf tournament, Sunningdale, 1912

developed a technique of hitting on which the modern golf swing is based. He became the trend-setter of his day to such an extent that even the overlapping grip of the club, by which both hands are linked, became known as the Vardon Grip even though many successful golfers were using the style long before he arrived on the scene.

What Vardon did was to bring a truly professional approach to the playing of the sport. He not only devised a repetitive technique that could be relied upon but he then demonstrated it successfully in money matches, exhibitions and championships throughout Britain and the United States. He became the first international superstar and, in setting a lifestyle for himself, encouraged others to follow and improve so that a direct line of succession can be traced from Vardon to Walter Hagen, Bobby Jones, Henry Cotton, Ben Hogan, Arnold Palmer, Gary Player and Jack Nicklaus, each of whom developed a new aspect of the sport and earned the mantle of greatness.

In 1882, when he was twelve years old, Vardon entered domestic service in one of the larger households at Grouville on the island of Jersey in the English Channel, first as a pageboy and later as a manservant. By the time he was seventeen he was working as an under-gardener for an affluent member of the Royal Jersey Golf Club and, while not terribly interested in the sport, felt obliged in common with other servants to play occasionally. But not until his brother Tom won the enormous sum of £12 in a professional event in Scotland did Vardon, a better player, reason that he too could earn that sort of money. So, at the age of twenty he turned professional. He had played no more than twenty rounds of golf in his life.

Vardon was self-taught and copied the methods of those around him, amending their styles to produce his technique. Quite by chance he developed the concept of the all-air shot in which the ball flew high and landed softly, thereby giving greater accuracy. It was a strength which formed the basis of Jack Nicklaus's supremacy more than half a century later. Vardon stood to the ball with his feet narrowly apart, which caused his backswing to be upright so that he struck the ball with a steep descending blow which forced it quickly into the air. The style was completely at odds with the traditional St Andrews swing, a wide-stanced flailing motion, whose object was to achieve low-level distance against the savage winds that assailed the Scottish links where the game was played.

But Vardon's style emphasised an obvious truth that while the ball was airborne it was free from the perils of terrain. His steep hitting action also had the effect of imparting backswing on the ball so that it landed and halted very quickly. The combination of these two features was to make him unbeatable for many years. He achieved such reliability with this method that he could strike the ball 200 yards with a brassie (two-wood) within fifteen feet of the flagstick and even nominate which side he intended the ball to land. Even so he had to compensate slightly for the

Opposite: Harry Vardon in 1926

narrowness of his stance and achieved a wider arc to his swing by bending his left arm at the top of the backswing so that it straightened with the momentum of the downswing to give him the sweeping action for the power he needed.

He had taken much of the chance out of golf, and proved the value of his method by winning the Open Championship six times over a period of eighteen years and only just missing the American Open title when he was fifty. His technique also remained undiminished through some dramatic developments in golf equipment. He won three Opens with the gutty ball and the remainder with the rubber-cored ball, though he was past his competitive peak when steel golf shafts were made legal in 1929.

Throughout his life he was assailed by tuberculosis which forced him out of the game for a period and certainly limited the scope of his achievements. He was a cautious, shy man, who nevertheless earned a public following as great as any theatrical performer of his day and his money matches attracted thousands of spectators.

In 1905 he partnered J. H. Taylor in a £400 challenge match against Alex Herd and James Braid that was to take many days and much travel to complete because it involved two courses in Scotland and two in England. After 36 holes at St Andrews, Vardon and Taylor were two up but became so dejected at the partisan behaviour of the Scottish crowds that they considered calling off the match and giving their rivals the cash. Instead, they moved on to Troon where they combined in devastating style to establish a 12-hole lead over the Scots. The match then moved to St Annes in Lancashire where Herd and Braid won back five holes so that they were only seven down by the time they reached Deal in Kent for the last part of the marathon match. The night before the contest Vardon became violently ill with his TB condition and there were fears that he would not play, but he insisted he would be ready and the next day he and Taylor beat the Scots by 13 and 12.

The Vardon era in fact began with a money match in 1896 when he challenged J. H. Taylor, the best golfer of the day, to a winner-take-all contest at Ganton and beat him by 8 and 7. Later that year Vardon was to win his first Open in a play-off with Taylor. Yet even then he demonstrated his legendary caution by preferring to take five on Muirfield's last hole and go into a play-off, rather than risk a dangerous shot to the green. There were sixty-four competitors in that championship, but it would be a mistake to conclude that his achievements therefore were minimal. The fact is that, even though more than 1000 contestants set out to play in the modern championship, the matter of winning is still resolved by a handful of golfers who are better than the rest and know they are playing one another.

Unquestionably Vardon and Ted Ray were the all-conquering stars of golf when they visited the United States in 1913 for the American Open at

Brookline, Boston. It promised to be yet another exhibition of British golf supremacy which had existed since hundreds of young Scots had emigrated at the turn of the century – 300 from the village of Carnoustie, for example – to teach and play golf mainly in the United States. The championship was therefore dominated by British professionals and the Americans had not produced a champion of their own. But that US Open was to become a milestone in the development of golf because it marked the awakening of golf in America. Francis Ouimet, a 20-year-old sports shop clerk from nearby Boston, was to tie with Vardon and Ray and beat them in a play-off when Vardon, a notoriously bad putter, lost his touch and Ray played erratically.

Francis Ouimet

The bespectacled American's historic achievement overshadowed the efforts of another young man who had drawn level with the leaders with nine holes of the last round to play, but had gambled and lost on a recovery shot and so finished well down the field. But the gesture was typical of the man who was to emerge as the next major influence in golf. His name was Walter Hagen.

Hagen was a flamboyant character who gave the sport style and sophistication. He possessed a great talent, but his greatest contribution to the sport was the emancipation of his fellow professionals from their 'second-class citizen' status which prevented them from even entering golf clubhouses. It was a crusade that brought him into conflict with authorities on both sides of the Atlantic. But his philosophy was very simple: he was the best and he expected to be treated as such. If he was forbidden to enter a club, then he would park his chauffeur-driven limousine outside and order his butler to serve champagne and oysters in the car park. He persuaded one Scottish club to allow him entry when he warned that if he won the Open Championship that week he would accept the trophy only in the nearby pub to which he and his fellow professionals had been banished. He was a bon vivant who never wanted to be a millionaire but just preferred to live like one. He captured the madcap spirit of the twenties when he dominated the sport with his cavalier style and would occasionally arrive on the first tee straight from an all-night party still wearing his dinner jacket.

Hagen was influenced by the self-made millionaires at the Michigan club where he was professional. All of them, Ford, the Chryslers, the Fishers, came from humble origins and judged a man on merit, not background or class. He transformed golf into box-office success because he was the complete entertainer. He hit more bad shots than any other top golfer, but this was part of his appeal because he was also the master of the recovery shot and could extract the full drama of any situation, going through a charade of worry but knowing exactly how he would play the stroke. He was the first professional to break away from the safety of a club job and he made a fortune from exhibition matches, prize money and contracts, yet spent it as rapidly as he earned it. He gave his winning cheque from one Open Championship to his caddie. He gave a staff journalist his complete fee for a series of articles when he learned the newspaper was not paying the writer for his assistance. He once threw a lavish party and hired an orchestra aboard a liner and then had to borrow $25 to tip the crew as he disembarked.

As a young man he seemed destined to become a baseball player with the Philadelphia Phillies but realised there was more money to be made from golf. Yet he never lost his baseball style, and his wide-stanced, free-swinging way in which at times he lost sight of the ball on the backswing was the cause of the inconsistency that prompted him to become such a

Above left: The life-style of Walter Hagen
Above: Hagen wins his fourth British Open, Muirfield, 1929
Left: Gene Sarazen, Hoylake, 1924

great recovery player. He won ten major championships including four British Opens and four American PGA titles in succession over a period of fifteen years. Yet it is for his contribution to the status of the golf professional that Hagen will be remembered. Gene Sarazen, himself winner of seven titles during the Hagen era, stressed Hagen's historical importance with customary eloquence: 'Whenever a tournament pro stretches a fat winning cheque between his fingers, he should give silent thanks to Hagen.'

The peerless Bobby.
Right: Jones plays a mashie in the British Open at St Andrews, 1927

Yet the diminutive Sarazen himself set standards for this sport which few have equalled. He was the first professional to win all four major world titles. In fact his collection included three American PGA Championships, two American Opens, one British Open and one American Masters, and it was the manner in which he won the 1935 Masters, only a year after the event had been established by Bobby Jones at Augusta, that earned Sarazen another niche in the history of the game. Craig Wood was already being hailed as the winner that year when Sarazen holed his second shot on the 485-yard par five fifteenth to draw level. He struck a four-wood 220 yards across the water and into the hole and went on to earn a place in the 36-hole play-off in which he beat Wood by a five-stroke margin the following day.

The legendary Bobby Jones was to give golf an intellectual dimension, and not simply because he was a brilliant scholar with degrees in law, engineering and English literature, who emerged as the champion golfer of his day. The Jones contribution to the sport was twofold. As an amateur, he set standards and records before he was twenty-eight that even to this day have not been equalled, and he was the first champion to articulate about his sport and its demands on the character and skill of its participants.

Jones is remembered primarily for his astonishing record over a seven-year period in which he won thirteen national titles in Britain and the United States, yet his contribution to the understanding of the game through his own literature was considerable and some of his works are masterpieces of insight. In 1930 he completed the Grand Slam of winning the amateur and Open titles of both the United States and Britain in the same season, after which he decided to retire. He was twenty-eight and there was nothing left for him to achieve as a competitor. He had beaten all the professionals at their own game while he played only on a part-time

Bobby Jones receives the key to the City of New York after winning the British Open, 1930

basis. It was a staggering achievement and one that was not even attempted seriously by those who came after him, because standards of professionalism grew keener. Indeed, since that day no amateur has ever won the US Open or the British Open, although Jack Nicklaus came very close to the US title in 1960 at Cherry Hills while still an amateur.

Jones was also prompted to retire because the years of competitive strain had taken their toll on his sensitive, fragile temperament. He was born of wealthy parents in Atlanta, Georgia, in 1902 and took to golf at the age of six when the family rented a holiday cottage at a golf course just outside their home town. By the time he was fourteen he had been hailed as a prodigy, but was not to win a major title until he was twenty-one.

With no formal golf training, Jones's technique was completely natural. He adopted a narrow stance to the ball and employed a long, easy swing that seemed to have more rhythm than power. His technique was described thus at St Andrews in 1927:

> Mr Jones stands to the ball as if engaged in conversation. There is no straddling of the legs, no tying of the muscles into a knot. The swing commences slowly as to suggest it is indolent. It is not a blow in the sense that it takes place and is done with. There is a glorious follow-through with the clubhead finishing round the neck and the hands held high.

The method may well have been God-given and effortless, but its application had to be learned the hard way and Jones endured many years of failure, largely because of his own temperamental weaknesses, before he succeeded as a competitor.

Indeed, the paradox of his astonishing career was that he was never really a sound competitor and was always liable to squander a golden chance of victory, or at least make the task much harder than needed. In 1923 in the US Open at Inwood, he was three strokes clear of the field with one round to play, but dropped four strokes in the last three holes to go into a play-off which he duly won. Much the same thing happened in the 1928

US Open but this time he did not win the play-off. A year later he was three strokes clear going into the last round of the championship but took seven at two holes to fall back into a play-off which he won.

It was evidence of the problem he struggled with throughout his career – his temperament. In his early days he had been an uninhibited club-thrower and in one US Amateur played a golfer of similar disposition so that it seemed the winner might be the one left with a club to strike the ball! During his first visit to St Andrews he became so exasperated with its demands that he tore up his scorecard and threw the pieces away, and admitted: 'To the finish of my golfing days, I encountered golfing emotions which could not be endured with the club still in my hands.'

Despite his lapses in stroke-play, he still preferred this form of competition to match-play in which the better player did not always win over eighteen holes. Indeed, Jones himself was to bring a rare philosophy to match-play golf in that he insisted he 'played the course and not the man'. Yet one of his greatest victories was a complete contradiction of that strategy when, in a stroke-play situation, he was obliged to 'play the man' to win the Open Championship at Royal Lytham in 1926.

He was level with fellow American Al Watrous as they stood on the seventeenth tee of the last round but hooked his tee shot into a bunker. Watrous was perfectly placed in the middle of the fairway and found the green safely with his approach. Jones was some 170 yards from the green and struck a magnificent recovery with such accuracy that it finished close to the flagstick – Watrous was so astounded that he three-putted and Jones went on to become champion. Indeed, that historic stroke is commemorated by a plaque at the edge of that bunker on the seventeenth hole at Royal Lytham.

By the end of that 1926 season Jones began to see the possibility of a Grand Slam. For a brief period during that summer he held the American and British Open titles while still the US Amateur Champion from the previous year. Thus he had evidence of his own ability against the opposition, but whether fortune was on his side was another matter. He was not a regular transatlantic commuter. His attempts at all four titles, therefore, were few and far between. He failed miserably in the 1926 British Amateur, for example, and did not try again for another four years – and only then because he was back with the American Walker Cup team to play in Britain.

In this context, therefore, the Grand Slam of 1930 represents more than an unparalleled athletic feat because he suffered intensely during competitive play. In one championship he lost 18 lbs and at times he would be reduced to inexplicable tears. On frequent occasions he would ask a friend to walk inside the ropes with him at a championship just for moral support. More than this, he endured the worries of simply getting to the championship venues safely during that historic year of 1930. In fact,

Bobby Jones with Mayor Jimmy Walker, New York, 1930

during the period between championships he narrowly missed being struck by lightning on a golf course and later was almost knocked down by a car in Atlanta.

The Grand Slam began at St Andrews when he won his way through to the final of the Amateur Championship to meet Roger Wethered, a genial, if casual, golfer who treated his golf so lightly that in 1921 he had to be persuaded to remain on to compete in a play-off for the Open Championship against Jock Hutchinson rather than return home to play for his village cricket team. (He lost the play-off.) It had been a precarious journey to the final for Jones. With five to play he had squandered a four-hole lead against one opponent before winning on the last green. He had been two down with five to play against another opponent before winning, and he had stymied Cyril Tolley at the 19th to win another match. In the final, however, Jones brought new purpose to his golf to overwhelm Wethered by 7 and 6.

Thus armed with the trophy Jones moved immediately to Royal Liverpool, Hoylake, for two weeks of preparation before the start of the Open Championship. At that time two rounds were played on the final day. Jones held the lead but lost it at lunchtime to Archie Compston and added to his own misery by taking a seven on the eighth hole. His chance seemed to have gone but he resolved to persevere and, true enough, Compston crashed to an 82 in the afternoon so that Jones became Open Champion and was halfway towards the Grand Slam.

He sailed back to New York and went directly to Minneapolis where he had two weeks to prepare for the US Open at Interlachen, and it was here during the second round that he struck what became known as the 'lily pad shot'. He topped his shot into a lake at the ninth but the ball bounced off the water and on to the green where he sank the putt for a birdie. It was held that his ball had bounced off a lily pad but in fact it simply ducked-and-draked like a pebble across the water. Yet it was a reminder that luck as well as skill was needed if Jones was to achieve the Grand Slam.

He was five strokes clear as he went into the last round but seemed in wastrel mood as he dropped six strokes at three short holes and believed that his chance of victory had gone as he stood over a 40ft putt on the last green. The ball curved on perfect line into the hole for a birdie. Only then did Jones learn that all his rivals were out of it and he was US Open Champion. Only the Amateur title remained to be won, but he would have to wait until the autumn for that.

Even so there seemed an inevitability about it although Jones progressed to the final in his customary erratic style, losing a few leads and giving himself and his fans some anxious moments. But once he faced his last opponent, Gene Homans, all self-doubt vanished and he triumphed by 8 and 7. The Grand Slam had been achieved. Future generations might argue the playing merit of that achievement, but as the venerable Tommy Armour, himself a champion on both sides of the Atlantic, said: 'It is nonsense to talk about who was the greatest golfer in the world. All you can say is there have been none greater than Bobby Jones.'

His legacy extended beyond the record books because Jones was to build one of the world's greatest golf courses at Augusta and stage what was to become a major championship – the US Masters – although he never called it a championship and established the contest initially for his friends and rivals from his playing days. Since then the Masters has become one of the world's four major events and part of the modern Grand Slam along with the US Open, US PGA and British Open. Only four players – Gene Sarazen, Gary Player, Jack Nicklaus and Ben Hogan – have won all four titles. Hogan won three of them in 1953, and Jack Nicklaus came very close to a Grand Slam in 1972 when he won the US Masters and US

Open and missed the British Open and later the American PGA title by only a few strokes.

The ultimate tragedy of Bobby Jones was that this great athlete who set so many sporting records was to spend the last years of his life as a cripple, the victim of a disease that wasted his muscles.

When Jones retired in 1930, the American domination of world golf was complete. The British missionaries who had brought the game to the United States had faded and nobody from their own land had reached world-class. Indeed, no home-based professional was to win the British Open for eleven years, until a former London public schoolboy by the name of Henry Cotton decided to make a career in golf.

It was a momentous decision in social terms because the professional sportsmen of the early twenties were still regarded as little more than gifted artisans and were not allowed to mix outside their class. Hagen and the rest of the American professionals had arrived in Britain and disregarded these attitudes, but it was still impossible for the British professional to break through those barriers when he lived with them all the time. Cotton confused the issue in that he came from the middle class, yet chose a career which until then in Britain had been the domain of the working class. But Cotton was to drag his profession out of this subtle bondage in what was a long and hurtful struggle in which at times neither side thanked him. His task was always to get what he thought his talent deserved and in so doing he elevated the status of his fellow professionals just as Walter Hagen had done in the United States. He became such a famous public figure that he even topped the bill at theatres throughout Britain with an act of golf trick shots.

Henry Cotton topping the bill at the Coliseum, 1938

Cotton plays an exhibition match at the Glasgow club, 1939

Cotton was a regular visitor to all the fashionable resorts throughout Europe. He lived well and employed a large staff and at one time lived in a penthouse suite in the Dorchester Hotel in London. He spoke fluent French, Spanish and later Portuguese. He brought style and sophistication to sport in general and not just to golf. But his struggle for status made him extremely controversial and, while he might please his fellow professionals by parking his limousine outside a club from which they were banned, he would irritate his colleagues by walking out of a tournament if he was not playing well enough to win a reasonable cheque. He was always prepared to criticise sponsors if he believed they were not offering enough prize money, and at the presentation for the French Open one year he declared that his cheque was an insult, adding: 'If you want the best golfers in the world, then you must pay for them.'

He could only carry on this campaign with any success so long as he had the talent to remain in big demand with sponsors and the public. That required a standard of dedication that has not been matched by subsequent generations of British professionals. As a young assistant in Kent, he was to practise with such intensity to perfect his golf swing that his spine was permanently twisted. All his life he waged a battle with his own vulnerable temperament and was to suffer from agonising stomach troubles during the peak years of his career.

The trouble during the early years was that, while he appeared to be one of the best golfers in the world and certainly in Britain, he could not deliver the ultimate proof by winning the Open Championship. Not until

1934, when he was under the steadying influence of Argentinian heiress Maria Isabel Estanguet – known as Toots – did Cotton fulfil his destiny. At the start of the last round of the Open Championship at Royal St George's that year it seemed he would at last win the title, and he was so far ahead of the field that thousands of fans arrived to watch him triumph. But even then there was a crisis as he was assailed by stomach cramps as he began his round. He stumbled over the outward nine holes in 40 strokes and only just managed to re-establish some control over his fickle temperament in time to win the title with a final round of 79.

In his own opinion his greatest victory was in 1937 at Carnoustie, when he beat the full-strength American Ryder Cup side which had stayed on to contest the Open. But his loyal admirers believe that his 1948 victory at Muirfield paid real tribute to the enduring qualities of a style and technique that had been learned and retained through hours of unrelenting toil. The truth is that Cotton never really believed he had a natural talent for the game. His method was based on the importance of the hands in controlling the swing. He believed that strong hands determined the flight and distance of the ball, and that any player could develop such strength given the required amount of application. More than this, such a method would allow a golfer to play to a reasonable standard long after his body had lost much of its suppleness. Cotton himself played to a single-figure handicap well into his seventies.

His style therefore attached much less importance to body positions and movements in the swing, because he felt that the proper hand action caused correct posture, but at times his own swing looked slightly mechanical and artificial. Above all, he was the first to prove that total dedication was essential for success in the new world of professional golf. The rip-roaring days of Hagen were over and it was no longer possible to carouse all night and still emerge as the winner next day. Winning at golf needed a high degree of mental and physical preparation.

A few visionary men were obsessed with the thought that absolute control of the golf ball could only be achieved by total discipline of the body muscles and the technique required to propel it. Ben Hogan, from Texas, may well have had more interest in a method of striking the golf ball than winning tournaments with it. To him it could become a truly mechanical action, capable of precise repetition if all muscles and limbs were controlled. It became his life's work and made Hogan himself a very aloof man who liked to keep the rest of the human race at arm's length. There was a mystic quality about him as he became absorbed in his own game for the purpose of studying how best to control it.

He would banish himself for hours to the practice ground to study some aspect of his swing. He once noticed his fairway wood strokes lost some of their accuracy when he tired, so he deliberately fatigued himself on the practice ground to ponder on his condition and rectify it. He once admitted: 'I think I must get more satisfaction out of just hitting the golf ball than any man who ever lived. I must be alone. Way to hell out there on the practice ground by myself. I love it.'

The paradox of Hogan was that his fame was an unwelcome price of his success. Crowds would flock to see the 'Ice Man' play, but they never dared to ask for his autograph. At his peak he insisted that an attendant accompany him during his rounds carrying a 'No Cameras' banner. He shunned all personal contact and never bothered too much about hurting the feelings of others. When Gary Player, then a great champion, phoned Hogan for some advice on the golf swing, he was told to try elsewhere.

Hogan captained the 1967 Ryder Cup side at Houston, Texas, and treated his most distinguished team member, Arnold Palmer, in dismissive manner. When Palmer asked his captain for a ration of smaller-sized golf balls on which to practise for the match, Hogan seemed angry that Arnie had not bothered to prepare before arriving for the contest and barked cynically: 'Did you remember to bring your clubs? Anyway, who says you're going to play?'

Hogan's own standards and scale of preparation for a tournament, particularly a championship, were exhaustive, and he was the first to analyse a course, check its yardages and locate landmarks so that he was never in doubt about any distance he had to play. The procedure is now standard practice among tournament professionals who even have card indexes of venues to save time in learning how to play them.

In 1949 he was involved in a car crash that almost claimed his life and seemed at the time to have ended his golf career. He was then at his peak and only a year earlier had won thirteen events on the American tour, six of them in succession including the US Open. When rescuers pulled him from the wreckage, they discovered he had a broken shoulder, leg and ankle, plus a fractured pelvis and many cuts and bruises. Later a blood clot formed and caused major complications in his legs. Had his career ended at that moment, Hogan would still have been remembered as a major figure in golf. It had taken him ten anonymous years of effort before he was to win a tournament. Yet his late arrival at the top may have been caused by his obsessive desire for perfection in himself. A man of modest stature, he swung the club in a wide arc to generate formidable power which made him one of the longest hitters of his day.

In his early pioneering days on the American tour, Hogan and his colleagues were frequently hard up. His close friend Jimmy Demaret, himself a Masters champion, recalled a time when they deliberately hit out of bounds into nearby orange groves just to stock up with cheap food for the week. He himself had once been obliged to throw his clubs out of the hotel window and stroll casually through the front door because he could not pay the bill, although it was settled later when he was in funds.

In 1940 Hogan had been on the circuit for ten years when he won his

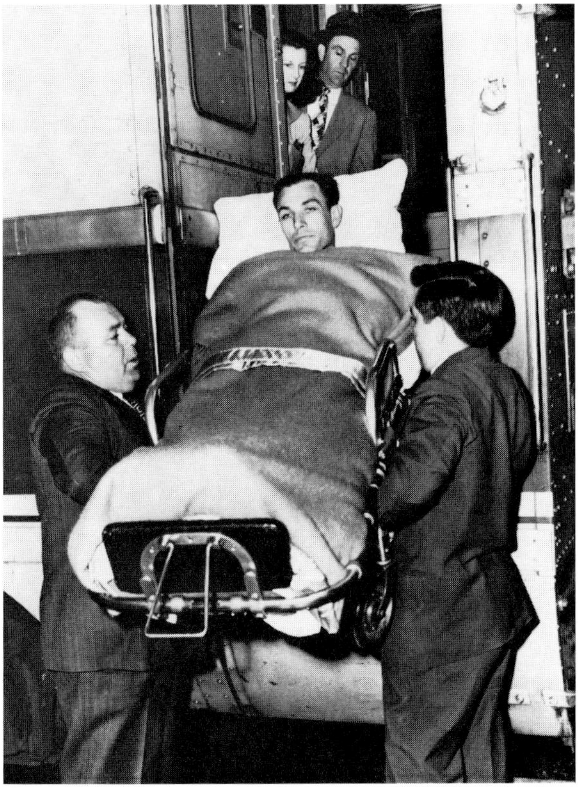

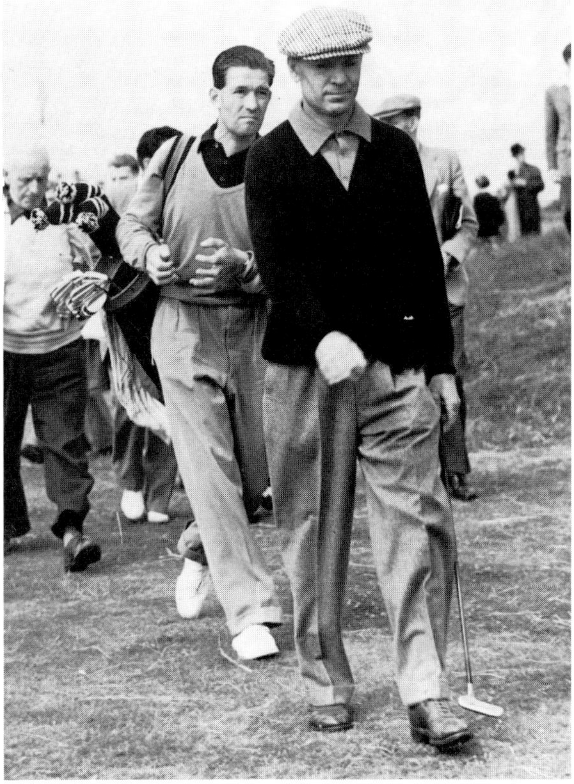

Left: Ben Hogan returns home to Fort Worth after his accident – his weight had dropped to 95 lbs
Right: Hogan's only appearance in the British Open, Carnoustie, 1953

first tournament and struck such tremendous form that year that he had amassed $100,000 by the end of it. Then World War II overtook his ambitions and he joined the Army Air Corps, so that he was in his thirties when he was demobilised, not yet having won a major title. Indeed, he was thirty-four when he became American PGA Champion, yet missed putts on the last green of both the US Masters and Open Championships that year that would have forced him into play-offs. In fact Hogan, in common with so many of the great golfers, was a less than average putter and compensated for this deficiency with his superior striking power. He concluded sadly that putting was a game within a game, and one that he could never master.

When the accident occurred in 1949 Hogan was concentrating largely on the major championships, but his injuries, in the medical view, put a full-time sporting career out of the question. American golf officials were so convinced that his playing days were over that they appointed him non-playing captain of the Ryder Cup side as soon as he came out of hospital later that year. But Hogan had other ideas and was already planning a comeback. He began to practise in secret at his home in Fort Worth, Texas, and while his first efforts at a swing were pathetic, each day brought new strength and what emerged was a new controlled style.

Hogan winning the British Open, Carnoustie, 1953

Less than a year after the accident Hogan astonished everybody by turning up to play in the Los Angeles Open and almost won the title. He scored 73–69–69–69 and had three-putted 11 times to lose to Sam Snead in a play-off. Though still assailed by leg cramps as a result of the accident, he was back to the only life he wanted, and confirmed his recovery by winning the US Open that year in a play-off with George Fazio and Lloyd Mangrum, the latter literally 'blowing' himself out of the title by unthinkingly picking up his golf ball to blow off an insect. The action cost him a two-stroke penalty so that he was never able to match the 69 Hogan produced in the play-off.

The following year Hogan won his first American Masters title, then arrived at Oakland Hills, Michigan, to defend the US Open. For much of his life Hogan gave the impression that the contest was always between himself and the course while the other players looked on, and he confirmed this attitude at Michigan when he opened with a 76, then scored 73–71–67 and remarked that he was always determined to bring 'this monster to its knees'. He was Open Champion again.

By 1953 he was forty years old and seemed to be nearing the end of his career when he pulled off another astonishing golfing feat that nobody has yet equalled. It began when he won the American Masters, then travelled to Oakmont, a massive course amid rolling countryside outside Pittsburg, for the US Open. Once again it was Hogan against the course and he opened with a 67, then seemed incapable of letting up even though his rivals were far behind. In the last round he drove the seventeenth green and two putted for his birdie, then attacked the last hole with a drive and one-iron for another birdie to win by six strokes.

Hogan's friends persuaded him to tackle the British Open, which that year was scheduled for Carnoustie, perhaps the toughest course in the British Isles, and he arrived two weeks before the championship to begin intensive preparation. He mastered the smaller-sized British golf ball, then he charted the golf course, learning the safe areas to land the ball and studying the subtleties and speeds of the greens. In the evenings when he had finished playing he would walk the course from greens to tees to gain another perspective. By the time the championship started, Hogan was better prepared than any other rival and again it was a duel between himself and the course as with each round Hogan forced himself to take more advantage, so that he scored 73–71–70–68 to win his third title of the season. It was his own version of the Grand Slam.

He never returned to defend his title and he just failed to equal the Bobby Jones record of five US Opens when he lost the 1955 play-off to Jack Fleck. But the true testimony of Hogan's skill remains that in the fourteen US Opens and Masters in which he played he never finished outside the top ten. His legend even overshadowed the exploits of such distinguished contemporaries as Sam Snead and Byron Nelson. But if Hogan had set standards of achievement that extended beyond the sport itself, it was Byron Nelson who was regarded by many professionals as the Father of the Modern American Golf Swing.

Byron Nelson

Until Nelson's time the great players hit *against* a firm left side so that this resistance gave their arms and club the impetus to hit the ball. But Nelson devised his own method in which his left knee seemed to buckle at impact so that he hit *with* his left side. It was a lateral body shift instead of the traditional rotation. The method served him well because in 1945 he won nineteen tournaments out of the thirty he entered, including eleven in succession with a stroke average of 68.33. Perhaps the best appraisal of Nelson came from Bobby Jones himself, who admitted: 'At my best, I never came close to the golf that Nelson shoots.' By 1946 Nelson had retired and went on to become a distinguished golf commentator for television. His swing lives on as a model for other golfers, and he was acknowledged by Arnold Palmer to be the major influence on the modern game. Yet although he won two US Masters, two PGA titles and one US Open, but never the British Open, he never quite captured the public's imagination nor received the acclaim his achievements deserved.

Sam Snead remained an athletic phenomenon throughout a career which spanned several eras, so that even at the age of sixty-two he was still playing well enough to finish third in the 1974 American PGA Championship. He was always superbly fit and had a suppleness that kept his swing long and leisurely all his life. The key to his swing was that he concentrated solely on returning his arms and club to the address position in the downswing. Indeed, most of the great players set themselves at the address in the hitting position they hope to achieve. Snead won the British Open in 1946 and the American PGA and the American Masters three times each. It was a sad and unjust omission in such a distinguished career that he never won the American Open.

Sam Snead

Once Hogan decided not to return for the Open Championship, his fellow countrymen saw no need to make the journey, so that a forceful American challenge was not revived until almost a decade later. Even so, the British professionals found themselves dominated by another overseas group as South African Bobby Locke and Australian Peter Thomson began to share the title.

The absence of an American challenge during this era has led some critics to minimise the achievements of these two golfers, yet Locke had proved himself on the American tour in 1947, when he won seven tournaments and finished second in the money list even though he joined the circuit for a summer period only while his American rivals had toiled all year. Locke was banned from the 1949 American tour for breaking commitments, but in fact he declined to play because he was refused the kind of appearance money American professionals received. He was allowed back in 1950 and won five tournaments, but though he made a

Left: Bobby Locke with British Open trophy
Right: Locke at Royal Lytham, 1954

spirited challenge, he never won the Open. The American experience may have soured him, because his greatest achievements were reserved for the British and European circuits.

Some critics mocked his swing but he won four British Opens with that famous unorthodox style by which he hooked every stroke. He aimed to the right of the target and hooked the ball back into the middle of the fairway. This strange-looking style was perfectly consistent with his philosophy on golf which, he concluded, was a game won or lost on the greens, and therefore putting was the greatest art and the one which he perfected. His golf swing accordingly was just a method to get him from tee to green where he could then demonstrate his great talent.

Never a great shot-maker in the Hogan tradition, he simply sought the green where he could start his work. He had the essential imperturbability of a great putter and his painstaking manner at times infuriated his playing partners and rivals. Yet it was never done for distracting effect but solely to maintain a personal state of tranquillity, vital for his work with the putter. He would take twenty minutes to put on his golf shoes. He could spend five minutes getting a golf ball out of his bag. On the practice ground he would strike one ball every ten minutes. Slow play never bothered him. He surveyed greens in ponderous manner because he believed that most putts failed because they were misread and not mishit.

Peter Thomson's greatest achievement was to gatecrash an era from which he seemed to have been excluded. In the mid-sixties he had been overtaken by the dynamic stars from the American tour who had returned to Britain. Thomson had won four British Opens in the fifties, three of them in succession and one in a play-off with Welshman Dave Thomas. Yet the great Americans had been absent from those championships so that Thomson's achievements seemed qualified somewhat because of it. But they were all present in 1965 at Royal Birkdale when he won his fifth title. It was a clash of philosophies as much as skill as Thomson took on the Americans.

Opposite: Arnold Palmer

Gary Player

Jack Nicklaus

Right: Tom Watson

Opposite
Top left: Lee Trevino
Top right: Johnny Miller
Bottom: Bill Rogers

Left: Nancy Lopez-Melton

Opposite
Top left: Severiano Ballesteros
Top right: Isao Aoki
Bottom left: David Graham
Bottom right: Tom Kite

LILY OF FRANC

Peter Thomson

Thomson was fiercely critical of the artificiality they had brought to golf through watered greens which gave the game a dartboard docility totally at odds with its traditional nature. He also disliked the slide-rule aspect of the game in which courses were measured and analysed, so that a player knew exactly how far he had to hit the ball just by arithmetic and not judgement. He did not like the changing face of golf. He preferred to use the smaller 1.62-inch diameter golf ball and was probably the best player of it the world has ever seen. He was also the last great player to use it because the American 1.68-inch diameter ball swept through golf and was later accepted by the Royal and Ancient Club for standard use in their Open Championship. The authorities also accepted it, because the Americans had become superior players through using it, and the Open would thereby maintain an attraction to the American professionals who would not be obliged to make the painful transition to the small ball for a week and then revert to their normal golf ball when they returned to the United States.

Thomson saw golf as a test of intelligence as much as physical skill and once said:

> Muscular strength is not particularly advantageous in golf. Control and direction pays off better . . . Plan your round before you tee off. Plan each hole and stick to that plan. Golf is at least 50 per cent a mental game and if you recognise that the mind prompts us physically, you can almost say golf is entirely a mental effort.

He had a textbook style which lacked power but he compensated with outstanding control and a kind of stepping-stone strategy, choosing his landing areas on the fairways, never attempting a stroke whose outcome might be in doubt. It was the obvious result of his traditionalist attitude, born of fast-running, unwatered golf courses that had not changed since golf began. But his attitudes were swamped by the new image of professsional golf which insisted the sport was public entertainment and that courses should be styled to encourage better and lower scores and not remain exhaustive, overpowering tests of man and his golf.

Opposite
Top left: Jan Stephenson
Top right: Beth Daniel
Bottom: Laura Baugh

The summer of 1965 had been hot and rainless so that Royal Birkdale's fairways were hard, and Thomson knew his lack of power would be no handicap against the Americans and that he had the advantage of being able to play the more essential pitch-and-run shots to greens while the Americans relied on their customary high-flying wedge play.

So it proved, because Thomson was six strokes behind defending champion Tony Lema after the first round but drew closer on the second day with a 68, so that they were paired together on the final day when two rounds were played for the last time in the history of the Championship. By lunchtime it had began to rain and Thomson was one stroke clear in the contest that had developed into a duel between himself and Lema. It was Thomson's instinct that was to make him champion, and the moment came on the short fourteenth when Lema was following the modern trend and checking his notes, while Thomson sensed a subtle shift in the direction of the breeze from the morning round. Lema overlooked the fact that the tee was shielded by a high sand dune and he missed the green with his tee shot, but Thomson found the mark. He had demonstrated his artistry in conditions that had proved too much for the mighty Americans, with Arnold Palmer taking 79 in that last round and Jack Nicklaus 77. Thomson was champion but already a new kind of golf star had emerged and the Australian was the last of the old breed.

In historical terms, Arnold Palmer ranks with Harry Vardon and Walter Hagen as a major figure in the development of the sport. While Vardon turned the playing of professional golf into a career and Hagen emancipated his colleagues from second-class citizenships, it was Palmer who transformed the sport into a national pastime and a television sport, and made himself a multi-millionaire.

For a start, Arnie was the epitome of the American dream. He was an ordinary country boy who became world-famous, who mixed with presidents and kings but never lost the common touch. At the height of his fame he still lived undisturbed in a modest house in his home town of Latrobe, Pennsylvania. It was his style of play as much as his success that drew the crowds who would rather watch him score an 80 than others shooting in the low 60s. He brought excitement, aggression and drama to the sport. If Hogan's contest with the golf course had the calculation of a chess game, then Palmer stepped on to the first tee as if spoiling for a fight.

His technique did not commend itself to the aficionados, nor did anybody really attempt to copy it. He had been brought up to hit the ball hard, in the belief that all other faults could be rectified. That lesson came to him from his father, Deacon Palmer, a stern professional at the nine-hole Latrobe club where young Arnold worked on the course and in the shop. On paternal orders he was never allowed to fraternise with the children of club members, nor was he allowed to use the club swimming pool. Indeed, years later when he became one of the richest sportsmen in

Opposite: Arnold Palmer

the world and bought out the golf club, he confessed: 'I still haven't used that pool.'

But the real secret of the Palmer phenomenon was that he had star quality – a charisma that strikes a chord with the public and sets one man apart from all the rest. It can be identified but not analysed, and Palmer showed that the supreme fame depended on this quality as much as any collection of titles. In championship terms he endured only seven years, one of the shortest reigns for a great player. He won his first US Masters in 1958 and collected his last major title in 1964. He won four Masters titles, two British Opens and one American Open, but never earned the American PGA. Thus the greatest modern influence on the game could not match the achievements of other members of that rare group – Hogan, Sarazen, Player and Nicklaus – who had won all four major titles. Yet in many respects Palmer stood above them all.

Part of his excitement was that he would erupt from anonymity to win tournaments in what became known as the Palmer Charge. In 1960 he was seven strokes behind the leader in the last round of the American Open but scored a 65 to win the title. Earlier that year he had collected the American Masters in similar style with birdies on the last two holes. But what transformed him from an important sporting figure into a major personality was that he happened to be the right man at the right time. He came on the scene at just the moment when President Eisenhower's patronage of golf set an example to millions of leisure-minded Americans.

The two men became close friends and Arnie's success marked the complete metamorphosis of the professional golfer from skilled artisan to national figure, and indeed Palmer himself was urged to enter American politics but decided against the move. Only Jack Nicklaus ever reached the same peak of fame and esteem as Palmer, and it took him the best part of eighteen years, even though he was a champion in his first year as a professional.

Palmer's public esteem was translated into hard cash by a shrewd young Cleveland lawyer called Mark McCormack, who took over Arnie's business affairs and made him the richest sportsman of his time. Indeed, the Palmer–McCormack partnership ushered in the age of the millionaire superstars. The other factor in Palmer's success was that he emerged just as television interest in the sport dawned and he was a figure whose performances – even his failures – were electrifying on the screen. His greatest achievement came in 1960 when he almost equalled Hogan's Grand Slam. He already had the American Masters and Open titles under his belt when he arrived at St Andrews for the British Open, but lost by a stroke to Australian Kel Nagle.

Even so he vowed he would keep coming back until he won and he did not have to wait long. The following year at Royal Birkdale he put on a superlative display to win the title and in so doing earned himself a

Palmer at Wentworth, 1965

commemorative plaque on the old fifteenth hole (now the sixteenth). In the final round he drove into a bush and decided against a safe jab back on to the fairway. Instead he reached for a five-iron and lashed so hard that the bush was wrenched from the ground and the ball finished on the green. He two-putted for par and, even though his pursuer Dai Rees birdied three of the last four holes, Palmer won the title by a stroke and remains convinced it was because he decided to risk all on that historic swipe.

That, too, was part of Palmer's charisma. He was invariably enmeshed in drama and sometimes its victim. In 1961 he needed a par four from a perfect drive in the middle of Augusta's last fairway to win the Masters title for the second year in succession, and even permitted himself a wave to the crowds who cheered their hero home. But he pushed a seven-iron approach into a bunker, thinned his recovery over the green and took six, so that South African Gary Player won the title.

In 1966 he was involved in a drama that probably finished his championship career. He was seven strokes ahead of the field with nine holes of the US Open remaining at the Olympic club in San Francisco and not only lost his lead but was beaten in a play-off the next day by Billy Casper. He never won another major title. Yet he had set standards: he won the 1962 American Masters title and could reflect that but for his last-green error in 1961 he would have made a hat trick of titles, and he had been very close to a hat trick of British Opens because, after failing to Nagle, he won in 1961 and 1962.

Palmer had a short, fast swing which befitted his manner and which he made workable with very strong hands and arms, but throughout his career he fought hard against hooking the ball, so that the left hand resisted strongly against being overpowered by the right and caused a high-handed flourish to the finish of the Palmer swing. It was a punishing swing and one that caused him some back trouble, but it was effective while it lasted and, indeed, it became more orthodox in later years. But by then he had lost his inspirational putting touch which had helped to make him a champion.

Opposite: Palmer in the sand

'A high-handed flourish' during the 1970 Masters

Palmer was such a beloved figure that anybody who succeeded him was bound to be regarded as an unwelcome intruder. When Jack Nicklaus emerged as the next great champion he had to fight this public hostility, which at times reached such hurtful proportions that spectators stood in the rough holding placards which urged: 'Hit it here, Jack.'

But then Nicklaus was everything that Palmer was not – an indulged, fat, privileged youngster from the country club set who seemed to find the game very easy, had very little charm, and almost won the US Open when still an amateur. Even before he was twenty-one he headed a flourishing insurance business. His unpopularity only hardened his resolve, particularly after he had turned professional (much to the disappointment of Bobby Jones who felt that Nicklaus had the ability to win all the major titles as an amateur as he himself had done). In his first year as a professional he won the US Open title and over the next eighteen years had collected eighteen championships. It was one of the longest winning spans of a champion – certainly the most productive – and bore witness to an enduring talent and a desire to keep winning even when there seemed no further need for money or glory.

The phenomenon of Jack Nicklaus reveals many different qualities. His strong back and legs allowed him to develop immense but controlled power, and nobody since Hogan did his homework so thoroughly before playing a golf course. But perhaps the prime reason for his success was that Nicklaus was a perfectionist and, from the moment he took a club in his hands when he was ten years old, he wanted to get it right and would hit more than 300 golf balls a day to drill his swing. This obsession with perfection drove him to unprecedented heights and those around him to occasional distraction. When he built his famed Muirfield Village course outside his home town of Columbus, Ohio, he insisted on many changes to the clubhouse before it was complete and he ordered a massive lake in front of one green to be filled with earth because players were not accepting the challenge of the hole and playing short of the water.

His golf technique was clearly leg-orientated and it was possible to see the immense power generated and transmitted to arm and club as they were dragged into the ball in whiplash fashion. For this reason he had to 'hang on' to the club tightly and used an interlocking grip because he felt his hands were too small to work effectively with Vardon's overlapping grip. For this reason, too, his flying right elbow at the top of the backswing, which offended the laws of orthodoxy, never really presented a problem for a swing that was controlled by his legs. In many respects Nicklaus's style was an important milestone in the development of the swing because it offered identifiable similarities with techniques used by javelin and discus throwers, all of whom employed the strong back muscles and legs to generate power. More than this, it was a technique in which very little could go wrong.

Jack Nicklaus in the 1960s (*left*) and 1970s

Yet Nicklaus's towering talent seemed to have a curious reverse effect on a public who resented him for it, and the great personal achievement for him was to gain public acceptance by 'humanising' his image. It happened when he seemed to have declined as a champion and came to St Andrews in 1970 without a major title to his name for almost three years. It looked as though he had missed out again when Doug Sanders, who had prequalified amongst the faceless hopefuls that year for a place in the Championship, stood over a putt on the last green to become champion. But Sanders made perhaps the most famous and saddest miss in the history of the game and went into a play-off the next day with Nicklaus. The match between them was so delicately balanced that Nicklaus was obliged to deliver a match-winning stroke and drove the last green to birdie the hole and become champion. But it was his unashamed jubilation as he threw his putter high into the air that really endeared him to the crowds all over the world. It proved that Big Jack was human after all and plagued by the same fears and doubts as the rest of the human race.

Nicklaus blasting his way to victory in the Piccadilly World Match Play Championship, Wentworth, 1970

Their beloved Arnie had shown his fallibility through his errors and Big Jack – no longer alluded to as the 'Golden Bear' though it remained his trademark – was just as human through his joy.

Nicklaus's greatest achievement occurred in 1972 when he came within a stroke of holding all four major titles at the same time. He was American PGA champion from 1971 when he won the American Masters and Open titles, but was then beaten by a stroke for the British title at Muirfield by Lee Trevino. That year also marked a significant change in the fortunes of Tony Jacklin, still a world-class player, who lost that British title to Lee Trevino at Muirfield when the American chipped into the 71st hole. There is a theory that this defeat when victory seemed to be assured ruined Jacklin's self-belief and thwarted his development from a good to great player. But Jacklin, the first British player for fifty years to win the US Open, confessed it was Nicklaus and not Trevino who ended his ambition. Jacklin, the 1970 US champion, wanted to be the best golfer in the world but felt inadequate alongside the accomplishments of Nicklaus.

Indeed, Nicklaus dwarfed all his contemporaries and likened himself at times to an old gunfighter from the Wild West who became the target of every young newcomer anxious to make a name. Not many of them lasted long.

It would be incorrect to regard Lee Trevino as a young hopeful when he broke through to snatch the 1968 American Open title at Oak Hill from the game's greatest and most experienced players. Yet he was twenty-seven years old and had resigned himself to a career as a club professional

Another show of strength from the Golden Bear in the World Match Play, 1970

until a year earlier when he decided to make his first attempt on the tournament circuit. He was therefore the oldest rookie on the American tour and had financed his attempt only because of a high finish in the 1967 Championship when he earned $6000 dollars. Over the next decade, however, he was to establish himself as a major force in golf by winning two American Opens, two British Opens and one American PGA Championship. The American Masters eluded him during this time because he felt that his type of stroke-making, a low-flying fade designed to beat the winds of Texas where he learned his golf, was ill-suited for the rolling countryside and plateau greens of Augusta.

But Trevino's imperishable contribution was that he, more than any other golfer, including Arnold Palmer, broadened the appeal of golf by his own background, struggle and attitudes. The son of poor Mexican parents, he had been brought up by his grandfather who was a gravedigger in El Paso. He came to golf, first as a caddie at the local club, then on municipal courses, and ultimately as an assistant professional on a par-three course where he supplemented his income by playing the customers for money. They could use clubs but he limited himself to a soft-drinks bottle swathed in adhesive tape . . . and rarely lost.

Trevino took the stuffiness out of golf and put the fun back into the game. But his happy-go-lucky public image hid the hardened soul of a fierce competitor who had come up the hard way and gatecrashed the upper echelons of the sport. He was a liberating influence, a free spirit, who felt under no obligation to observe any values and customs in which

Opposite: Lee Trevino with the British Open trophy

Trevino at Wentworth, 1972

he did not believe. He once turned down an invitation to the Masters because he did not agree with the club's policies. That breach was subsequently healed.

He was the best shot-maker of his day and capable of fashioning the precise stroke to suit the task. His method was ungainly and imposed immense strain on his back, for which he had to undergo surgery. It was a 'money swing' – a method in which little could go wrong, limited in movement and producing a fade which minimised the risk of the ball running into trouble. Thus he found himself most times 'in the money'. In three glorious weeks in 1971 he won three major titles. He took the American Open for the second time by beating Jack Nicklaus in a play-off at Merion – the experience prompted Nicklaus to remark in admiring tones that once Trevino realised just how good he was, then 'Lee could be unbeatable'! A week later Trevino won the Canadian Open, then moved on with only a few days to prepare for the British Open at Royal Birkdale which he also won. He retained the British title at Muirfield in 1972 but was never in serious contention for a hat trick of victories at Troon a year later.

Left: Johnny Miller
Right: Severiano Ballesteros

By the mid-seventies professional golf offered such massive rewards to the best golfers that the need, and perhaps desire, to stay at the top was diminished and the important knack – which seemed to elude the likes of Johnny Miller and Tony Jacklin – was to ignore the riches and play for glory. For a period golf lost some of its excitement until the emergence of Tom Watson and Severiano Ballesteros, both of whom were motivated by intense pride and sustained by prodigious talent.

Ballesteros, the Spaniard, demonstrated an artistry and daring that seemed to have been lost to the game as everybody played safe percentage golf to reap financial rewards. He was not afraid to miss fairways nor find trouble among the trees, because he had a superlative talent for recovery strokes which at times seemed to be the only challenge he relished in a game he had learned as a part-time caddie on the Royal Pedrena golf course in Northern Spain next to his parents' modest farm. By the time he was twenty-three he had captured the British Open and American Masters titles within a year.

Tom Watson was a different phenomenon who of all the great players seemed to suffer the kind of agonies of competition that assailed Bobby Jones. He earned a good degree in psychology at Stanford University, California, and toyed with thoughts of a medical career until his

Tom Watson

extraordinary golf talent developed during his student days. Yet it was a talent which, in the early years, he seemed unable to direct towards specific titles in the manner of an athlete training to hit peak form for a certain race. But even though Watson was to waste several golden chances, particularly in the American Open, he achieved such a high level of consistency that after nine years as a professional he had won the British Open three times, the American Masters twice and topped the US money list for four successive years.

Yet it is a comment on the influence of Jack Nicklaus that two of Watson's finest victories involved the Golden Bear himself. Their epic duel over 36 holes for the British Open at Turnberry in 1977, when Nicklaus escaped from a bush down the last fairway and holed from the front of the green but still lost, ranks as an imperishable moment in golf. Earlier that same year Watson had triumphed over Nicklaus at the US Masters in rather dramatic circumstances when he mistook a wave of delight by Nicklaus as a personal taunt. Watson's misplaced anger bore him to victory but he later admitted his mistake and apologised to Nicklaus. It was an untypical error by Watson, whose level-headedness and sense of proportion allowed him wider horizons beyond golf itself.

If longevity is proof of talent and dedication, then the remarkable South African Gary Player stands alongside the great champions. He won the British Open for the first time in 1959 and was still in champion's form twenty years later when he won the US Masters in 1978. All of which underlined his basic philosophy that the golfer is an athlete and needs to train and be fit in the manner of a runner. His diminutive stature (5 ft 7 ins and 150 lbs) meant he had to develop his strength to match the power players who emerged in the sixties, and he was willing to try any health-giving aid if it made him play better golf.

Gary Player

His keep-fit antics were legendary and not only did he try all manner of diets including bananas, raisins and peanuts, but he took to wearing black clothes because he believed they absorbed the sun's rays and gave him additional strength. His training programme was rigorous and his excess baggage charges enormous because he brought his own weight-training equipment wherever he played. He would perform hundreds of finger-tip press-ups (even with weights on his back). He would run for miles every evening and urge fellow professionals to join him. He believed that a healthy body promoted an alert and quick mind which was essential for successful golf, whose psychic aspect had never been fully explored. There was also, in Player's case, a hint of mysticism as though he had a duty in life which could be fulfilled only through his golf.

Gary Player was not stirred by overt missionary zeal, although there is no doubt he felt bound to perform well for his country as much as for himself. No golfer, perhaps no sportsman, has ever had such demands put upon him. Not only did he travel thousands of miles around the world annually to compete, but wherever he went he was generally called to task for South Africa's political situation in relation to apartheid. Indeed, in the 1969 American PGA Championship at Dayton, Ohio, he needed an armed guard in the final round after demonstrators had attacked him on the third day. Even so he almost won the title, finishing runner-up to Ray Floyd.

It is a measure of Player's skill that many of his championships were won on the most demanding golf courses in the world. He won three British Opens and, while Royal Lytham, the scene of his last triumph in 1974, placed more emphasis on accuracy (though Severiano Ballesteros was to confound that theory by ignoring the fairways in winning the 1979 title), there is no doubting the formidable nature of both Carnoustie and Muirfield on which he won his other two titles. Two victories in the US Masters underlined his capacity to adapt his technique to whatever kind of strokes were needed.

Gary Player's reign was to touch three decades, during which he joined Gene Sarazen, Jack Nicklaus and Ben Hogan as the only men ever to win all four major titles. Player won the US Open in 1965 and took the American PGA title in 1969 and 1972. He was the master of practice and perhaps nobody since Hogan spent more time improving his technique. His power came from a suppleness born of his physical-fitness routines. He became the best bunker player in the world and the confidence this talent gave him instilled an authority through the rest of his game. He possessed an indomitable spirit which kept him at the top for so long and was never better demonstrated than when he fought back from five down with nine to play to Tony Lema during the 1965 World Match Play Championship at Wentworth to win at the first extra hole. He showed then just how important self-belief and stamina can be to a golfer's success.

Thus has each great champion made a different but vital addition to

Player on his way to winning the British Open, Carnoustie, 1968

the game and thereby enriched it. Each depended on those who had gone before in that standards were set to be matched and bettered. Vardon gave the world a golf swing from which all else stemmed and his record of six Open Championship victories still stands. The great Bobby Jones can rest easy that his Grand Slam record is secure since no amateur has proved himself good enough to win an Open title in modern times – though some have come close – let alone win on both sides of the Atlantic in the same years as well as taking the amateur titles. Both Walter Hagen and Henry Cotton gave professional golf a status and prestige from which Arnold Palmer and his explosive talent created the age of the millionaire professionals.

Yet the game is about winning and about personal achievement on a golf course and in particular in a championship when it matters. That remains the eternal target for those who wish to prove their excellence. Being champion is the ultimate dream and ambition. One man has been champion more times than anybody. Thus for enduring skill and that obsessive desire to remain the best, Jack Nicklaus remains the greatest of them all. Like Bobby Jones he set standards and records for others and already they are out of reach.

CHAPTER SIX

Golf is Big Business

by Renton Laidlaw

If you are in doubt that golf today is a big-money sport consider these facts. It takes over £1 million to run the Open and it makes a profit; Arnold Palmer Enterprises had a turnover last year of $40 million; Jack Nicklaus heads a golf-course design and construction firm which, along with real-estate development, will gross him an estimated $300 million over the next few years; Severiano Ballesteros makes $1 million a year; Lee Trevino estimates that real-estate deals that went wrong have cost him $8 million. And what about this? Golf ball sales around the world annually represent a turnover of £240 million – twenty million dozen balls.

When the Open Championship began at Prestwick, Scotland, in 1860 the winner, Willie Park, received no financial reward. The glory of winning and custody for a year of the Open Championship belt was his prize. Now money rules golf. Big business has taken over. Today the Open champion receives a £32,000 first-prize cheque, but that is just the tip of the iceberg or rather of a golfing gold mine. Winning the Open, if the player is in cold, calculating, business terms 'marketable', is a springboard to millionaire status. Tony Jacklin won the title in 1969 and within three

Tony Jacklin and his wife Vivien on their way to a million, British Open, Royal Lytham, 1969

years he had netted a million dollars in contracts – helped, of course, by the fact that he went on to add the US title to his victory list. Imagine, then, what a British winner of the title would make today – and how quickly he would make it.

Prize money just keeps going up and up and up. Last year there were $40 million on offer on the major circuits of the world – America, Europe, Japan, the Far East, Australia and New Zealand, and South Africa. Richest first prize in America is the $100,000 cheque that goes to the winner of the World Series at the Firestone Country Club in Akron, Ohio. In the winter of 1981 the booming golfing calendar included a new $1 million event in Bophuthatswana just north of South Africa. The field comprised only five players, with the winner, Johnny Miller, netting a cool $500,000. Incidentally Jack Nicklaus, who played in it, turned down a $1.5 million winner-take-all challenge match in the mid-1970s to play 18 holes against the same Johnny Miller. Nicklaus felt it was not in the best interests of the game.

In this chapter we shall examine the rapid growth of prize money, the ever-spiralling cost of equipment as raw material costs soar in an inflationary economic climate. We shall examine, too, just how much it costs these days to play golf here in Britain, in America and in Japan where five million golfers will, incredibly, never get the chance to step on to a golf course! We shall look at the cost involved in running a club here, and in America where some complexes, like the Pinehurst development in North Carolina, have six courses.

It is estimated that, worldwide, around twenty-five million people are members of golf clubs and that another twenty-five million play golf, making fifty million altogether. In the sixties when Arnold Palmer was at his peak there was an annual seventeen per cent increase in the golfing numbers. Now it has slowed down to five per cent a year but, as more and more people become interested and want to play, facilities for them to do so cannot cope. The high cost of building golf courses means construction has been hit as the recession bites. It means more and more existing courses are becoming log-jammed from dawn to dusk. In some parts of America it is not unusual for golfers to queue through the night to get a starting time. Such is the grip of the game, however, that even all that hassle does not deter the intrepid enthusiast. Golf is addictive.

Building a new course means high capital expenditure. The cost involves a number of imponderables – how much you pay per acre of land and how much you pay to develop it, especially if the terrain is initially unsuitable. In Britain building just one hole will set you back more than £10,000 – and that's the minimum. Not that poor terrain is always a stumbling block to development. At the Aga Khan's course at Pevero in Sardinia hundreds of tons of rock were blasted – at tremendous expense – to cut a tough championship course through the mountains. Within the

House-owner Isao Aoki

last couple of years a new desert course has been opened in the Middle East, with greens laid on earth flown in from Greece. They must be the most expensive putting surfaces in the world. Just think of the air-freight charges alone.

Over the years golf has always had a big-money tag in one respect or another. In Scotland, way back in 1849, Allan Robertson and Tom Morris played a challenge match against the Dunn Brothers for £400 – a fortune then. Nearly 200 years earlier King James VII/II played with an Edinburgh shoemaker against two English noblemen. The King and the shoemaker won and with his winnings the tradesman was able to buy a house for himself in Edinburgh's famous Royal Mile. To this day there is still a building there – appropriately named Golfer's Land. In more modern times Japan's Isao Aoki won a £55,000 condominium at Gleneagles for just one shot. His bonus came when he aced the second hole in the 1979 World Match Play at Wentworth. Golf can be a crazy game, too.

The really big money in golf began with Arnold Palmer and Jack Nicklaus. When in 1960 Palmer asked Mark McCormack, a young Cleveland lawyer and himself a keen student of the game, to represent him, a multi-million-dollar empire was born – an empire that has reaped huge rewards for player and manager, an empire that, like Topsy, just grew and grew and grew. McCormack, whose massive International Management Group now handles top sportsmen and women in all fields of activity plus show business personalities, can justifiably bask in the glory of being recognised as the world's top manager-organiser-entrepreneur. He has even been called in to mastermind the arrangements for the Pope's travels abroad.

McCormack has come a long way from the days in Cleveland when he was earning $5400 dollars a year and taking the bus into work. When he shook Arnold Palmer's hand to clinch their partnership it was in every sense a golden handshake. To this day there is no written contract between them. McCormack's success story is the result of selfless dedication and hard work. His timetable is a punishing one. If he is not at his Cleveland headquarters he could be at his London office, or in Sydney, Buenos Aires or New York. McCormack men around the world are signing contracts, arranging tournaments, satisfying clients twenty-four hours a day. With very few exceptions McCormack's cut is usually a quarter. No one complains about that – 75 per cent of the income McCormack can generate for a client is usually far more than the 100 per cent a client could arrange for himself. In modern parlance McCormack is a workaholic – and proud of it. Twenty years on he still loves what he is doing, never more than when he is working on a new deal for Arnie – the flagship of the organisation.

Top man Mark McCormack

In his book about Palmer, published a few years ago, McCormack, detailing just how well he marketed his client, wrote:

It is possible to play golf with Arnold Palmer clubs, to dress from head to toe in Arnold Palmer clothes. You can buy your golfing insurance from the Arnold Palmer agency, stay in a Palmer motel, buy a Palmer lot to build a home, push a Palmer-approved lawnmower, read a Palmer book or newspaper column, be catered to by a Palmer maid [yes, he ran a domestic help service at one time], listen to Palmer music on gramophone records, have your suit dry-cleaned at a Palmer laundry. You could shave with his lather, spray on his deodorant, drink his favourite soft drink, fly his preferred airline, buy his approved corporate jet, eat an Arnold Palmer candy bar, and order your stock certificates through him.

That's marketing! In 1979 – fifteen years after he won his last Masters, his last big one – Palmer's income from golfing and business sources was £2.5 million and it is even more now per annum.

Today Arnie may be over fifty, have grey hair, be a little thicker round the waist, but he is still as popular as ever. He is something of a folk hero. His business success has been the result of a combination of McCormack's astuteness and his own personal charm. He oozes honesty and sincerity. He is down-to-earth, likeable, friendly – superbly marketable. At the Masters each year at Augusta he always films a commercial in front of the clubhouse door for Cadillac who help sponsor that very special tournament. On television he is just as likely to pop up on-screen recommending a certain brand of oil, or it might be the latest in business machines. Every article he promotes is carefully vetted. His reputation must be protected. In the early days he was involved in a cigarette advertisement but now that kind of ad is banned. The organisation turns down on average one lucrative offer a week because the product does not fit the Palmer image, the money is not right, or Arnie just does not have the time to fit it into his crowded schedule, a schedule in which, these days, playing golf takes second place.

Multi-millionaire Arnold Palmer

Palmer's operation alone has a gross annual turnover of $40 million. Six hundred people work for him to keep his business interests ticking over. He has his motor-car agencies and dealerships; he is into hotels in a big way. There are the real-estate, golf-course construction and commercial developments like the 60-acre Palmer Corporate centre in Charlotte, North Carolina. He may not tee it up so often these days but whenever he does (and wherever) he still has an army of fans to follow him around.

Arnold Palmer literally has millions of admirers. His greatest is McCormack who, just as Arnie revolutionised golf, has turned sports management on its head. Now he not only manages players, he runs tournaments (although not in America where the rules prevent that) and finds sponsors. His organisation grossed $25 million in the mid-seventies. The wage bill for his staff of 400 is colossal but then they include the top experts in the business: he does, after all, provide his clients with the complete service – accountants to deal with tax problems, lawyers to handle contracts, experts from the stock market to handle investments. He makes millionaires of his larger clients, grossing half a million dollars himself annually.

If McCormack has cashed in on Palmer's charisma and uncomplicated all-American image, he has done the same for others on a more modest scale. Gary Player, who spends only about twelve weeks in America in each year, does not have anything like the business interests of Arnie but his gross turnover from agriculture, his expanding racing stables and real estate is $4 million a year. Severiano Ballesteros, who will gross a minimum $1 million a year for the next ten years, with most of the money going into a special account in Nevada, is not in the McCormack camp but International Management Group maintain a fully-operational file on him just in case he ever does switch managers. That's all part of the meticulous way McCormack does business. McCormack saw the potential of sports management and exploited it – although exploitation is not a word in the IMG vocabulary.

Yet McCormack's success has meant sacrifices too. He spends little time at home – how could he, clocking up 250,000 miles a year in travel? (He can confirm that figure each December, by the way.) Just as he is punctilious in business, so he is in private life. A confirmed jogger, he does half a mile a day to loosen up; he sleeps on average only five hours a night. He has been fortunate that he has an iron constitution, although he did get a nasty scare in 1974 when, after a fall in Spain, he developed a clot on the lining of the brain. He needed very delicate surgery; five holes were drilled in his head to relieve the pressure.

Some of his associates thought that that would be the end of the jet-set, globe-trotting, life-style for Mark Hume McCormack. They were wrong. Five weeks later, after a recuperative stay at the fashionable Gleneagles

Hotel, McCormack was back at his office desk doing what he likes best – working. He still makes every minute of the day count. No matter what time of the day (or night) he flies in, a car and a secretary are at the airport to meet him. En route to the office memos are dictated, letters written, orders rapped out. By the time of his first appointment he is ready for a busy round of meetings with all the office routine taken care of. Even when he is at home with his wife Nancy and their three children there is little chance of his missing out on any business development. He has eleven phones in his Cleveland home.

Such a hectic life – busier than that of many top golf professionals – would have sidelined most people years ago. Not McCormack. He enjoys the frenetic life-style and loves being not only the behind-the-scenes, 24-hour dynamo but also the front man of the organisation. At the World Match Play, for instance, he is always in evidence throughout the week at Wentworth, and not just because he signed up the sponsor, his company runs the event, the field comprises mostly players under his management, his film company makes the official film of the tournament or because he arranges the worldwide television rights. He is there because he wants to be, getting his biggest kick out of his golf business. During the week he even finds time to keep his hand in at commentating on BBC Television. He is Mr Incredible who, when he started in golf management, admits he felt like a modern Robin Hood. In the 1960s top sportsmen, he alleges, were being ripped off. Not any more!

McCormack's first big business venture with Palmer was to organise, in the early sixties, the 'Big Three' golfing challenge games for television – Palmer, Player and Nicklaus, whom he signed up as an amateur but who left him after ten years to do his own thing. Nicklaus set up the Golden Bear organisation which grosses more, annually, than even the Palmer empire. Big Jack has made over $3.5 million in prize money on the US circuit (almost $5 million worldwide) in the past fifteen years, but he will make much more from his business interests over the next fifteen. His earnings potential from golf-course building, land development and real estate is estimated at 100 times what he earned playing golf – a staggering $300 million.

The transition from player to designer and developer began about five years ago. Nicklaus is so much in demand that he just cannot cope, himself, with all the potential business and now works on occasion with Tom Watson. Nicklaus does not come cheap but that is no deterrent. People do not mind paying up for the Nicklaus connection, expertise and style. His fee for a basic course design in America is $150,000, for one elsewhere in the world $250,000. Add on another $50,000 if an interpreter is required. If the client wants Nicklaus himself to supervise the construction add on a further $100,000 and, of course, the post-construction maintenance programme is virtually obligatory at $50,000

Preparing for the big prize: Tom Watson and Jack Nicklaus (with Nick Faldo in the background), British Open, Sandwich, 1981

. . . and a spade has not gone into the ground yet! Once the course has been completed the Nicklaus organisation will, if you wish, appoint a professional and stock his shop, even appoint a club manager and run the club too. The service is all-embracing.

That is only one branch of the Nicklaus empire. There is the real estate – not least at his own development, Muirfield Village, in his home state, Ohio, a multi-million dollar project on which Nicklaus has spent a fortune to get it right. It's a showpiece project well suited to a man who, five years ago, had assets estimated at $15 million. Another development scheme he is working on is at the St Andrew's Golf Club near New York. Nicklaus is modernising the Club, maintaining all the traditions of the course but building £100,000 villas around it!

His real-estate operation is so big that when the famed Pebble Beach complex on the Monterey peninsula just south of San Francisco was up for sale recently Jack was in the market. On that occasion he lost out, but only to the huge 20th Century Fox Corporation. Like Palmer he has major contracts with quality firms – Hart, Schafner and Marx, the largest producers of men's clothing in America, with a turnover of over $100 million a year in Nicklaus clothing; American Express; MacGregor Clubs, which he now owns. He is a golf consultant to a top television network, has motor-car dealerships like Arnie – the list is endless. But his lasting legacy to a game that has been tremendously good to him and for which he has also given so much are his courses. Long after he has stopped playing they will still be there as a permanent memorial to, arguably, the greatest golfer ever. He is proud of his achievements on the course, the records he has made, many of which may never be broken, but he is just as proud of his golf courses – and not because of the income they generate.

Tony Jacklin has, since the war, been Britain's most successful golfer, managed of course by Mark McCormack. Jacklin joined up with 'Mark the Knife' in 1967 because he believed McCormack could make him a millionaire. Over the years he *has* made a million – not bad for a former apprentice fitter earning less than a fiver a week in Scunthorpe. Today, thirteen years after his Open success that July afternoon at Lytham, he still earns £100,000 a year from various contracts. Like Ballesteros, Nicklaus, Palmer and company he has wide-ranging connections in Japan where big-money contracts are still available for him. He has a marvellous home in tax-haven Jersey where he fled, unwillingly, when government tax changes meant he would have to pay high British tax even on money earned abroad where tax levels can be lower.

Even if he retired tomorrow, however, Jacklin is financially set up for life. The multi-million dollar sport has served him well and his crowd appeal and popularity have put hundreds of pounds in his fellow professionals' pockets. In the mid-seventies, when John Jacobs was skilfully pulling together the European circuit as we know it today, he encouraged sponsors to pour money into the game by dangling 'the Jacklin carrot'. If international star Jacklin was in the field sponsors did not mind increasing the prize kitty and, as a reward, Jacobs permitted Jacklin to accept appearance money as well. In the early seventies European prize-money for the season was around the £300,000 mark. Now it is over £2 million and rising. What Palmer did for the American circuit, Jacklin and Jacobs did for the European professional scene.

Even in difficult inflationary times most of the golfing tours remain buoyant. There is no shortage of sponsors ready to come forward. Indeed, they are being turned away in America. Exposure on television has done much to boost sponsor interest in the Royal and Ancient game. Television coverage in America has been worth $30 million to the US Tour over the past three years, and more than half the events on the British circuit are 'on the box'.

Most sponsors, wherever in the world, see golf as a quality vehicle for a quality product. Some years ago Cadillac did a research survey which revealed that the basic audience for golf (in America certainly and, I suspect, elsewhere too) is up-market. The viewers were, in general, the men and women who were highly educated, who were between the ages of twenty-four and forty-five, and all of whom lived on an above-average income. They were, in short, the professional and managerial types, the decision-makers. Cadillac saw the potential and decided to sponsor the US Masters, golf's quality springtime promotion. They signed up Arnold Palmer for their commercials – stylish commercials which boosted car sales considerably.

That was a shrewd business move, aimed directly at a special quality market, but there were other reasons why Eastern Airlines opted for a partnership with Doral Country Club near Miami to run a tournament. The airline, based in Miami, were well aware, of course, of the free advertising benefits they would get from coast-to-coast television coverage. Because the event is staged in March in warm Florida sunshine, Eastern did indeed find their ticket desks received considerable extra business just after the event. Their golf sponsorship not only increased business, however, it also gave them a community involvement which pleased their regular Miami commuters.

The Kemper insurance company moved into golf sponsorship because they wanted to sell more insurance policies to men – and did so well that they even started the Women's Kemper to sell more insurance to women. The Industrial Valley Bank of Philadelphia benefits, too, from its involvement with golf in that area. The money spent on official spending and entertaining during the week of the IVB tournament would finance a million advertisement hoardings or twenty television slots, but the bank believes it gets better value from the tournament, where officials can meet potential local investors at grass-roots level. Business has done well.

Fifteen years ago United Airlines started the Hawaiian Open in the hope of stimulating air traffic from the mainland. Just how successful that operation has been can be judged from the fact that fifty per cent of all United's flights now go to Hawaii and now account for half the company's income. Take another example, Michelob beer. That company knew everyone enjoys a glass of something after a round. They felt they had a quality product well suited for the game of golf. Their campaign was so successful that they formed an advisory staff of professionals who now represent the company in appearances for charity and at local tournaments. The professionals also carry a Michelob sticker on their bags.

In British terms the situation is similar. Martini, Dunlop Sports, Cacharel, Lancome, Haig, White Horse are all in golf because they want a quality product advertised in the right circles. Lawrence Batley, the pawky Midland millionaire who runs his own tournament each year, does so in partnership with Bradford Council, who are keen to attract new industry to the area. Jersey run their tournament to attract summer visitors to the honeymoon island. Corals, who now operate on-course betting at some golf tournaments, promote their Classic in order to advertise the service they provide and at the same time be seen to be putting something back into the game.

Sponsors clearly feel it is all worthwhile or they would not keep coming back. Hard-headed marketing men cannot all be wrong. Without sponsorship the tour would die in Britain and wither considerably in the States, but they are doing nicely. The European circuit snakes its way up and down and across the continent and throughout Britain from April until November. Full-time expenditure on the tour can amount to nearly £6000 a year for a professional, not living lavishly but ensuring he has a proper caddie, regular and protein-packed meals, a comfortable room in an average hotel and reasonably planned travel arrangements. A week on the continent can cost £500 although it is cheaper in Britain. When, each year, young hopefuls enter for the qualifying school in Portugal to get a Tour card, they are warned that if they think the £250 package is too costly they are unlikely to be able to afford to play the circuit full-time!

The rewards for the successful players are, of course, considerable. Bernhard Langer, the young German who won the Order of Merit in 1981, scooped not far short of £100,000 – that, incidentally, is eight times what top money-earner, Neil Coles, won in 1970. If the circuit is worth £2 million you can be sure it took at least a further £2 million, probably three, to stage the various events. The £100,000 Bob Hope Classic, which is a highly popular pro-am event featuring top professionals and show business stars, takes £600,000 to run once advertising costs, course preparation fees and appearance money and expenses have been worked out.

Appearance money has been banned on the American circuit, but it has not been possible to do that in Europe and Japan, where Lee Trevino can command $40,000 or even $50,000 just to turn up. That is about the going rate for one-day exhibitions for the superstars as well. Severiano Ballesteros may be restricted in what appearance fees he can command on his home circuit but he can pocket £40,000 for a two-week stint in the land of the rising sun – and, incidentally, the land of booming golf business. More staggering statistics from Japan later. Money alone, of course, could not persuade Jack Nicklaus or Tom Watson to head for Britain, except for the Open whose prestige is second to none in world golfing terms. Top stars require more unusual inducements – the

Opposite: Golfing matador Seve Ballesteros

Left: Europe's biggest money-winner 1981, Bernhard Langer
Right: Globe-trotter Greg Norman

opportunity for some deep-sea fishing, the chance to go on safari, the possibility of a week in Paris for the wife. You will seldom see a top star crossing the Atlantic these days in a Jumbo. They all travel Concorde, eliminating jet lag. Nicklaus sometimes uses his own jet although he does not fly it. Palmer flies his, however, and when he is not using his plane (in fact he has two) he hires it out at $1000 an hour. It is just another money-spinner for him.

Although the European tour has grown dramatically in the past seven years, to the point where it can now attract top international fields, it is only the third largest in the world. The Japanese tour is twice as big, but the American is the biggest – over $14 million worth of prize money on offer in 1982.

The US tour first broke the $1 million mark in 1958, the year Palmer was top money-winner with $42,000. Tom Kite was top money-winner last year, but the most prolific earner in America recently has been Tom Watson. He was No. 1 for four years from 1977, grossing half a million himself in 1980. In the last five years Watson has earned on American golf courses a staggering $2,014,185 and 42 cents. He made a million of that between 7 May 1978 and 25 May 1980 – the quickest million in the history of the tour. It took Palmer, golf's first $1 million prize-winner, thirteen and a half years to amass that total, but then golf was not the big-money business in the sixties that it is today.

Million-dollar men
Left: Bruce Lietzke
Above: Tom Kite

Thirty-two players on the US Tour have made at least $1 million – Kite, Bruce Lietzke, Jerry Pate, John Mahaffey and David Graham of Australia joining the exclusive club in 1981. Only Watson, Trevino and Hale Irwin have made more then $2 million, only Nicklaus has topped $3 million. In 1972 Nicklaus made over $300,000 in one season. He did so again in 1973. Johnny Miller was the big earner in 1974. Watson in 1977, 1978, 1979 and 1980, when he was joined above the $300,000 mark by Lee Trevino. Last year five players made more – Watson, Kite (who won only once but had twenty-one top-ten finishes out of twenty-six

Million-dollar men
Above: David Graham
Right: Jerry Pate
Below: Bill Rogers

starts), Ray Floyd (who had the distinction of winning over $500,000 in two weeks for back-to-back wins at Doral and the Tournament Players Championship thanks to a local bonus offer), Lietzke, and Open Champion Bill Rogers, who was America's player of the year. Thirty-eight golfers in 1981 earned more than $100,000 on the US circuit. Even sixtieth place on the money list grossed Vance Heafner $73,000, but remember weekly expenditure is high. Peter Oosterhuis, whose victory in the 1981 Canadian Open – his first tour success – was worth $63,000, budgets on $25,000 in expenses each year – and that is the least it could be. Frankly, the above-the-line profit of Barney Thompson, who finished 100th last year with $36,000, would have been marginal. It's a tough school.

The biggest winner on the US Tour is not a player at all. It is charity.

Million-dollar men
Above: Hale Irwin
Left: Ray Floyd
Below: John Mahaffey

Many of the events on the 45-week schedule are organised on a community basis to help local funds. The Bing Crosby at Pebble Beach each year has raised nearly $5 million; the Bob Hope Desert Classic can top that with $6 million over the years, most of it going to a local hospital. Community pride ensures that locals not only give their time to help run tournaments, they also plough in some of their own cash. At Phoenix each year the 'greenskeepers' – 330 local businessmen – chip in $500 apiece to ensure the tournament is a financial success. Overall, last year, charity benefited to the tune of $5 million on the US circuit or an amount equal to forty per cent of the prize-fund kitty. In the past twenty-five years $50 million has been raised on the tour for hospitals, medical research and youth programmes.

The average weekly attendance at an American event is 80,000, but many more than that attend the US Open, where gate-money amounts to $750,000 during the week; a season ticket costs $80. Even the programme is a money-spinner: it costs $150,000 to produce, has over 300 pages, weighs about a pound and a half, and sales gross nearly $1 million. Most of that goes to the host club. Even the local club professional at the American Open can boost his gross takings by $80,000 during the Championship by selling souvenirs – jerseys, coasters, bag tags, hats, rainwear, umbrellas, shooting sticks and folding chairs, glasses, commemorative plates, books and ties. Concessionary stands selling soft drinks, hot dogs and hamburgers at the biggest American golf event of the season (the US Masters is a refined, all-ticket, garden-party affair with its own character and style) will net upwards of $30,000.

The television fee for exclusive coverage is a staggering $1.75 million. Actually that is for a package involving all the events the US Golf Association handle, but the big one is the Open and that gets the big treatment. Last year ABC, using thirty-one cameras, covered every hole on the course. No shot was missed because sixteen of the cameras were mobile. Producer Roone Arledge utilised over sixty camera positions, and high above Merion hovered the Goodyear blimp with a camera crew on board to give the occasional bird's-eye shot. Over 300 people worked on the telecasts over the last two days – 120 technicians, thirty staff and 150 local residents used for spotting, scoring and other duties. Logistically ABC Sports used 150,000 feet of camera cable, 300,000 feet of sound cable, 25,000 feet of video cable supplying the closed-circuit feed to every corner of the course, and ten miles of communication cable to ensure a fail-safe scoring system – and . . . whisper it . . . even then they got a score wrong. If normal US television tournament coverage costs on average $500,000 a time, the ABC operation must have cost double that – $1 million plus the television rights fee – $2.75 million – massive but much of it recoverable from prime-time advertising. At the Masters, where advertising is limited to seven minutes in any one hour, a minute costs around $50,000 these days. It's just another example of big money in golf.

At the American Open they are learning, too, from Britain's Royal and Ancient Golf Club of St Andrews about successful tournament staging. Hospitality tents, first featured at the Open in Britain, are sprouting up now at major American events. The US Open bosses are beginning to provide more seating accommodation and better scoreboards but they are still a long way from matching spectator facilities like those provided at the Open in Britain. Without a doubt the British Open is the best-run, best-managed golf event in the world. New standards are being set each year.

Keith Mackenzie has masterminded the Open since 1967. He is the secretary of the Royal and Ancient and it was he who revived the Championship, with the help (in fairness) of a useful twosome – Palmer and Nicklaus. After World War II American Sam Snead had come over to win the title; so too had Ben Hogan, but more and more in the fifties the Championship was losing its international status. Without detracting in any way from the marvellous victories of Bobby Locke and Peter Thomson, they won most of their titles when the American challenge was not at its strongest. In 1960 Palmer came to the Centenary Open and finished second to Kel Nagle. Two years later Jack Nicklaus made his first appearance and finished down the field at Troon. But the support these two (and Gary Player) gave the event was enough to set it alight again. With Keith Mackenzie enthusiastically whipping up interest, the Championship was restored to its rightful place on the golfing calendar. It *is* number one! In the truest sense it is the most open of all Opens and, with secretary Mackenzie in recent times turning his efforts to attracting Japanese participation, it is the most cosmopolitan.

In 1972 the Open cost just over £150,000 to run and income was £190,000 which included £60,000 for the television rights. In 1981 the production costs were £1,250,000, the income £1,500,000 – a third of that coming from television rights. It seems incredible that just over twenty years ago the BBC's contract to cover one and a half hours of Open golf was a paltry £450. Indeed the BBC were not even all that interested in televising it! At that stage there was no mass-appeal player and the cost of getting the Open on the screen, in the Corporation's opinion, was far in excess of its potential viewer interest. Last year thirty-six million people watched the Open live in Britain and America. Millions more watched in Japan and fourteen other countries hooked into same-day if not live coverage.

When Roberto de Vicenzo, that gentleman golfer from Buenos Aires, won the title in 1967, Mackenzie's first year 'in charge', 29,000 people paid to watch the action. At Lytham in 1980 over 130,000 spectators travelled to the course during Open week. In 1967 the total prize-fund was £15,000 – that's £17,000 less than the winner gets today! What profit the Open makes each year is ploughed back, incidentally, into golf in one way or another. The members of the R and A do not benefit at all. Indeed, most years they have to pay for their own tickets.

An economic survey carried out in 1978 at St Andrews, when the Championship was won for the third time by Nicklaus, indicated that during Open week £3 million was spent in the area. On average each visitor spent £47, not including their gate entry money. Hotels benefited; so too did restaurants; and in the long term everyone in the area had some reason to be pleased that the Championship was in town, even if, for a few days, the place was crowded.

Four caterers are needed now each year to cope with the job of feeding 25,000 hungry people a day. Gallons of tea are drunk, hundreds of meat pies and sausage rolls are consumed, and in the hospitality tents

Above: The tented village, British Open, Sandwich, 1981
Right: Inside the press tent, Sandwich, 1981

companies entertain clients lavishly at about £45 a head to a champagne lunch with all the trimmings and a seat in a reserved stand around the eighteenth green. And for every five spectators at the Open each day there is someone there to work. Each day 5000 people pass through the turnstiles to assist with scoring, catering and stewarding. A medical unit copes with 500 cases during the week and the physiotherapy unit is in demand as much from the players as from those spectators who have twisted an ankle or pulled a neck muscle craning to see their hero in action. Not that much craning is needed with so many stands sited at vantage points to aid spectators. At the Open nothing is left to chance. Even a team of youngsters operates from early morning to late evening on litter patrol. From the moment the greenkeepers sign in at 5 am each day to the moment when the last card has been handed in and the draw for the following day made, the Open runs like a well-oiled machine.

Still staggered at the expense of running the Open? Well, ponder these

LEADER BOARD
HOLES
PAR
PLAYER
SCORE
WATSON T
TREVINO
CRENSHAW
NICKLAUS
MASON
BROWN
STADLER
BEAN
GREEN
NEWTON
MORGAN
275
277
280
280
282
282
282
282
283
283
POSITION AFTER 71 HOLES
PLAYER
SCORE FOR ROUND
BROWN
WATSON
CRENSHAW
TREVINO
69
69

Watson winning the British Open, Muirfield, 1980

figures: stands around the course £200,000; the Tented Village £135,000; scoreboards and their operation £40,000; spectator controls £20,000; litter control £22,000; mobile toilets £20,000; prize money £250,000; qualifying events £35,000; press tent £35,000 . . . and those are just some of the larger sums. In the days before Keith Mackenzie and Palmer and Nicklaus, the press tent was a homely unit with a blackboard and some chalk, which the secretary used from time to time to scratch up some leading scores. At most, probably fifty people were there to cover the Championship. How it has changed! Four hundred journalists now jet in to a press centre which is almost as big as a soccer pitch. The scoreboard is forty feet high and twice as long.

In 1860 when there was a field of eight professionals, thirty or so

Golfing goddesses
Left: Kathy Whitworth
Right: Beth Daniel

Opposite
Left: Donna Caponi
Top right: Nancy Lopez-Melton
Bottom right: Laura Baugh (from the 1982 calendar)

spectators and one pressman were present. Today there are now women professionals with their own circuits in Japan, Britain and, of course, America where the 1982 prize fund is $6.2 million – more than the European men's circuit can offer. Yet as recently as 1958 the American Ladies' professional tour was worth a total of just $158,000. That year the leading money-earner, Beverly Hansom, made $13,000. Last year Beth Daniel, first in the money table for the second year running, Jo-Anne Carner and Donna Caponi banked around $200,000 each; Pat Bradley, Jan Stephenson and Nancy Lopez-Melton were not far off that mark.

The LPGA of America is booming so much that they plan to move their headquarters from New York to an $11 million development in Houston, Texas. They have edged ahead of their male rivals, too, by initiating a pension plan for members – the first time this has been organised in a non-team sport. Veteran Kathy Whitworth, who has been on tour since 1959, was the first woman golfer to make a million. Carner and Caponi have also broken that barrier. Television coverage of the ladies' tour has increased too. More people watched the women golfers on television last year than in the first twenty-five years of the circuit put together! It is easy to understand why. Not only do the ladies play a brand of golf more readily comparable to that played by most men, they also look attractive doing it.

The average age of the golfing tourist after all is just twenty-three. Attendance records were broken at almost every event in 1981, and there are moves to make the tour much more international with regular stop-offs in Japan, Australia and Europe.

Until Beth Daniel came along, Nancy Lopez-Melton had been the most recent golfing goddess with the Midas putting touch. She won nine tournaments on the US Tour in 1978, including five in a row. She won a further eight in 1979. She has shot a 64 and impressed Lee Trevino greatly when he played an exhibition with her. But you do not need to be a winner to make big money on the women's tour. Take Laura Baugh, the petite blonde with the attractive, dimpled smile, a neat figure and the right manager – yes, Mark McCormack. He saw Miss Baugh's potential in Japan as long ago as 1974. That year the Laura Baugh calendar was produced – a series of attractive pin-up pictures of Laura. The Japanese queued up for copies and still do so every year. That earned Laura a Japanese fortune; so too did a toothpaste contract which netted her £150,000. There have been 'Learn English with Laura Baugh' cassettes which sold like hot cakes, photo albums and every conceivable sports fashion item with the Laura tag. At one point she was the highest-paid woman in golf – and she still hasn't won a tournament. She is a winner, however, with her looks.

It has been estimated that America's sixteen million golfers were involved in 350 million rounds last year. A $1 million programme is operating at the moment, geared to introduce one million more players to the game. In Florida Chi Chi Rodriguez from Puerto Rico is involved in a $2 million youth project designed to help potentially delinquent children. The scheme envisages a new course for children, built by them and run by them under supervision. In Britain the Golf Foundation, a non-profit-making organisation which provides coaching in schools, introduces 20,000 golfers to the sport every year.

The problem is that once a golfer knows how to play the game it may be tough for him to find a course on which to put what he has learned into action, because building a course is exceptionally costly. It is difficult to quantify exactly, but in Britain you could not build a course for under £200,000, and that's the bottom line. It is necessary to take into consideration how much the land on which the course is to be built costs per acre, how much work has to be done on the land to make it suitable to construct the course – at Woburn, near London, they had to remove 9000 trees. Sometimes massive drainage is required before a start can be made on the construction of a course which, once laid out, will take up to five years in Britain to mature. Not for the British the luxury of laying out a course in the spring, sowing the seed and playing on it in late autumn, as they do in Florida or southern Spain. Play a course too soon in Britain, skimp the preparation, and a high-cost outlay may be lost for ever. There is no quick way to make a course – and no cheap way either.

If it costs £10,000 a hole, then £7000 of that will go on the construction of the green. Gone are the days when the green was just a more closely cut extension of the fairway. Now greens are built to very modern dimensions. After excavating to a depth of about two feet the foundations are laid, drainage is installed and the whole thing topped off with high-quality soil, frequently from another part of the country altogether. So far, no one in this country has suggested greens of artificial turf – the so-called astroturf – probably because they would be difficult to drain, but it may come yet as every move is made to cut down course maintenance costs. The new Wee Links – courses for young children – in America are already using synthetic grass reasonably successfully.

But back in Britain remember that, once you have built your course for £200,000 on ground that probably cost you £250,000, you will still have to dig into the money box for £50,000 of machinery and £250,000 for the clubhouse. When you consider that much of this money will be borrowed at high rates of interest, it is no wonder that clubs are looking for instant return on outlay, just to pay back the interest. Cost effectiveness in modern planning will try to ensure wherever possible some additional features as standard to any new complex. There should be a covered driving range and a short hole or par 3 course where golfers with an hour to spare, but not three, can have a game. Such facilities would ensure more people use the club, and in the long run keep costs down. Running a club is an expensive business. The turnover at a private two-course club in the London area will be a staggering £700,000 – almost half of that coming from bar and catering sales. Keeping a course in good order is a £30,000 annual expense.

Compared to other countries, golf in Britain is still remarkably cheap. Too cheap? One golf secretary reports that, if every one of his members bought a daily ticket just once a week, the club's financial situation could be made completely secure. But that ticket bought fifty-two times a year is the equivalent of a £500 subscription and the club's sub is actually half that! Entry fees in Britain are far lower than the American average of £1000, but the Americans can put their club dues down on their tax form as a deductible expense. The club managers of America announced, when there was a suggestion a year or two ago that the tax benefit would be scrapped, that 1500 clubs would have to close down, a further 4000 would be financially impaired, and 117,000 jobs would be lost because so many people would, as a result, be unable to afford their golf. The tax threat was removed.

While it would cost £800 a year to be a member of a more exclusive club in the United States, golf there is not nearly as expensive as it is in Japan. Golf is a religion to the Japanese. Their golfing mecca, their Old Course, is a driving range in the middle of Tokyo that grosses $3.5 million a year. It is built on land which is worth $6 billion, but there is no suggestion of it being sold to a developer. There would be an outcry. The range operates thirteen hours a day with typical Far Eastern efficiency. Each stall on each of the three tiers has a self-operating ball machine. Insert a card and start hitting as the balls pop out. You are charged according to how many balls you hit, and you could run up a £10 bill in just over half an hour. There are 1.3 million club members in Japan playing on 1400 courses, but five times that number of golfers never have the opportunity, the luxury, of hitting balls on a real course. They are confined to the range because that is all they can afford!

The reason there are not more courses is simply the scarcity of land and the cost of developing what there is available. If Scotland is the land of cheap golf, Japan is the land of soaring prices. Entrance fees to golf clubs range from £10,000 at the lower end of the market to £70,000 at the top end. It is generally accepted that membership of one exclusive club in Japan involves a £250,000 entrance fee – if you could get in, but you cannot. Club memberships are so sought after that they are sold on the open market. Regular listings appear in the golfing magazines. But joining a club is just the start. Being a member involves considerable expense, too. There are monthly dues, caddie fees, green fees. The caddies, mostly women, used to carry the bags, but now they use electric carts and

The enthusiasts: Shiba Park driving range, Tokyo

operate with four bags. Their life-style has been upgraded, too. Their wages have increased substantially and, instead of living in club dormitories, they have their own homes away from the course and enjoy full pension and medical rights underwritten by a tax imposed on each round played at the club. A guest at a moderately priced club in Japan could expect to pay £100 for a round at the weekend all in. That is even more expensive than Pebble Beach in California, where your £30 ticket does include hire of an electric cart.

Those electric carts are big business in the States. A recent survey pinpointed that over 50,000 carts are produced annually. At £1000 a cart that is £50 million worth of business right away. There are about 400,000 carts available for hire and that is revenue annually of £125 million. A top club can expect to make £50,000 a year from cart hire alone.

In order to keep club membership costs down new courses are tied into real-estate development. Take the new Tournament Players' Club at Sawgrass, just south of Jacksonville, Florida. The development is geared to providing 150,000 condominiums on 1300 acres. Eighty million dollars is involved and most of the homes and plots have already been sold. Buying yourself into an expensive slice of golfing real estate, however, does not necessarily provide you with trouble-free golf. The first tee at some quality projects in Florida is busier most of the day than Manhattan during a traffic jam. The only way to ensure some privacy, some exclusivity, is to join a course which has no planned development. That is when your golf becomes exceedingly expensive, but there are plenty of golfers willing to pay for the luxury.

Those that have not got the 'wherewithal' may have to make do, however, with golf at a municipal course. This can be a hair-raising affair because many of the golfers are intent simply on 'getting round' and are not too worried about the rules. At one New York municipal course the starter was reported to have said rather wearily, 'Stepping off the first tee here is like trying to cross a ten-lane highway at rush hour. You take your life in your hands.' In order to cram in as many rounds as possible, to give as many people as possible the opportunity of playing, public links are invariably fenced in and there could even be fences between fairways to ensure no one ever has to look for a ball. That would be time-wasting. The rough is minimal. Often there are no bunkers because getting in and out of them slows up play. In order to get a tee time you might have to turn up the night before.

Arguments about who was where in the queue when the starter arrives in the morning forced some local authorities to bring in the police to keep control, and then to operate a book-a-week-ahead system. One problem on municipal courses is theft. Nimble-footed youngsters dash on and off the courses snatching balls and making a profit reselling them. One old-timer said that he considered his ball lost when, and if, it stopped rolling. At a New York course they used 4000 feet of wire one year repairing holes in the fence where ball thieves had cut their way in. It sounds ghastly but golfers still turn up to play in their droves, spurred on by their enthusiasm for a game which demands patience and resilience and a sense of humour. Even the greenkeepers at one New York course have to have a sense of humour. When they take out the pins to cut the greens play continues with the golfers aiming at them!

Have you ever thought how much you pay for your golf every year? In Britain the average annual expenditure, according to a golf magazine survey last year, was £340 – expensive, but the magazine, *Golf World*, revealed that this was just a tenth of the expenditure per head in Japan, a third of what it cost in Germany and half the cost in France. How is the £340 made up? Last year, on average, a golfer paid out £91 on his membership, £52 on green fees, £15 on golf instruction, £19 on equipment, £11 on magazines and books, £14 on competitions, and £38 on caddies and trolley hire. In the survey the highest amount spent on these items by an individual was a mammoth £2530 in a year. He must have lost a lot of balls.

Which brings us to another massive money-spinner. How is this for a staggering statistic? Two million dozen golf balls are sold in Britain each year, three out of four of them made in this country. Since the average cost of a ball is now £1 this represents £24 million in sales. In Japan sales run at 20,000 dozen balls a day six days a week, or six million dozen a year. In America the figure is double that. In all, twenty million dozen golf balls are sold annually – £240 million worth.

If the United States caters for half the market in golf balls it is the same with clubs, which are more difficult to cost accurately because of the price variation. Dunlop, whose golf-ball production is the most extensive throughout the world – they have factories in Britain, America, South Africa, New Zealand and Japan – monitor sales of clubs costing at least £6 and as high as £35 or £40. Total club sales in Britain are 1.5 million a year or £21 million in sales, and this represents just one fifth of world trade. Clubs gross annually £400 million for manufacturers. In Britain 250,000 of the 1.5 million clubs produced are putters, and a further 200,000 are wedges of one kind or another. Of course, it is far cheaper to buy a set of clubs in Britain than it is in Japan. A set of Ben Hogan clubs there will cost you £300, and a graphite-shafted driver as much as £350! I wonder how many of these are bought simply to hit balls on a driving range in the centre of Tokyo?

Clubs and balls account for £640 million in sales each year and we have not touched on all the other equipment – shoes, shirts, sweaters, golf bags, caddie carts, sun-visors, caps, golf gloves. Equipment of that kind will send the cash registers ringing up £30 million a year in Britain alone, at a very conservative estimate. So whatever branch of golf you explore these days, big money is involved. Somehow through the jungle of multi-million-dollar deals, appearance-money wrangles, massive take-over bids and super new multi-million-dollar developments, the game remains the same. Its character remains intact. It is a game of trust, a game where politeness is part of the creed, where hooliganism is unknown. It is a game seldom affected by politics. It is a game apart – a game which in the last twenty years has lost its élitist tag – even in some countries, like Spain, where the rich might have liked to have preserved it for themselves. Severiano Ballesteros and a booming holiday-trade market to the sun-drenched golfing resorts on the Costa del Sol have seen to that.

Because of the current economic recession, development may have slowed down temporarily but it will pick up again. As we get more and more leisure time to ourselves so golf will keep growing in popularity. It is a game with a great many advantages. You can play it from the cradle to the grave. Players of different standard can play it and enjoy the competition thanks to a unique handicapping system. Its popularity today around the world is due, however, in no small measure to Arnold Palmer and what happened in the sixties. He made thousands who would otherwise have been unaware of golf conscious of the game. Hubert Green, the former US Open champion, echoes the view of every one of the tour men in America when he says that there is nobody on tour who does not feel he really owes Palmer 25 cents of every dollar he earns. Not that Palmer needs it! We have all benefited from the era of Arnold Palmer and Jack Nicklaus and of Tony Jacklin here in Britain. Low figures win big money in golf – but the business of golf these days is all about telephone figure finance. Golf is big business is big money.

CHAPTER SEVEN

St Andrews is still the Mecca

by Michael Williams

Bobby Jones was already a sick man in 1958 when he was the USA's non-playing captain in the inaugural World Amateur Team Championship for the Eisenhower Trophy at St Andrews. The victim of a progressively debilitating muscular disease he was, still thirteen years before he died, already largely dependent on an electric golf cart for getting around.

By then Jones was an adopted son of St Andrews. He had first played there in the 1921 Open Championship when, maddened by the many perplexities of the Old Course, he had torn up his card in the fourth round. Six years later he returned, to win the second of his three Open Championships. It was also at the home of golf in 1930 that he took the Amateur Championship in his year of the Grand Slam.

St Andrews in the railway age: Bobby Jones on the seventeenth tee on his way to winning the British Open, 1927

Bobby Jones with the Australian winners of the Eisenhower Trophy, 1958: Peter Toogood and (*behind, left to right*) Doug Bachli, Bruce Devlin and Bob Stevens

Jones at once retired from competitive golf, but in 1936, en route to watch the Olympic Games in Berlin, he joined some friends for a few days at Gleneagles and, being so near, felt that he could not let the opportunity pass of having just one more game at St Andrews. His friends made the necessary arrangements, and soon the word that Jones was back was passed from house to house and shop to shop in the 'old grey toon', as St Andrews is called. Jones was quite unsuspecting, but by the time he had made his way from his hotel to the first tee some 2000 people were there to welcome him.

In his book, *Golf is My Game*, Jones later wrote:

I had not been playing very much golf and had not really expected to play any on this trip. I had brought my golf clubs along because of an ingrained habit. What golf I had played had been very bad, and I was certainly not pleased with the prospect of exhibiting my game in its present state, especially to the people of St Andrews.

But for reasons he was at a loss to explain, 'and very much to my astonishment', he recalled, 'I played as well that afternoon as I ever played in my life, at least for 10 holes'. He was out in 32 and at one point received a compliment that he was to treasure for the rest of his days. At the eighth, a flat, short hole measuring then some 160 yards, he faded a four-iron neatly beyond a mound behind which the flag was tucked. His ball came to rest seven or eight feet from the hole. As Jones replaced his club in the bag, his caddie murmured under his breath: 'My, but you're a wonder, sir!'

Those sentiments were very much shared by the people of St Andrews and in 1958 when he returned with the American Eisenhower team Jones was approached beforehand by the Town Clerk asking if he would be prepared to accept the Freedom of the Town. To an unsuspecting American this meant almost nothing; but not many more than a dozen people, great figures all in the world of politics and literature, had previously been so honoured. The ceremony, before a packed audience in the Younger Graduation Hall and with thousands waiting outside, was one nobody fortunate enough to have been present would have missed for the world. Jones scrapped the notes he had written beforehand, spoke naturally and movingly for some ten minutes and, near the end, said: 'I could take out of my life everything except my experiences at St Andrews and I'd still have a rich, full life.'

No golfer's life, whether he be Jones or Nicklaus, Cotton or Jacklin, Player or Locke, Von Nida or Thomson, or your most humble club golfer, is complete without at least one visit to the home of the game. Only Hogan, of golf's great masters, never played the Old Course. It was an omission he might always regret, for St Andrews has a quality about it that is different, in a golfing context, from anywhere else in the world. As you make the last turn on the A91 from Cupar, and see for the first time the grey-bricked university town climbing a gentle gradient on the horizon,

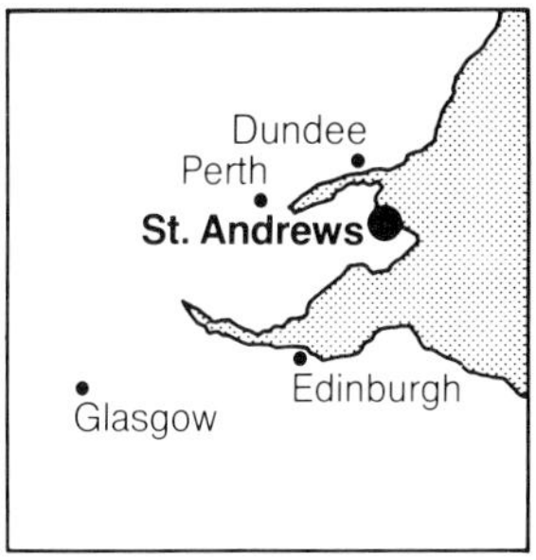

St Andrews, with the first and eighteenth holes of the Old Course in the foreground

the church tower sharp against the sky and, to the left, the low line of whin bushes that conceal the four courses – the Old, the New, the Eden and the Jubilee – the past and the present are suddenly rolled into one.

Each year thousands of golfers make such a pilgrimage, some for the first time, some for the umpteenth time. Strangely, it would seem, for so historical and exclusive a golfing domain it is a course that anybody may play. Each year some 42,000 rounds are played on the Old Course alone, for which the green fee in 1982 is £8. Each Sunday it is closed. The demand for the other three courses is only slightly less. In 1972 a fifth course, the Balgove, was opened, though this is very much for the use of beginners and children and golf here is free. For one month each year, usually March, the Old Course is shut completely for much-needed rest and maintenance, and the others – though never more than two at a time – enjoy similar breathing spaces.

While St Andrews is also the home of the Royal and Ancient, golf's governing body whose four-square clubhouse stands sombre and grey immediately behind the first tee (see page 71), which is also but a few yards from the eighteenth green, the R & A do not directly control the courses. They are owned by the District Council and run by the St Andrews Links Trust and Management Committee, on which the R & A and the local authority are equally represented. These bodies were formed as the result of a Links Order Confirmation Act in 1974, when a reorganisation of local government in Scotland threatened to put the links in the control of more distant and less sympathetic hands.

This was regarded as ominous for, while the origins of golf have never conclusively been pinpointed, St Andrews was indisputably one of the first places where it was played and has long been regarded as its home. The first documented evidence of golf there came in 1552, though this tended only to confirm rights already established – together, incidentally, with permission for the townsfolk to graze their sheep on the links.

First impressions of the Old Course are misleading. Few people fall in

The Old Course
6578 yards (Medal) 6933 yards (Open Championship)
Par 72

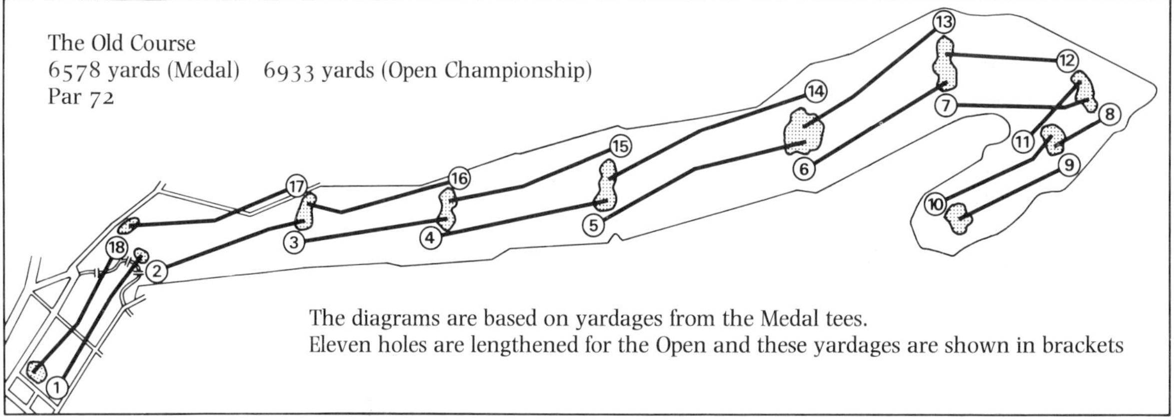

The diagrams are based on yardages from the Medal tees.
Eleven holes are lengthened for the Open and these yardages are shown in brackets

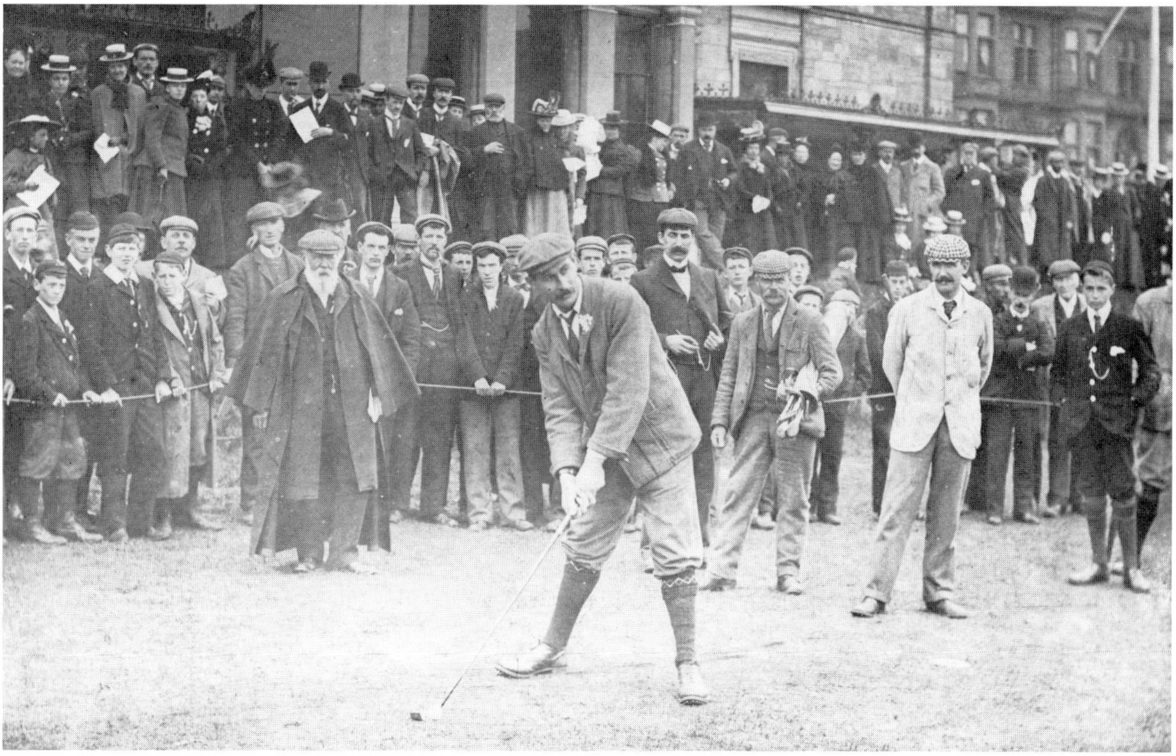

love with it at first sight, any more than Jones did. The broad acres of the first and eighteenth fairways, which are all one, sweep away from the clubhouse without a patch of rough to be seen. It appears a target impossible to miss from the first tee or, in the other direction, from the eighteenth tee, though many players have had it proved otherwise. Only a pencil-slim line, the Swilcan burn, which crosses the whole of the fairway and, most critically, just in front of the first green, hints of trouble ahead.

Harry Vardon teeing off at the first under the watchful eyes of Old Tom Morris

That opening drive is nevertheless intimidating. One is massively conscious of all the world-famous golfers who have stood on that very strip of immaculate turf and played the hole exactly as it is today. Behind is the clubhouse and, somewhere beyond the long windows of the Big Room, are the members of the Royal and Ancient critically watching the

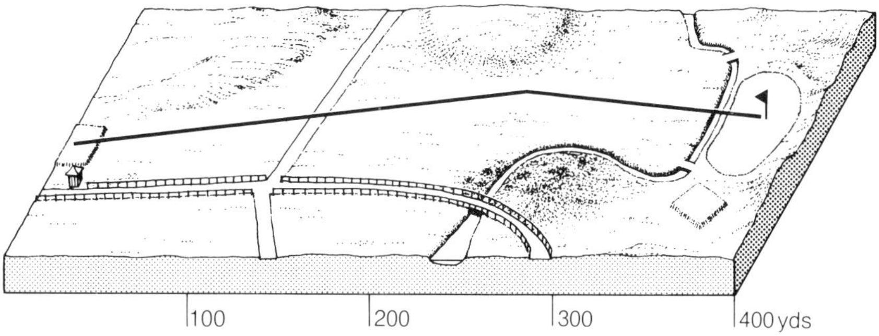

Hole 1 Burn
370 yards Par 4

execution of the shot. There is a story of one unfortunate, hopefully not apocryphal, whose opening drive shot off almost between his legs and finished in the hole at the eighteenth. 'Round in one, sir,' remarked his caddie.

But if it is good to have that opening drive away, one is soon faced with a second shot that, in its way, is even more daunting. Though the hole measures a by no means unreasonable 370 yards, the second shot must, if it is to reach the green safely, also pitch on the green. Anything fractionally short is almost certain to end up in the burn. Depending on the wind and individual ability, this can vary from a wedge to a long iron, and it is invariably 'one more' than you suspect. I have a friend who wore the broadest of smiles when his partner feebly topped his opening drive at foursomes. It meant that he could play the second shot with total freedom for both green and, more important, the burn were still out of range.

In the 1970 Open Championship Tom Shaw, an American professional, was a little strong with his approach and finished on the back of the green. He then putted back too hard and into the burn. In the 1980 European Amateur Team Championship, with Scotland playing England in the final, Ian Hutcheon had to go down the nineteenth against Peter Deeble in the decisive match, and in rapid succession became both a villain and a hero as he pitched his second into the burn, picked out under penalty and then chipped in for a half in four. But he lost the game at the twentieth and so did Scotland.

The feature of the Old Course is that so little has changed. It was designed by nature. Here and there a new tee has been added to give the hole some extra yardage, but not by much and, though some argue that it is not the test it was, Kel Nagle's 278 in the 1960 Open Championship – 10 under par – is still the record.

After the first hole the course swings right, parallel with St Andrews Bay where long lines of breakers come rolling in from a grey North Sea, and follows roughly the shape of a hockey stick with a sharp loop at the far end. At some points the course is no more than 100 yards in width and because of this most holes share fairways just as they do some huge double greens. Only the first, ninth, seventeenth and eighteenth holes have their own greens. The second shares with the sixteenth, the third with the fifteenth, the fourth with the fourteenth, the fifth with the thirteenth (which is quite enormous and some eighty yards across), the sixth with the twelfth, the seventh with the eleventh and the eighth with the tenth.

To begin with there were twelve holes running out to Eden Estuary. Golfers drove off from beside the home green, played eleven holes to the far end and then came back again, playing the same holes but in the reverse direction. There were therefore twenty-two holes in all, but in 1764, ten years after the club was founded, it was suggested that the first four holes should become two, thus converting the last four into two as well. A round

St Andrews and its Links courses

of golf was consequently reduced from twenty-two holes to eighteen and this became the accepted distance.

In those early days the fairways were even narrower than they are today, but as the number of golfers increased, so it became necessary to broaden them to avoid golfers being hit as they advanced from the opposite direction. Two holes were cut on the now double greens and, by its very layout, St Andrews gave birth to the expression 'out' and 'home'.

Until the recent introduction of fairway watering, which has made placement of shots easier than on hard, sun-baked turf, it was very necessary for players to have caddies to pilot their way round. When in doubt the policy is still to aim left, for the Old Course is dotted with so many hidden bunkers that even those who play there regularly often stumble across a bunker they could swear had never been there before, some big enough to accommodate, as Bernard Darwin once wrote, 'only an angry man and his niblick'. The wind also plays a major part in the defence of the course and many are the times a golfer goes to the turn with the wind against and then finds, as he heads for home with a sigh of relief, that the wind has swung 180 degrees and is against him all the way home as well.

While it may in many instances be safer to drive to the left, it can also mean a more difficult shot. For instance, at the second, a par four of just over 400 yards, a deep bunker burrows into a green that slopes from front to back. The easier approach is from the right but that is an area of unseen bunkers and encroaching whin.

The third, comparatively one of the shorter par fours, gives some respite, but the fourth, 463 yards from the Championship tee and forty

Hole 2 Dyke
411 yards Par 4

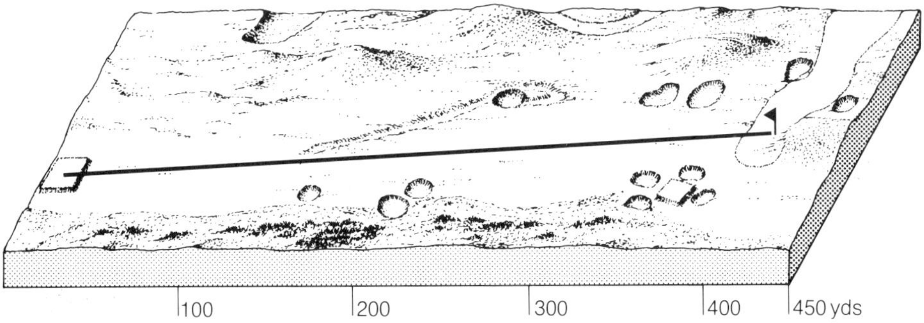

Hole 3 Cartgate
352 (371) yards Par 4

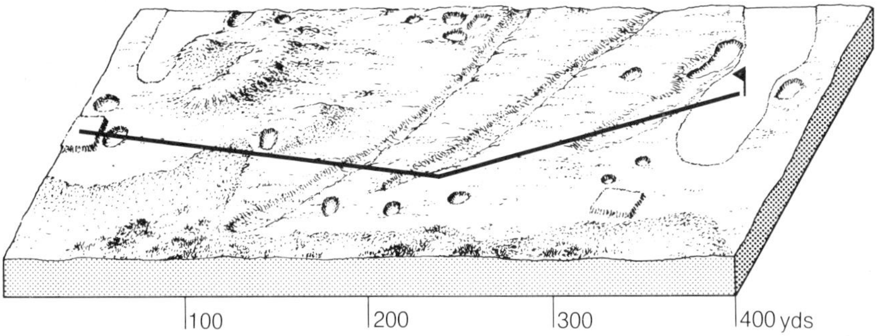

Hole 4 Ginger Beer
419 (463) Yards Par 4

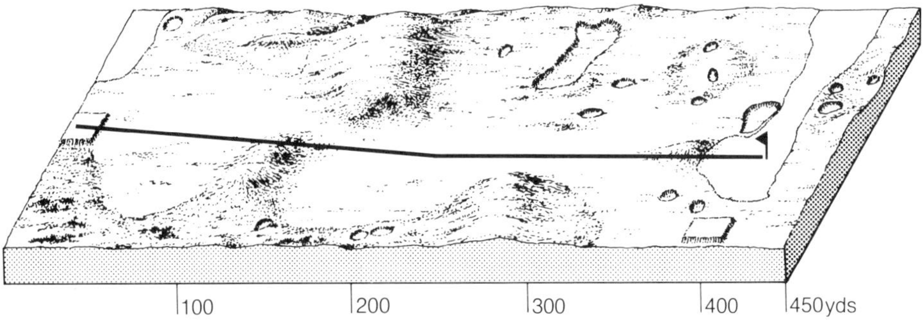

yards shorter from the medal tee, is probably the hardest hole going out. It is known as Ginger Beer, after a character known as Old Daw who used to sell refreshment there.

All the holes have names but some double up because of their shared greens. Thus the par five fifth, or Hole o'Cross, bears the same name as the thirteenth, the only distinction being that the former is 'going out' and the latter 'coming home'. The fifth is said to be less formidable than it used to be for the drive is now more straightforward. The testing shot is the second, for it has to be threaded between two bunkers set in a suddenly rising and narrow fairway to a green hidden beyond the crest. In the 1933 Open Championship these bunkers were some 420 yards from the tee but, with a gale behind him and the fairway like concrete, Craig Wood drove into one of them. That would not happen today with the fairways

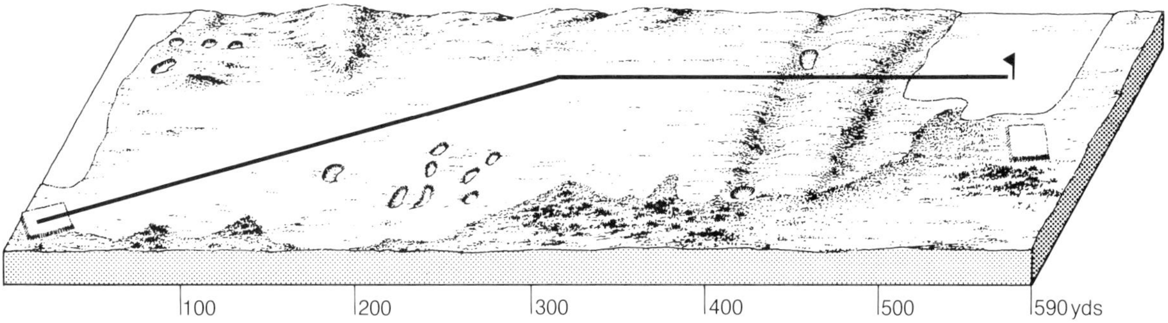

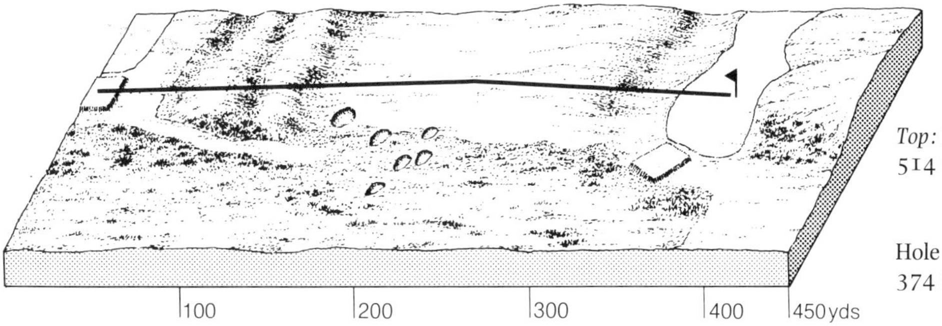

Top: Hole 5 Hole o'Cross
514 (564) yards Par 5

Hole 6 Heathery
374 (416) yards Par 4

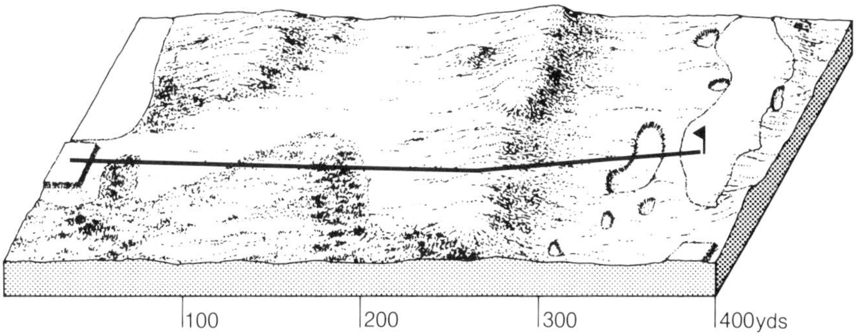

Hole 7 High
359 (372) yards Par 4

artificially watered, and in any case the hole has been lengthened to well in excess of 500 yards. The huge green also invites three putts.

The sixth is deceptive because a bank close to the green makes the flag look nearer than it is. The seventh demands a rather blind drive between dunes and, once negotiated, there is still the big Shell bunker to be cleared with the second shot.

There are only two short holes in the Old Course and the first of them, the eighth, comes at the beginning of the famous loop. It is in this sequence of four holes that a player will hope to make his score. The ninth and tenth have both been driven but they are so flat and without landmarks that it is the easiest thing in the world to underclub the second shot. Neither measure much more than 300 yards from the medal tee.

The eleventh is a marvellous short hole. The green tilts sharply

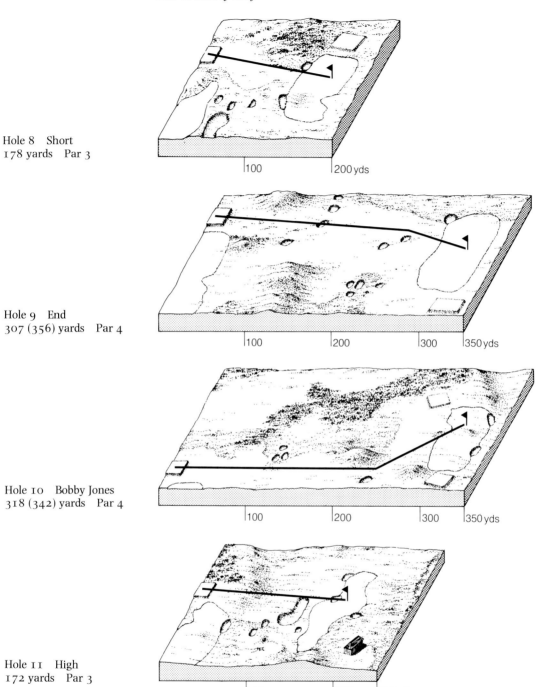

Hole 8 Short
178 yards Par 3

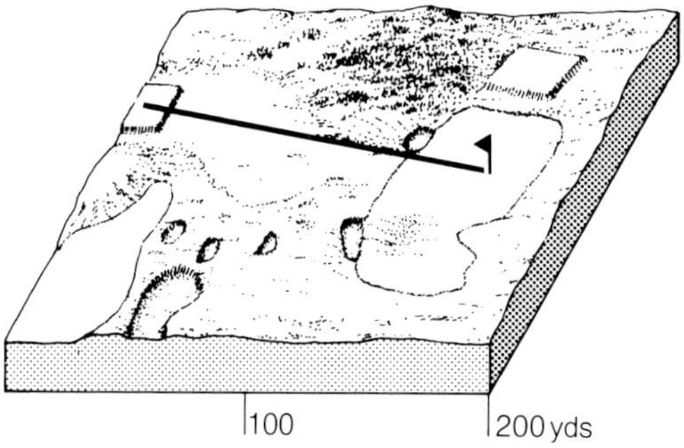

Hole 9 End
307 (356) yards Par 4

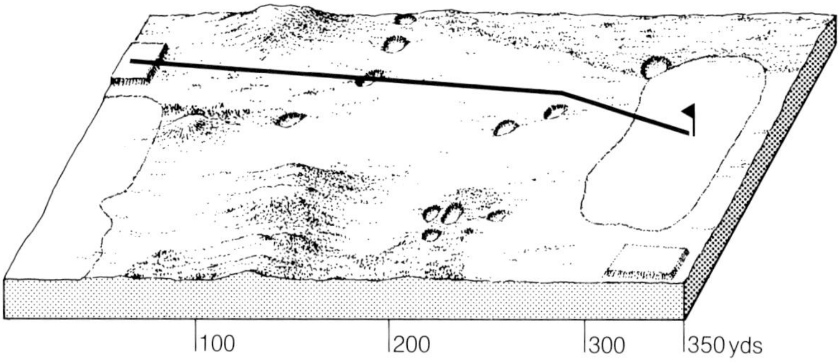

Hole 10 Bobby Jones
318 (342) yards Par 4

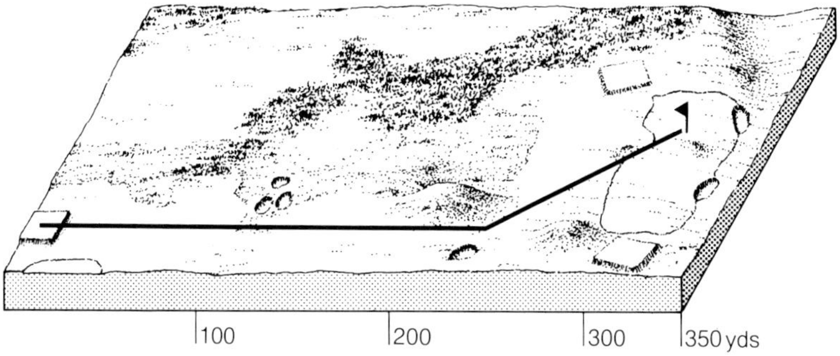

Hole 11 High
172 yards Par 3

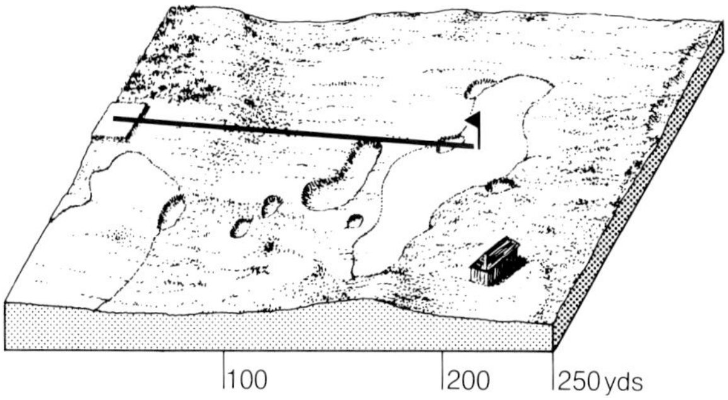

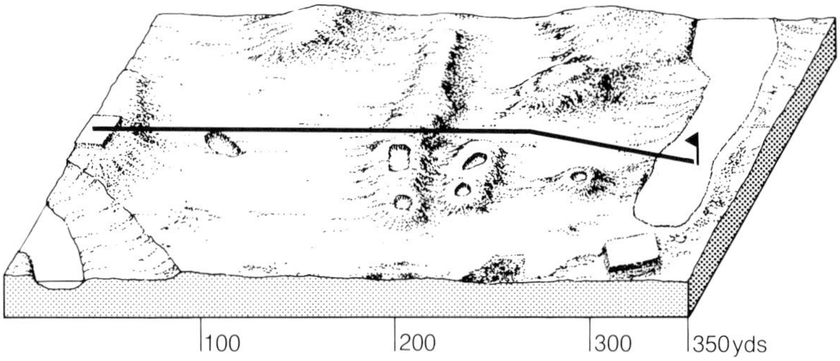

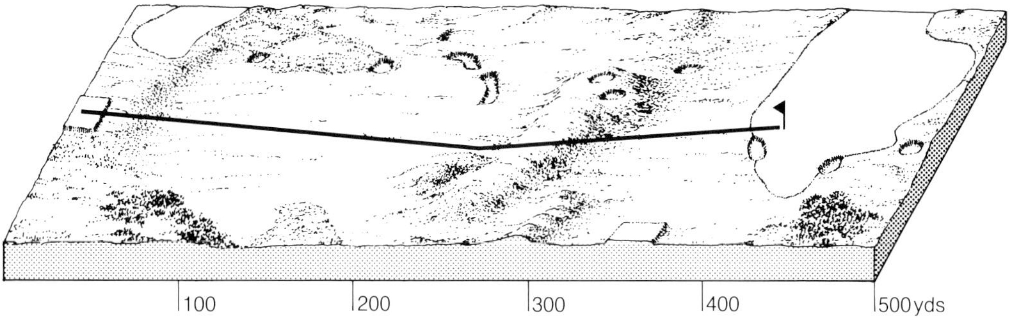

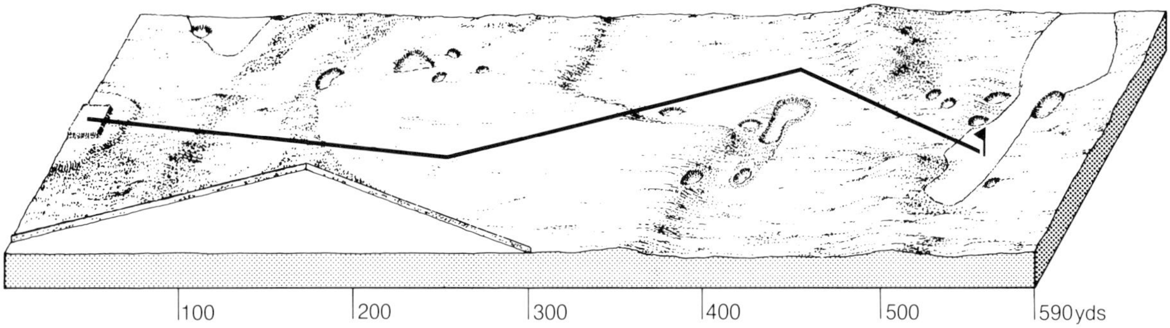

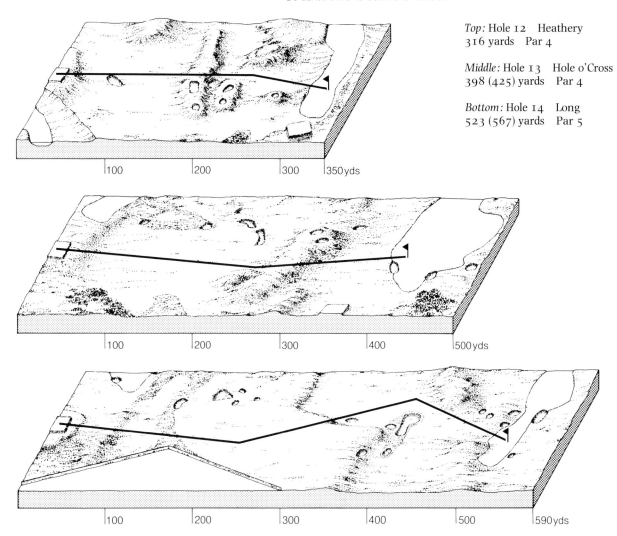

Top: Hole 12 Heathery
316 yards Par 4

Middle: Hole 13 Hole o'Cross
398 (425) yards Par 4

Bottom: Hole 14 Long
523 (567) yards Par 5

towards the golfer and at 170 yards there are a variety of ways of playing it. Sometimes it demands a long iron or wood into the wind, sometimes a pitch and run, and I have even heard of it being played with a putter from the tee. It is the little Strath bunker, immediately behind which the flag is invariably placed, that causes all the trouble. Clear it by too much and there is the very devil of a downhill return putt. The Hill bunker a little to the left has also claimed some famous victims. In the 1933 Open Gene Sarazen, who was defending the title, took six at the hole, three of them in that bunker. At one point he waved his club in anger and a steward interpreted it as a shot, reporting to the Championship Committee that Sarazen had in fact taken seven. The American's explanation was accepted but he was very hurt that anyone should have regarded him as a cheat.

The twelfth, coming out of the loop, is the last of the obviously potential birdie holes. Again not much more than 300 yards, it appears from the tee to be a fairway devoid of bunkers. In fact it is dotted with them but they are hidden in little swales. So hidden, indeed, that one day Rear Admiral C. H. G. Benson, as staunch a member of the Royal and Ancient as there has ever been, had his attention diverted as he walked from the tee by a trim female figure. So hypnotised was he that he failed to take note of the course he was charting. One moment steaming for the green, the next he had been sunk without trace, disappearing, clubs, trolley and all, into the sand below. From that day to this it has always been known as The Admiral's bunker.

Not only must the drive be well placed to avoid the many little craters, but the second is a classically teasing shot. The green is shallow but it has an oblong plateau running from left to right. A slightly hesitant pitch or chip will consequently roll back, or a bold one slip down the far side. And then it is difficult to get down in two more.

The three Coffin bunkers to the left threaten the drive at the thirteenth. Cat's Trap lurks beyond them, but even if they are avoided there is still a difficult and quite long second shot over broken ground to the big green that is shared with the fifth.

By now the Old Course is ready to set the hardest part of its examination, particularly for those trying to protect a good score. It happened notably to Tony Jacklin as he began his defence of the Open Championship in 1970. On a grey listless day, with a host of players already under 70 and Neil Coles in with a 66, Jacklin reached the turn in 29, started back with another birdie, and was eight under par as he drove off at the par five fourteenth. At that moment a violent storm broke out of the stillness. Jacklin's second through the deluge found a bush, but with the course in minutes becoming unplayable it had to remain there overnight. When, at first light the following morning, he resumed, he had to pick clear under penalty, took six, finished in 67 and lost all momentum.

The drive, particularly from the Championship tee, demands both nerve and a true swing. A low stone wall, which separates the Old from the Eden course, angles in from the right and is a constant reminder to the golfer that a slice or excessive fade will almost certainly finish out of bounds. On the other hand, a hook or too much draw will flirt with a cluster of bunkers known as the Beardies and, like most bunkers at St Andrews, so deep that it is enough just to get out. Thus a sigh of relief follows a good straight hit onto that broad sweep of fairway known as Elysian Fields; which only leads up to another problem. Dead ahead is the distant green, but in between two more graveyard bunkers, Kitchen, which is small, and Hell, which is not.

To avoid them many opt for a line on the church tower, which seems

Hell bunker

ridiculously left for the ultimate destination. It also leaves a longer shot into the green, which is further protected by a steep, fronting bank. It is not easy to get the ball close to the hole and many are those who have taken six or seven without hitting a bad shot.

There is some respite at the fifteenth, a more straightforward par four of around 400 yards. But many an apparently good drive has found its way into a lonely little bunker by the name of Sutherland. Some of its victims once decided that it should be filled in, so unfair did they believe it to be. But overnight it was mysteriously opened up again and has remained so ever since.

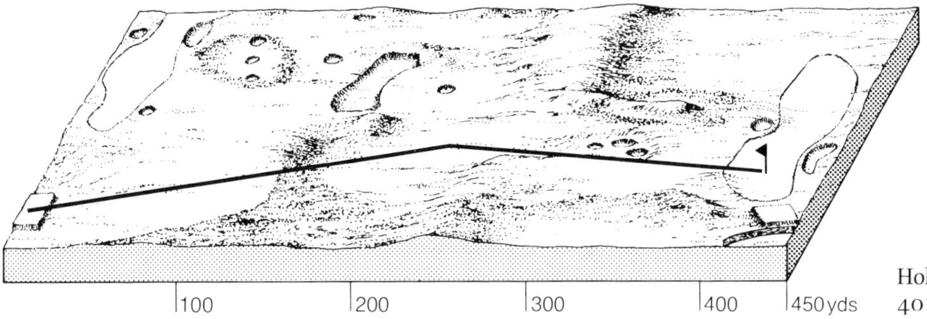

Hole 15 Cartgate
401 (413) yards Par 4

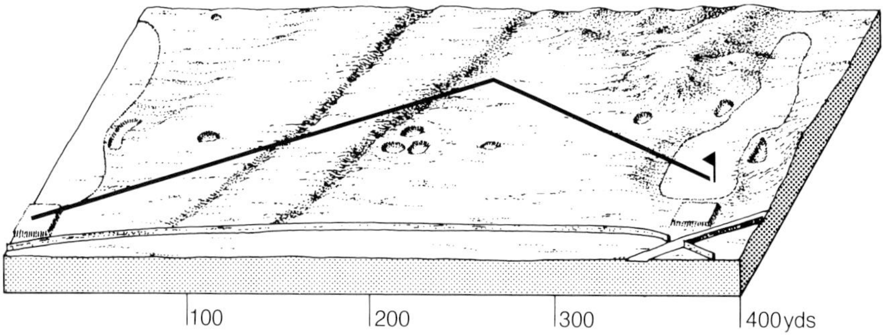

Hole 16 Corner of the Dyke
351 (382) yards Par 4

Just where one feels one ought to be aiming off the sixteenth tee, another famous bunker, the Principal's Nose, lies in wait. In fact it is a cluster of three little bunkers, one on the tee side and two more the far side of the bulge. A safer line is therefore to the left for, though an inviting corridor runs between the Principal's Nose and the fence on the right that used to run parallel with the old railway line, such a line flirts dangerously with out of bounds. So it is prudent to aim left, though then the second shot must be played over Wig, another strategically-placed bunker set in the mouth of the green and ready to swallow anything which is fractionally short.

It was here that Jack Nicklaus played his winning ace in the 1978 Open Championship. Simon Owen, a New Zealander, had just chipped in at the fifteenth during the final round for the lead. With the wind at his back Nicklaus was pinning his faith in his spoon from the tee, and the nine-iron second he was able to play before Owen hit his approach was therefore critical. Not only did it leave him close enough for a birdie, it put the pressure on Owen who went through the green and took five. Thus did the lead change hands for the last time.

By common consent the Road Hole is the greatest seventeenth hole in the world. It comes at a crucial stage in the round and poses the problem of whether to attack or defend. A right-hand dog leg of nearly, but not quite, par five length, it is necessary, if the green is to be reached in two, to drive over the corner of the out of bounds and what used to be some rather ugly, black railway sheds. But in many eyes they were infinitely more beautiful than the modern Old Course Hotel which has sprung up in recent years. There was a request to call it the 'Royal and Ancient' but the good sense of the Scottish Office, who were approached with the request, prevailed. A pyramid of wire netting now protects unsuspecting guests from a direct hit as they enter or leave the hotel, and I know of at least one visitor who had to take hasty evasive action when he leaned out from one of the balconies to watch a drive from the tee in the 1981 Amateur Championship.

A safer line is to the left, but that leaves a very long second shot to a raised, angled green protected on its left by a small, deep bunker shown as

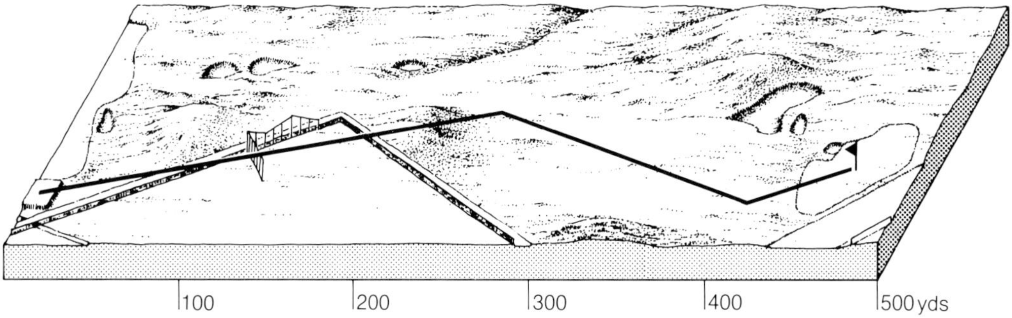

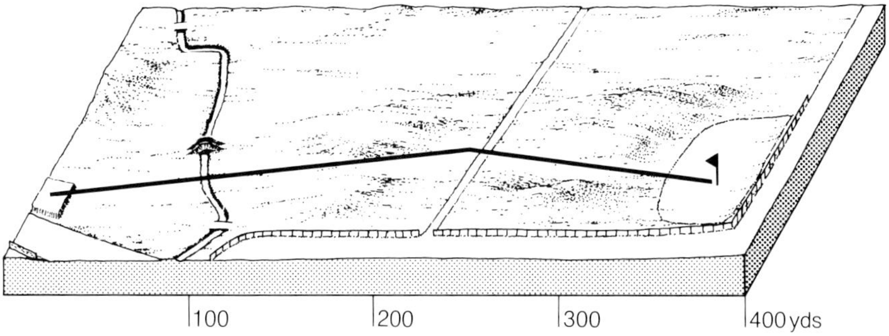

Top: Hole 17 Road
461 yards Par 4

Hole 18 Tom Morris
354 yards Par 4

the Road Bunker. In fact the road is on the far side of the green and a shot which climbs the bank too swiftly will tumble off the far side and on to grit or tarmac from where one takes one's life in one's hands with any sort of chip shot. Many opt for the putter and just hope to bumble the ball back on to the green. As often as not it rolls back down again.

In the 1971 Walker Cup Vinny Giles of America holed out from off the road against Michael Bonallack. The shot hit the stick a foot above the ground and fell straight in. It was the only time I have seen Bonallack react to the many injustices of golf, as a promising position for Britain seemed suddenly to erode. He hurled his own ball to the ground in disbelief. But he quickly recovered himself with a rueful grin and, in the long run, all was not lost.

It is a moot point whether a shot off the road is easier than a shot out of the Road Bunker. In fact, there are those who now refer to the bunker as the 'sands of Nakajima', after a Japanese professional who, in the 1978 Open, was on the green in two, caught the wrong slope with his approach putt and was in the bunker in three. He finally made the green again with his seventh shot and took two putts for a nine.

The eighteenth, by contrast, poses only one problem. The drive, over the tiny stone bridge that looks to have been there as long as time itself, is to a fairway as wide as it is inviting. Terraced houses, hotels, shops and the New, St Rule and St Andrews Golf Clubs flank the right-hand side and, however humble the players, there is always a handful of curious

The notorious Swilcan burn snaking its way across the first and eighteenth fairways

Joyce Wethered and Glenna Collett lead the way over the old bridge across the Swilcan, Ladies Amateur Championship, 1929

spectators looking on. An unlucky drive can sometimes end up on the road which crosses the last and first fairways and, with no relief, that becomes a second shot of some chance. But the solitary, seemingly innocuous defence of the hole is the Valley of Sin, a deep swale eating into the front of the green.

The approach looks one of the simplest in golf. But it is also a most deceptive one, whether it be pitched high or struck low so that it runs through the valley towards a flag invariably perched not far beyond. The very vastness of the green lulls the golfer into a false sense of security, and

The most famous miss in the history of St Andrews: Doug Sanders on the eighteenth green, British Open, 1970

of all the three putts there, none were more tragic than those by Doug Sanders in the 1970 Open.

A golfer of colour, in manner as well as style of clothes, and with an unusually short backswing, Sanders had come to the eighteenth needing a par four to beat Nicklaus. A drive and pitch behind the flag negotiated the first part of it comfortably enough, but the approach putt, never as fast as it looks, came up just about a yard short. Golfers of all ages have, in fantasy, told themselves in a variety of situations, 'This for the Open'. That putt by Sanders was, however, the real thing and all the world now knows that he missed it and then lost the play-off to Nicklaus the following day. One of the game's most tragic photographs is of Sanders crumpling almost to his knees as he watches his putt leaking past the edge of the hole, his right hand already off the club in perhaps the classic pose of a man whose nerve has failed him under the ultimate pressure.

Jack Nicklaus is congratulated by Doug Sanders at the end of the play-off, British Open, 1970

Nicklaus had once remarked that 'one can feel so lonely at St Andrews missing a putt', and this is undoubtedly true. Spectators at the Championships are no longer allowed to walk the fairways and have to be marshalled to the touchlines, as it were. On top of that, the vast rolling greens may not be difficult to find but they are difficult on which to get down in two. It is not enough simply to be on the green, as at many courses. In places it is difficult to get down in three, let alone two, and a man who is not on terms with his putter has little hope.

The eighteenth green at St Andrews was also the stage for a rather odd finish to the Open Championship. This was in 1957 when Bobby Locke won and, for the first time, the closing holes were televised live. Needing only a short putt to take the title by three strokes, Locke first marked his ball because it was in the way of his partner's putt. But when he replaced it he had forgotten that he had moved his marker the length of the blade of his putter. Consequently he holed out from the wrong place. No one noticed it at the time and, though the matter was subsequently brought to the attention of the Championship Committee, they sensibly took no action.

The most unforgettable shot I ever saw on the Old Course was played by Dr David Marsh at the seventeenth with the Walker Cup of 1971 hanging in the balance. Marsh had come to the hole one up on Bill

Hyndman and, with Great Britain and Ireland having rallied magnificently to turn impending defeat into possible victory, the whole place was seething with excitement. I recall wandering out on to the course that final afternoon to watch the last rites as the Americans, who had lost the opening morning's foursomes by an unprecedented 4–0, had come back to win both the afternoon's singles and the next day's foursomes so that they led 9–7 with just eight singles to play. Nor were the indications any better when Lanny Wadkins and Michael Bonallack, the British captain, came sprinting past in the opposite direction with Wadkins well in charge and about to make the score 10–7. But somewhere out at about the thirteenth green a scoreboard hinted at better news. Britain were up in six matches, square in another, and one blinked, looked again and wondered.

The next two hours fled by in a blur of pounding heartbeats, first Stuart beating Giles, then Humphreys holing two monstrous putts on, I think it was, the fourteenth and fifteenth greens to crush the very life out of the massive Melnyk, a week later to win the Amateur Championship at Carnoustie. Then came Green and young Roddy Carr, son of Joe Carr, one of Ireland's great amateurs, proving himself the inspired choice of the selectors as he won his third game out of four, the other being halved. Suddenly, with the evening sun casting lengthening shadows over the Old Course, the improbable became probable with Macgregor one up going to the last and now Marsh the same against Hyndman coming to the seventeenth.

Spectators hung from every window they could find, a roar greeted Macgregor's win, and then, clear against the blue sky, came Marsh's ball, a three-iron shot from the centre of the fairway right to the heart of the green. Hyndman still got his four but Marsh got his the more easily and at that moment he could neither be beaten nor Britain fail to win. Strong men wept at that moment as the Lancashire doctor was engulfed when he still had a hole to play. He won one up, Britain by 13–11, and older memories than mine went back to the same scene in 1938 when the only other British Walker Cup victory was recorded.

Every one of that side was present thirty-three years on and only the circumstances had changed. In those days the match was still being played by 36-hole foursomes on the opening day and 36-hole singles on the second. Indeed, some were regarding this as the watershed of the Walker Cup, so one-sided had the contest become. But a clean sweep of selectors and a new captain, John Beck, worked wonders at a highly successful trial match during the spring which, above all, served to unite the team. The belief was born that the possibility of victory was there, particularly with a young Irishman with a highly individual swing, Jimmy Bruen, at its head.

However, just as the 1971 side won 'despite its captain' (these were Bonallack's words as he lost three times out of four), so also did the 1938 team succeed without a major contribution from Bruen, its strongest card. He halved his foursome in partnership with Bentley, and then in the singles lost to Charlie Yates, winner at Troon that year of the Amateur Championship. By avoiding defeat Bruen and Bentley had nevertheless ensured a British lead at the end of the first day since two of the other pairs, Peters and Thomson and, at the bottom, Pennink and Crawley, had won well. There were thoughts overnight that Kyle, rather than Bentley, would be the man to be dropped for the singles, but the captain thought otherwise and was proved absolutely right. Kyle's 5 and 4 defeat of Haas in the bottom match was the one that clinched overall victory and the first since the series had begun in 1922.

The Walker Cup is only one of the many responsibilities of the Royal and Ancient. The club organises the match every four years in Britain and also provides the selection committee, though strictly speaking only the chairman, who serves for four years, has to be a member of the R & A. He is also responsible for selection of the British team for the Eisenhower Trophy and the St Andrews Trophy, a 'Walker Cup'-type match between Britain and the Continent.

It is a private members' club and came into existence in 1754 as the Society of St Andrews Golfers. Twenty-two men were at its formation, all being 'admirers of the anticient and healthfull exercise of the Golf'. They adopted at once the code of rules compiled by the Honourable Company of Edinburgh Golfers ten years earlier, and, in essence, these thirteen rules have stood to this day. With the passing of time, however, they have been lengthened many times over, such are their complexities.

The present clubhouse was opened in 1854, by which time William IV

The Royal & Ancient clubhouse with the eighteenth green

The R & A's trophy case

had already granted permission for the name of Royal and Ancient Golf Club to be used. Meanwhile the Honourable Company of Edinburgh Golfers was moving its headquarters, first from Leith to Musselburgh, later from Musselburgh to its present site at Muirfield, and by degrees golf clubs generally were turning more and more to the R & A for leadership and guidance. In 1860 the Prestwick Golf Club in Ayrshire decided to hold an Open Championship, but it was not until 1873 that the Open was first played at St Andrews.

By 1897 the club was invited to become the governing authority on the rules of golf and has held that position ever since. Other countries soon sought affiliation until now the number is more than fifty. The rules are overhauled regularly by a committee of twelve, in consultation with the

United States Golf Association. Not their least task, however, is to make decisions on the interpretation of the rules. These have proved as multiple as many have also been complex. There is another committee which deals with implements and balls for, while golf clubs are of basic design, there have been many inventions which have been declared illegal.

Also under R & A jurisdiction is amateur status. In recent years an increasing number of players have turned professional in search of a fortune, quickly found it wishful thinking, and then asked for reinstatement as amateurs. A committee now deals with some 200 applications a year and these are invariably granted, though the wait will depend on how long the player has been a professional. Sometimes it takes years and never less than six months.

Before the First World War a small number of clubs had been involved in the running of the Open Championship and also the Amateur Championship. But in 1919 it was agreed that the Royal and Ancient should take over responsibility for both events. In 1949 they also assumed responsibility for the boys' championship, in 1963 the youths' championship, and in 1970 the seniors' championship.

Not the least of the club's responsibilities lies with its members, who now number 1800, nearly half of them from overseas. No one can apply for membership; they can only be invited to join the club by an existing member, seconded by another and supported by a sufficient number of the others to indicate that he is of 'good standing'. The wait between proposal and election is normally about three years.

The highlights of the year for the members are the spring and particularly the autumn meetings, which now attract an entry of such size that the main competition, the King William IV medal, has recently had to be run over three days compared with only one a few years ago. Golfers from all over the world gather in a unique atmosphere that has to be experienced to be appreciated. Most acquire a considerable thirst on the links, though consumption of kummel, port, whisky and gin equals, if not exceeds, that of beer in the Big Roon where portraits of the Queen and famous old golfers look down on the hubbub below while students from St Andrews University bear the orders on silver trays. The students, wearing white coats, are female as well as male, but the wives of members are only allowed within the clubhouse on rare and special occasions.

Dress for the annual dinner and presentation of prizes in one of the university halls is still referred to as being 'black tie' (by which is meant dinner jacket), as is dinner in the clubhouse during the meeting. Every new captain has the ball with which he drove himself into office that morning subsequently encased in silver and then attached to two silver clubs. After many years these now look like large clusters of grapes and at the annual dinner all new members are invited to go up to the main table 'and kiss the captains' balls'.

GOLFER. 'You never caddied for me before?' CADDIE. 'Oh yes, Sir. But you wouldn't remember; it was after lunch.' (*Punch*)

Captain Hay Wemyss about to drive off, 1854. Old Tom Morris is on the extreme left and Allan Robertson in the centre with the clubs under his arm.

This is a more relaxed ceremony for the captain than the moment he drives himself into office. Previous captains nominate the new captain but this is not announced until the spring meeting. The new incumbent then has six months in which to contemplate how he will execute one of the most forbidding strokes man can be asked to play, at the hangman's hour of 8 am on the final day of the autumn meeting. The members gather with the public on the shale path before the clubhouse, past captains assemble on the tee, and the immediate captain accompanies his successor to his

The R & A's honorary professional, Laurie Auchterlonie, teeing the ball for the driving-in ceremony for the new captain, Hugh Neill, autumn 1981

moment of reckoning. The club's honorary professional, of recent years Laurie Auchterlonie, son of Willie Auchterlonie, the Open champion of 1893, then enquires of the new captain as to whether he would like a high, medium or low tee and adjusts it accordingly.

An old cannon stands beside the tee; a fuse is lit and, at the precise moment the captain hits his drive, so the cannon booms out, thus informing the town that the King William IV medal competition is under way, the course closed to the public, and will remain so until the last putt is holed or, in the case of a tie, the play-off complete. Then the cannon is fired again and the links become once more a public place.

Ranged across the fairway awaiting the new captain's opening shot of office is a cluster of caddies, some at a respectful distance, others rather closer at hand. The man who gets there first – and often there is a lively dash by two or three – then returns the ball to the captain, who traditionally rewards him with a gold sovereign. This is a long-standing custom and occasionally the successful caddie has been prepared to sell his sovereign back to the captain. These days he could expect to receive upwards of £50. In 1951, when Francis Ouimet became the first American to be elected captain of the R&A, he rewarded the successful caddie with a $10 gold coin.

A second American, Joe Dey, drove into office not only on a miserably wet morning, but also with the knowledge that the ceremony was being televised throughout the United States. He was up to the demands of the

Opposite
Top left: Caddie Tod Holmes retrieves the ball for the new captain, Hugh Neill, and receives his gold sovereign
Top right: Francis Ouimet, first American captain of the R & A, 1951
Bottom: Joe Dey, the second American captain, plays himself into office, 1975, watched by Laurie Auchterlonie

occasion but there is a tale of one new captain having a 'fresh air' shot, though the professional, with commendable quickness of mind, covered up the error by announcing just loudly enough for it to be overheard: 'That was a very good practice swing, now just hit it.'

Alec Hill, who played for Britain in the 1936 Walker Cup, maintained that as he walked down the stone steps to the first tee, he stubbed out his twenty-third cigarette of that still young day. Shortly afterwards, much relieved at having made contact with the ball at all, he went round the Old Course in 72 and won the medal, the only captain ever to have accomplished the feat. Gerald Micklem also had a unique distinction. Illness had prevented him from driving into office during the Autumn meeting in 1968, but he was not spared and instead fulfilled the ceremony at the Spring meeting the following year.

When Ronnie Alexander became captain in 1980, the head of his driver collided with the tee box in a practice swing. He seemed the only person unaware of what had happened and, when the moment came, he struck the ball straight and true. Major David Blair's drive in 1978 was, by all accounts, one of the best of modern times and in keeping with an amateur golfer of high class with no apparent nerves.

Yet the Royal and Ancient means only one thing to most people and that is their organisation of the Open Championship. World wide, this is regarded as the supreme event of the golfing year and through television, which conveys it to an audience of millions each July, it has also become one of the great occasions of sport. In such highly commercial days it is worth emphasising that the Championship Committee is composed entirely of amateurs, fronted only by the club's small professional staff, with Keith Mackenzie, secretary of the club since 1967, its main architect.

Keith Mackenzie has travelled many thousands of miles to all parts of the globe 'selling' the Open and, even accounting for inflation, it is testimony to the success the R&A has had that prize money rose from £15,000 in 1967 to £250,000 by 1982. Not the least reason for this was an approach by the American Broadcasting Corporation to Wilbur Muirhead, then chairman of the Championship Committee, at about the same time as Keith Mackenzie's appointment, to negotiate a contract separate to that of the BBC. This was a considerable boost to the income side of the balance sheet. Then, in 1977, Mark McCormack was appointed negotiating agent on behalf of the R&A, and through him television audiences in Japan, Australia and a number of other countries now enjoy live coverage of the Open.

The profit the R & A make out of the Open goes not to the members of the club but to the welfare of the other championships they control and the international match fund. It is the game that benefits. There have been many offers of commercial sponsorship but, while this would undoubtedly have been lucrative, it has always been resisted in the interests of golf.

In recent times one other man played an important part in the Open Championship's revival. Though a number of Americans, beginning with Walter Hagen in 1922 at Sandwich, had won, their interest in crossing the Atlantic to chase the oldest title in the game had waned from the mid-1930s. Nor was it revived by Sam Snead's success in the first post-war championship at St Andrews in 1946. But 1960 was the year of the Centenary Open, by which time the name of Arnold Palmer was causing a golf explosion in the States. He had just won the US Open, had twice triumphed in the Masters and, like all the great players, he believed that his golfing education would not be complete until he had succeeded in Britain as well. His arrival at St Andrews caused tremendous interest, though it was not at first triumphant.

Kel Nagle, the Australian, won the Centenary Open by a stroke from Palmer. Nevertheless, Palmer's appetite had been whetted and he was back the following year at Royal Birkdale, where he won, and again at Troon in 1962, when he won again. His support for the Championship over the next ten years and more was unfailing and, more important, he persuaded others to follow him. Tony Lema, Jack Nicklaus, Lee Trevino, Tom Weiskopf, Tom Watson, Johnny Miller and Bill Rogers have all in turn taken the trophy back home to America and, while the money is now

Kel Nagle on the eighteenth green winning the Centenary Open, 1960

undoubtedly worth winning, it is not for this that they come. Happily championships still carry more value than the biggest purses.

It is all very different from days gone by but the common denominators are both the courses the old masters also trod (increasingly it is to be admitted from different tees) and the trophy they have all held and treasured. Originally it was a championship belt of old morocco leather, but young Tom Morris put paid to that when he won it outright with three successive victories, all at Prestwick, between 1868 and 1870. That caused such a reappraisal of the situation that in 1871 there was no Championship. But the following year Prestwick, the Royal and Ancient and the Honourable Company of Edinburgh Golfers clubbed together to provide a silver cup, in return for which each should host the Open in turn. The cup has since been duplicated, the original remaining at St Andrews. The champion also receives a gold medal, which he keeps.

The first Open Championship at St Andrews was won by Tom Kidd in 1873, and altogether it has now been staged at the home of golf on twenty-two occasions. Kidd was a St Andrews man and other 'home' winners were Bob Martin in 1876, Jamie Anderson in 1879 (he also won it at Musselburgh in 1877 and Prestwick in 1878), Bob Martin again in 1885 and lastly Hugh Kirkaldy in 1891. This was the last time the Championship was played over 36 holes for the following year at Muirfield it went to 72 holes, which is now accepted as the classic distance for championships.

Golf was not all sweetness and light even in those days, and Martin's victory in 1876 was an example. David Strath, playing behind him, needed two fives to win but finished 6,5 which meant a tie. Martin's supporters, however, claimed that Strath's ball had been stopped from going on to the road at the seventeenth by spectators. They therefore lodged an official protest. The Championship Committee apparently had little idea of what action to take and ordered a play-off while still considering the protest. Strath took the understandable view that the protest should be settled first, for if it went against him there was no point in playing. Nor did he, and Martin simply walked the course for the title.

It was a shame that two of the most famous sons of St Andrews, Old Tom Morris, who won the Championship four times, and Young Tom, who was equally successful, took all their titles on other courses. Old Tom was at the height of his powers before the Championship roster was extended to include St Andrews, while Young Tom, who never recovered from the death of his wife in childbirth, only once contested the Open there, finishing third behind Kidd. The professionals of that time nevertheless played an important part in making the history of St Andrews, going back to Allan Robertson, the first man ever to break 80 on the Old Course. He also invented iron shots to the green (hitherto they were played with baffing spoons) but he died the year before the first Open.

Keen golf historian Ben Crenshaw examines one of Laurie Auchterlonie's hand-made putters

Old Tom Morris, once appointed to Robertson as a maker of clubs and feathery balls, was the first professional to be appointed by the Royal and Ancient. This was in 1863; his salary was £50 and his responsibility the upkeep of the golf course. He remained a loyal and devoted servant of the club for forty years. He played in his last Open Championship at the age of seventy-five and was succeeded by Andrew Kirkaldy, a blunt, dour Scot whose brother Hugh won the Open in 1891. Andrew himself was once runner-up and it is also claimed that he originated the phrase 'the door is shut' when a player becomes dormy. One up one day with one to play against J. H. Taylor, he announced in a loud voice: 'That's the door locked, Taylor, you canna beat me now.'

In 1935 Kirkaldy was succeeded by Willie Auchterlonie, whose Open Championship win in 1893 is the most recent by a Scotsman living in Scotland. He was a gentle, kindly man whose abiding passion was club-making. Along with James Braid and J. H. Taylor he was, in 1950, the first professional to be made an honorary member of the Royal and Ancient. Laurie Auchterlonie succeeded his father as honorary professional to the club and he also inherited his considerable skill as a club-maker. He once made four sets for Bobby Jones and he is one of the world's leading authorities on old clubs. His shop, around the corner from the eighteenth green, attracts a constant stream of visitors.

James Braid, by then an exiled Scot, won the Open Championship at St Andrews more than any other man – in 1900, 1905 and 1910 – while Bobby Jones (1927) and Densmore Shute (1933) began the American dominance we have come to accept as a matter of course. Dick Burton was

Open winners
Left: Bobby Jones, 1927
Right: Jack Nicklaus, 1978, with his daughter Nancy and wife Barbara

the last British winner at the home of golf in 1939, Peter Thomson (1955) and Bobby Locke (1957), both of whom dominated the Championship for many years, had their successes on the famous links, while Tony Lema's victory in 1964 was remarkable in that he had never played golf in Europe before, and moreover, allowed himself as little as thirty-six hours in which to get to know the Old Course. Two of Jack Nicklaus' three Open Championships, in 1970 and 1978, have been at St Andrews, and the sight of him on that last afternoon arriving in the grand arena of the eighteenth hole, the crowd on their feet and not a dry eye in the house, was something no one present will ever forget.

Nor will Nicklaus. If there is one place where a man would choose to win the Open Championship, it is unquestionably St Andrews. Indeed, it is the mecca for every golfer – professional, amateur, rich, poor, black or white. Regardless of whether he plays on a driving range in Japan, a luxurious country club in America, the deserts of the Middle East, or beneath the shadow of the local gasworks, each and every one has the same dream – that one day, driver in hand, he will step on to the first tee of the Old Course.

Results of the Four Majors

BRITISH OPEN CHAMPIONSHIP

Year	Winner	Score	Venue
1860	Willie Park, Sr	174	Prestwick
1861	Tom Morris, Sr	163	Prestwick
1862	Tom Morris, Sr	163	Prestwick
1863	Willie Park, Sr	168	Prestwick
1864	Tom Morris, Sr	167	Prestwick
1865	Andrew Strath	162	Prestwick
1866	Willie Park, Sr	169	Prestwick
1867	Tom Morris, Sr	170	Prestwick
1868	Tom Morris, Jr	170	Prestwick
1869	Tom Morris, Jr	157	Prestwick
1870	Tom Morris, Jr	149	Prestwick
1871	No competition		
1872	Tom Morris, Jr	166	Prestwick
1873	Tom Kidd	179	St Andrews
1874	Mungo Park	159	Musselburgh
1875	Willie Park, Sr	166	Prestwick
1876	Bob Martin	176	St Andrews
1877	Jamie Anderson	160	Musselburgh
1878	Jamie Anderson	157	Prestwick
1879	Jamie Anderson	170	St Andrews
1880	Bob Ferguson	162	Musselburgh
1881	Bob Ferguson	170	Prestwick
1882	Bob Ferguson	171	St Andrews
1883	Willie Fernie	159	Musselburgh
1884	Jack Simpson	160	Prestwick
1885	Bob Martin	171	St Andrews
1886	David Brown	157	Musselburgh
1887	Willie Park, Jr	161	Prestwick
1888	Jack Burns	171	St Andrews
1889	Willie Park, Jr	155	Musselburgh
1890	John Ball	164	Prestwick
1891	Hugh Kirkaldy	166	St Andrews
1892	Harold Hilton	305	Muirfield
1893	Willie Auchterlonie	322	Prestwick
1894	J. H. Taylor	326	Sandwich
1895	J. H. Taylor	322	St Andrews
1896	Harry Vardon	316	Muirfield
1897	Harold Hilton	314	Hoylake
1898	Harry Vardon	307	Prestwick
1899	Harry Vardon	310	Sandwich
1900	J. H. Taylor	309	St Andrews
1901	James Braid	309	Muirfield
1902	Alex Herd	307	Hoylake
1903	Harry Vardon	300	Prestwick
1904	Jack White	296	Sandwich
1905	James Braid	318	St Andrews
1906	James Braid	300	Muirfield
1907	Arnaud Massy	312	Hoylake
1908	James Braid	291	Prestwick
1909	J. H. Taylor	295	Deal
1910	James Braid	299	St Andrews
1911	Harry Vardon	303	Sandwich
1912	Ted Ray	295	Muirfield
1913	J. H. Taylor	304	Hoylake
1914	Harry Vardon	306	Prestwick
1915–19	No competition		
1920	George Duncan	303	Deal
1921	Jock Hutchison	296	St Andrews
1922	Walter Hagen	300	Sandwich
1923	Arthur Havers	295	Troon
1924	Walter Hagen	301	Hoylake
1925	Jim Barnes	300	Prestwick
1926	Bobby Jones	291	Royal Lytham
1927	Bobby Jones	285	St Andrews
1928	Walter Hagen	292	Sandwich
1929	Walter Hagen	292	Muirfield
1930	Bobby Jones	291	Hoylake
1931	Tommy Armour	296	Carnoustie
1932	Gene Sarazen	283	Prince's, Sandwich
1933	Denny Shute	292	St Andrews
1934	Henry Cotton	283	Sandwich
1935	Alfred Perry	283	Muirfield
1936	Alfred Padgham	287	Hoylake
1937	Henry Cotton	290	Carnoustie
1938	Reg Whitcombe	295	Sandwich
1939	Dick Burton	290	St Andrews
1940–45	No competition		
1946	Sam Snead	290	St Andrews
1947	Fred Daly	293	Hoylake
1948	Henry Cotton	284	Muirfield
1949	Bobby Locke	283	Sandwich
1950	Bobby Locke	279	Troon
1951	Max Faulkner	285	Portrush
1952	Bobby Locke	287	Royal Lytham
1953	Ben Hogan	282	Carnoustie
1954	Peter Thomson	283	Royal Birkdale
1955	Peter Thomson	281	St Andrews
1956	Peter Thomson	286	Hoylake

Year	Winner	Score	Venue
1957	Bobby Locke	279	St Andrews
1958	Peter Thomson	278	Royal Lytham
1959	Gary Player	284	Muirfield
1960	Kel Nagle	278	St Andrews
1961	Arnold Palmer	284	Royal Birkdale
1962	Arnold Palmer	276	Troon
1963	Bob Charles	277	Royal Lytham
1964	Tony Lema	279	St Andrews
1965	Peter Thomson	285	Royal Birkdale
1966	Jack Nicklaus	282	Muirfield
1967	Roberto de Vicenzo	278	Hoylake
1968	Gary Player	289	Carnoustie
1969	Tony Jacklin	280	Royal Lytham
1970	Jack Nicklaus	283	St Andrews
1971	Lee Trevino	278	Royal Birkdale
1972	Lee Trevino	278	Muirfield
1973	Tom Weiskopf	276	Troon
1974	Gary Player	282	Royal Lytham
1975	Tom Watson	279	Carnoustie
1976	Johnny Miller	279	Royal Birkdale
1977	Tom Watson	268	Turnberry
1978	Jack Nicklaus	281	St Andrews
1979	Severiano Ballesteros	283	Royal Lytham
1980	Tom Watson	271	Muirfield
1981	Bill Rogers	276	Sandwich
1982			Troon
1983			Royal Birkdale
1984			St Andrews
1985			Sandwich

UNITED STATES OPEN CHAMPIONSHIP

Year	Winner	Score	Venue
1895	Horace Rawlins	173	Newport, R.I.
1896	James Foulis	152	Shinnecock Hills, N.Y.
1897	Joe Lloyd	162	Chicago, Ill.
1898	Fred Herd	328	Myopia Hunt Club, Mass.
1899	Willie Smith	315	Baltimore, Md.
1900	Harry Vardon	313	Chicago, Ill.
1901	Willie Anderson	331	Myopia Hunt Club, Mass.
1902	Laurie Auchterlonie	307	Garden City, N.Y.
1903	Willie Anderson	307	Baltusrol, N.J.
1904	Willie Anderson	303	Glen View Club, Ill.
1905	Willie Anderson	314	Myopia Hunt Club, Mass.
1906	Alex Smith	295	Onwentsia, Ill.
1907	Alex Ross	302	Philadelphia Cricket Club, Pa.
1908	Fred McLeod	322	Myopia Hunt Club, Ill.
1909	George Sargent	290	Englewood, N.J.
1910	Alex Smith	298	Philadelphia Cricket Club, Pa.
1911	Johnny McDermott	307	Chicago, Ill.
1912	Johnny McDermott	294	Buffalo, N.Y.
1913	Francis Ouimet	304	The Country Club, Mass.
1914	Walter Hagen	290	Midlothian, Ill.
1915	Jerry Travers	297	Baltusrol, N.J.
1916	Chick Evans	286	Minikahda, Minn.
1917–18	No competition		
1919	Walter Hagen	301	Brae Burn, Mass.
1920	Ted Ray	295	Inverness, Ohio
1921	Jim Barnes	289	Columbia, Md.
1922	Gene Sarazen	288	Skokie, Ill.
1923	Bobby Jones	296	Inwood, N.Y.
1924	Cyril Walker	297	Oakland Hills, Mich.
1925	Willie Macfarlane	291	Worcester, Mass.
1926	Bobby Jones	293	Scioto, Ohio
1927	Tommy Armour	301	Oakmont, Pa.
1928	Johnny Farrell	294	Olympia Fields, Ill.
1929	Bobby Jones	294	Winged Foot, N.Y.
1930	Bobby Jones	287	Interlachen, Minn.
1931	Billy Burke	292	Inverness, Ohio
1932	Gene Sarazen	286	Fresh Meadow, N.Y.
1933	Johnny Goodman	287	North Shore, Ill.
1934	Olin Dutra	293	Merion, Pa.
1935	Sam Parks	299	Oakmont, Pa.
1936	Tony Manero	282	Baltusrol, N.J.
1937	Ralph Guldahl	281	Oakland Hills, Mich.
1938	Ralph Guldahl	284	Cherry Hills, Colo.
1939	Byron Nelson	284	Philadelphia, Pa.
1940	Lawson Little	287	Canterbury, Ohio
1941	Craig Wood	284	Colonial, Tex.
1942–45	No competition		
1946	Lloyd Mangrum	284	Canterbury, Ohio
1947	Lew Worsham	282	St Louis, Mo.
1948	Ben Hogan	276	Riviera, Cal.
1949	Cary Middlecoff	286	Medinah, Ill.
1950	Ben Hogan	287	Merion, Pa.
1951	Ben Hogan	287	Oakland Hills, Mich.
1952	Julius Boros	281	Northwood, Tex.
1953	Ben Hogan	283	Oakmont, Pa.
1954	Ed Furgol	284	Baltusrol, N.J.
1955	Jack Fleck	287	Olympic, Cal.
1956	Cary Middlecoff	281	Oak Hill, N.Y.
1957	Dick Mayer	282	Inverness, Ohio
1958	Tommy Bolt	283	Southern Hills, Okla.
1959	Billy Casper	282	Winged Foot, N.Y.
1960	Arnold Palmer	280	Cherry Hills, Colo.
1961	Gene Littler	281	Oakland Hills, Mich.
1962	Jack Nicklaus	283	Oakmont, Pa.

Year	*Winner*	*Score*	*Venue*
1963	Julius Boros	293	The Country Club, Mass.
1964	Ken Venturi	278	Congressional, Washington D.C.
1965	Gary Player	282	Bellerive, Mo.
1966	Billy Casper	278	Olympic, Cal.
1967	Jack Nicklaus	275	Baltusrol, N.J.
1968	Lee Trevino	275	Oak Hill, N.Y.
1969	Orville Moody	281	Champions, Tex.
1970	Tony Jacklin	281	Hazeltine National, Minn.
1971	Lee Trevino	280	Merion, Pa.
1972	Jack Nicklaus	290	Pebble Beach, Cal.
1973	Johnny Miller	279	Oakmont, Pa.
1974	Hale Irwin	287	Winged Foot, N.Y.
1975	Lou Graham	287	Medinah, Ill.
1976	Jerry Pate	277	Atlanta, Ga.
1977	Hubert Green	278	Southern Hills, Okla.
1978	Andy North	285	Cherry Hills, Colo.
1979	Hale Irwin	284	Inverness, Ohio
1980	Jack Nicklaus	272	Baltusrol, N.J.
1981	David Graham	273	Merion, Pa.
1982			Pebble Beach, Cal.
1983			Oakmont, Pa.
1984			Winged Foot, N.Y.
1985			Oakland Hills, Mich.

UNITED STATES PGA CHAMPIONSHIP

The Championship was decided by match-play until 1957, and thereafter by stroke-play

Year	*Winner*	*Score*	*Venue*
1916	Jim Barnes	1 up	Siwanoy, N.Y.
1917–18	No competition		
1919	Jim Barnes	6 & 5	Engineers, N.Y.
1920	Jock Hutchison	1 up	Flossmoor, Ill.
1921	Walter Hagen	3 & 2	Inwood, N.Y.
1922	Gene Sarazen	4 & 3	Oakmont, Pa.
1923	Gene Sarazen	1 up	Pelham, N.Y.
1924	Walter Hagen	2 up	French Lick, Ind.
1925	Walter Hagen	6 & 5	Olympia Fields, Ill.
1926	Walter Hagen	5 & 3	Salisbury, N.Y.
1927	Walter Hagen	1 up	Cedar Crest, Tex.
1928	Leo Diegel	6 & 5	Baltimore, Md.
1929	Leo Diegel	6 & 4	Hillcrest, Cal.
1930	Tommy Armour	1 up	Fresh Meadow, N.Y.
1931	Tom Creavy	2 & 1	Wannamoisett, R.I.
1932	Olin Dutra	4 & 3	Keller, Minn.
1933	Gene Sarazen	5 & 4	Blue Mound, Wis.
1934	Paul Runyan	1 up	Park, N.Y.
1935	John Revolta	5 & 4	Twin Hills, Okla.
1936	Denny Shute	3 & 2	Pinehurst, N.C.
1937	Denny Shute	1 up	Pittsburgh, Pa.
1938	Paul Runyan	8 & 7	Shawnee, Pa.
1939	Henry Picard	1 up	Pomonok, N.Y.
1940	Byron Nelson	1 up	Hershey, Pa.
1941	Vic Ghezzi	1 up	Cherry Hills, Colo.
1942	Sam Snead	2 & 1	Seaview, N.J.
1943	No competition		
1944	Bob Hamilton	1 up	Manito, Wash.
1945	Byron Nelson	4 & 3	Morraine, Ohio
1946	Ben Hogan	6 & 4	Portland, Ore.
1947	Jim Ferrier	2 & 1	Plum Hollow, Mich.
1948	Ben Hogan	7 & 6	Norwood Hills, Mo.
1949	Sam Snead	3 & 2	Hermitage, Va.
1950	Chandler Harper	4 & 3	Scioto, Ohio
1951	Sam Snead	7 & 6	Oakmont, Pa.
1952	Jim Turnesa	1 up	Big Springs, Ky.
1953	Walter Burkemo	2 & 1	Birmingham, Mich.
1954	Chick Harbert	4 & 3	Keller, Minn.
1955	Doug Ford	4 & 3	Meadowbrook, Mich.
1956	Jack Burke	3 & 2	Blue Hill, Mass.
1957	Lionel Hebert	2 & 1	Miami Valley, Ohio
1958	Dow Finsterwald	276	Llanerch, Pa.
1959	Bob Rosburg	277	Minneapolis, Minn.
1960	Jay Hebert	281	Firestone, Ohio
1961	Jerry Barber	277	Olympia Fields, Ill.
1962	Gary Player	278	Aronomink, Pa.
1963	Jack Nicklaus	279	Dallas Athletic Club, Tex.
1964	Bob Nichols	271	Columbus, Ohio
1965	Dave Marr	280	Laurel Valley, Pa.
1966	Al Geiberger	280	Firestone, Ohio
1967	Don January	281	Columbine, Colo.
1968	Julius Boros	281	Pecan Valley, Tex.
1969	Ray Floyd	276	National Cash Register, Ohio
1970	Dave Stockton	279	Southern Hills, Okla.
1971	Jack Nicklaus	281	PGA National, Fla.
1972	Gary Player	281	Oakland Hills, Mich.
1973	Jack Nicklaus	277	Canterbury, Ohio
1974	Lee Trevino	276	Clemmons, N.C.
1975	Jack Nicklaus	276	Firestone, Ohio
1976	Dave Stockton	281	Congressional, Washington D.C.
1977	Lanny Wadkins	282	Pebble Beach, Cal.
1978	John Mahaffey	276	Oakmont, Pa.
1979	David Graham	272	Oakland Hills, Mich.
1980	Jack Nicklaus	274	Oak Hill, N.Y.
1981	Larry Nelson	273	Duluth, Ga.
1982			Southern Hills, Okla.
1983			Riviera, Cal.
1984			Shoal Creek, Ala.
1985			

UNITED STATES MASTERS TOURNAMENT

Played at Augusta National GC, Ga.

Year	*Winner*	*Score*	*Year*	*Winner*	*Score*
1934	Horton Smith	284	1961	Gary Player	280
1935	Gene Sarazen	282	1962	Arnold Palmer	280
1936	Horton Smith	285	1963	Jack Nicklaus	286
1937	Byron Nelson	283	1964	Arnold Palmer	276
1938	Henry Picard	285	1965	Jack Nicklaus	271
1939	Ralph Guldahl	279	1966	Jack Nicklaus	288
1940	Jimmy Demaret	280	1967	Gay Brewer	280
1941	Craig Wood	280	1968	Bob Goalby	277
1942	Byron Nelson	280	1969	George Archer	281
1943–45	No competition		1970	Billy Casper	279
1946	Herman Keiser	282	1971	Charles Coody	279
1947	Jimmy Demaret	281	1972	Jack Nicklaus	286
1948	Claude Harmon	279	1973	Tommy Aaron	283
1949	Sam Snead	282	1974	Gary Player	278
1950	Jimmy Demaret	283	1975	Jack Nicklaus	276
1951	Ben Hogan	280	1976	Ray Floyd	271
1952	Sam Snead	286	1977	Tom Watson	276
1953	Ben Hogan	274	1978	Gary Player	277
1954	Sam Snead	289	1979	Fuzzy Zoeller	280
1955	Cary Middlecoff	279	1980	Severiano Ballesteros	275
1956	Jack Burke	289	1981	Tom Watson	280
1957	Doug Ford	283	1982	Craig Stadler	284
1958	Arnold Palmer	284	1983		
1959	Art Wall	284	1984		
1960	Arnold Palmer	282	1985		

The Contributors

PETER ALLISS

Golf is in the Alliss blood. Born into the game in 1931 in Berlin, where his father Percy was professional, Peter's natural talent resulted in his turning professional at the precocious age of fifteen. When he retired from the tournament scene in 1970 he had won twenty-two major tournaments, including the Open Championships of Spain, Italy, Portugal and Brazil. He played in the Ryder Cup on eight occasions, including a famous victory in 1963 at Atlanta where he defeated Arnold Palmer in the singles. But Peter has never been just a golfer and his retirement from the tournament circuit was as much inspired by his desire to fulfil some of his other business and sporting interests as by his legendary putting twitches. He is now much in demand throughout the world as a teacher, course architect and television commentator.

PAT WARD-THOMAS

Born in Cheshire in 1913 and educated at Wellingborough School, Pat Ward-Thomas is the doyen of golf correspondents. From 1950 until his 'official retirement' in 1978 he was the golf correspondent of *The Guardian*. For a time he was a colleague of the legendary Bernard Darwin at *Country Life* and, with the latter's death in 1961, Pat has been their regular golf correspondent ever since. He is a member of the Royal and Ancient, an overseas member of Pine Valley (USA), and in 1980 he was captain of Royal West Norfolk. In 1946 his handicap was four and even now it is still only sixteen. His books include *Masters of Golf*, *The Long Green Fairway*, *Shell Golfers Atlas*, *The World Atlas of Golf*, *The Royal and Ancient* and *Not Only Golf*, his autobiography.

PETER DOBEREINER

Peter Dobereiner is the golf correspondent of *The Observer* and *The Guardian*, consultant to *Golf World*, contributing editor of *Golf Digest*, and the author of numerous books on golf. He was born in 1925 of Anglo-Scottish-Canadian-Danish-Red Indian-German parentage and stubbornly resisted all attempts by King's College, Taunton, and Lincoln College, Oxford, to impart a rudimentary education. Hence his choice of journalism as a profession. His first ambition, to defeat Hitler and Hirohito, was completed in 1945, and in order to avoid hero-worshippers he went to India where he was involved in the distillery business, making gin of such vile quality that it made cirrhosis of the liver an endemic disease throughout the sub-continent. His reputation as a brilliant golfer is mainly self-confessed and totally imaginary. He is married and has children the way other people have mice.

ROSS GOODNER

Ross Goodner was born in Oklahoma in 1927. He received a degree in journalism from the University of Oklahoma and then wrote about sports for newspapers in his native state until 1962, when he joined the *New York Times*. He was subsequently editor of *Golf Magazine*, and did public relations work in the Bahamas and Bermuda before joining *Golf Digest* where he is Associate Editor. His books include *Golf's Greatest* and the *History of the Shinnecock Hills Golf Club*. He lives in Connecticut with his wife and an erratic 15 handicap.

LEWINE MAIR

Born in 1945, Lewine Mair was educated at the Convent of the Holy Child, Edgbaston. A keen tennis player, she switched to golf at the age of fourteen and represented the English girls' side for three successive years. In 1966 she played in an unofficial match between England and France and, that same year, started writing on golf for *The Times*. She is married to Norman Mair, golf correspondent of *The Sunday Standard*, but remains a regular contributor to *The Times* and is the author of the *Dunlop Lady Golfer's Companion*. For all that she is a mother of four, she is still very much in touch with the game, and has had first-hand experience of playing on the Women's PGA tour in Britain.

MICHAEL McDONNELL

Michael McDonnell has covered golf worldwide for the London *Daily Mail* for the last eighteen years. He has written four golf books, is a regular contributor to golf magazines on both sides of the Atlantic, and has scripted two television documentaries. He began his journalistic career as a local news reporter on the *Romford Times* in Essex and later joined the *Bristol Evening World* and reported golf events for both papers because nobody else wanted the job. An enthusiastic club golfer, he holds a nine handicap at Thorndon Park in Essex and is a former winner of the Golf Writers Championship. In 1980 his journalistic work was honoured when he received the Monsanto British Press Award for sports reporting. He is forty-six.

RENTON LAIDLAW

Renton Laidlaw is one of the exclusive band of sports reporters who travel the world covering golf – in his case by courtesy of the London evening newspaper *The Standard*. Born in Edinburgh in 1939, he began his journalistic career in the *Edinburgh Evening News*, after leaving Daniel Stewart's College where the headmaster had failed to convince him that his career lay in the more solid professions of insurance or banking. Now he admits he has the best of all worlds – a widely read newspaper column, a weekly commitment to report golf on BBC Radio, and regular commentary contributions to ITV's golf coverage. Not surprisingly he remains unmarried, and lives in the Sunningdale stockbroker belt where he plays golf to a handicap of 15.

MICHAEL WILLIAMS

Michael Williams has been golf correspondent of *The Daily Telegraph* since 1971 when, rather to his surprise, he was appointed to succeed Leonard Crawley. His ability as a golfer was not quite in the same class, though he has managed to keep a single-figure handicap for the best part of twenty-five years. In 1968, at the age of thirty-four, he was made the youngest captain of Chelmsford Golf Club and is now also a member of the Royal and Ancient. Educated at Ipswich School, his career stepping-stones were the East Anglian *Daily Times*, *Stratford Express* and *The Sunday Telegraph*, for which he wrote a column embracing all sports. His marriage has happily survived a rigorous travelling schedule and he has four children to prove it.

GORDON MENZIES

Born near Pitlochry in the Highlands of Perthshire, Gordon Menzies started his working life as a teacher of history. For the past twenty-two years he has been in the BBC, where he is a Senior Television Producer. When he produced television series, such as *Who are the Scots?*, *The Scottish Nation*, *History is my Witness* and *Play Golf*, he also contrived to produce successful books to accompany them. The *World of Golf* series, like *Play Golf*, was not only his idea but was scripted and directed by him. Regarded (kindly) by his colleagues as a workaholic, he is a former captain of Lenzie Golf Club, where he still plays to a single-figure handicap.